# The impact of Fair Trade

# The impact of Fair Trade

edited by

Ruerd Ruben



Wageningen Academic
Publishers

**Photos cover:**
**Solidaridad and**
**AgroFair (Geoff Crawford-Tearfund)**

**ISBN 978-90-8686-083-8**

**First published, 2008**

**Wageningen Academic Publishers**
**The Netherlands, 2008**

# Preface

It is time to look back. At the start of 1988, Solidaridad initiated the establishment of the Max Havelaar Foundation. In November of the same year, Professor Jan Tinbergen offered His Royal Highness Prince Claus the first package of coffee with the label of the foundation that was only young at the time. Three years of preparations by Solidaridad were rewarded with a successful launch of a new trade model that would gradually become known as *Fair Trade*. Nowadays, Fair Trade is a global player with a total turnover of over two and a half billion Euros. Thousands of coffee farmers, fruit producers, tea planters, and cocoa and cotton producers in developing countries have been certified. In 22 consumer countries, Fair Trade has become a way of thinking and it offers consumers a concrete possibility to opt for a sustainably produced product.

Fair Trade has always been ahead of its time and has gained many followers. Founded by the theory on making the economy more sustainable, the so-called Pyramid of Change, Solidaridad is at this moment working on the further growth of Fair Trade and organic in the top segments of the market, with concepts for corporate social responsibility in the middle segments of the market and sector-wide through round tables. It is not only about consumer goods such as coffee or bananas anymore, but it is also about raw materials such as cotton, industrial ingredients such as palm oil and bulk products such as soy and cane sugar. The dynamics are changing, and sustainable chain management is becoming an important economic value for the continuity of a business.

It's time to mark time; time for analysis and reflection. One specific question has to be central for Solidaridad: *What is in it for the producers?* Does Fair Trade indeed contribute to empowerment of producers in developing countries? Or, in other words; what is the impact for development?

For the start of an answer to that question, this book proves of great importance. It contains reports from independent research, executed by the Centre for International Development Issues (CIDIN) at the Radboud University Nijmegen, the Netherlands. Many relevant data have been gathered, and a clear research methodology has been used. Their results are surprising. The conclusions are a crucial contribution to a debate that has to lead to new policies and adapted strategies. But we can also be self-confident. We're on the right track.

I'd like to show my gratitude to Mr. Ruerd Ruben and his team. Ruerd has a fresh view on the matter and he is a reliable scientist. For many years already, this has made his work interesting. He knows how to involve many young scientists in his passion; investing in rural development of countries in the third world by including people, by increasing production possibilities, by strengthening the basis of existence for people and by optimizing the trade chains. Such scientific engagement has the future.

*Nico Roozen, Director Solidaridad*

# Table of contents

## List of figures

# List of Tables

## Abbreviations

| | |
|---|---|
| APBOS | *Asociación de Productores de Banano Organico de Salitral* (Peru) |
| ASBANA | *Asociación Bananera Nacional* (Costa Rica) |
| Asoguabo | *Asociación de Pequeños Productores Bananeros 'El Guabo'* (Ecuador) |
| APVCH | *Asosiación de Productores de Banano Orgánico del Valle del Chira* (Peru) |
| BANDECO | Banana Development Corporation (Costa Rica) |
| CEPCO | Central de Productores de Café de Oaxaca (Mexico) |
| CIPIBO | *Central Piurana de Bananeros Organicos* ((Peru) |
| CNOC | *Confederación Nacional de Organizaciones Campesinas* (Mexico) |
| Coopeetrabasur | *Cooperativa de Tabajadores del Sur* (Costa Rica) |
| COOCAFE | *Consorcio de Co-operativas de Caficultores de Guanacaste y Montes de Oro R.L.* (Costa Rica) |
| COPDEBAN | *Corporación Peruana de Desarrollo Bananero S.A.C.* |
| CORBANA | *Corporación Bananera Nacional* (Costa Rica) |
| EFTA | European Fair Trade Association |
| FEDECOOP | *Federación de Co-operativas de Caficultores R.L.* (Costa Rica) |
| FLO | Fair Trade Labelling Organization International |
| FT | Fair Trade production |
| FTPC | Fair Trade Premium Committee |
| GAWU | General Agricultural Workers Union (Ghana) |
| GEL | Golden Exotics Ltd. (Ghana) |
| Inmecafe | Instituto Mexicana de Cafe |
| MCCH | Maquita Cushunchic Comercializando como Hermanos (Qcuador) |
| Minka | Minka Comercio Justo (Peru) |
| Non-FT | Non-Fair Trade production |
| PSM | Propensity Score Matching |
| REPEBAN | *Red de Pequeños Productores de Banano Organico Comercio Justo* (Peru) |
| UEPC | *Unidad Económica para la Producción y Commercialización* (Mexico) |
| VREL | Volta River Estates Ltd. (Ghana) |

# Chapter 1

## The development impact of Fair Trade: from discourse to data

*Ruerd Ruben*

### 1. Introduction

Twenty year ago, the first Fair Trade initiative for democratic development by guaranteeing market access to (groups of) smallholder producers from Southern countries was initiated by the Dutch development organisation Solidaridad. Fair Trade programs started with coffee (Max Havelaar) and subsequently expanded to tropical fruits (Oké), and hereafter several new products have been included (i.e. cocoa, textiles, tea, quinoa, nuts, wine, etc). New partners and corporate agents have joined the Fair Trade movement and further upscaling has now become the major device.

Fair Trade (hereafter: FT) is an organised social movement which promotes standards for production practices and delivery procedures, working conditions and labour remuneration, environmental care and social policies in supply chains of certified goods. A widely recognised definition of Fair Trade presents it as a trading partnership, based on dialogue, transparency and respect, seeking greater equity in international trade. According to its supporters, Fair Trade contributes to sustainable development by offering better trading conditions and securing the rights of producers and workers in the South. Fair Trade organisations are also actively engaged in supporting consumers' awareness raising and in campaigning for changes in the rules and practice of conventional international trade.

Several studies have tried to capture the impact of Fair Trade for local producers and households, but sound empirical evidence regarding social, economic and ecological impact remains scattered and sometimes contradictory. Due to the notable absence of base-line studies and reference groups, it remains difficult to precisely assess the welfare impact at household and cooperative level. Therefore, a new methodological framework has been developed and applied in this study that permits to capture the tangible and less-tangible effects of Fair Trade involvement.

Impact studies concerning Fair Trade labelled products, looking at longitudinal changes in welfare and livelihood conditions are, however, notably absent. The European Fair Trade Association (EFTA) provides an overview of impact studies that were realised since 2000, but none of these studies rely on ample field work data, nor on a sound comparison with otherwise similar non-Fair Trade producers. Several studies (Calo and Wise, 2005; Milford, 2004) emphasise the positive effects on producers organisations – focussing on the process of capitalisation from the Fair Trade premium payments – while little attention is given to the individual and household-level implications. Other studies refer to the effects on prices and productivity and the role of Fair Trade for improving competitiveness (Bacon *et al.*, 2008). Some general constraints for deepening and widening Fair Trade that are identified refer to difficulties of involving farmers/workers in management decisions and the importance of public consciousness-raising for enhancing the size of the Fair Trade market.

Recent studies have shown various advantages and disadvantages of the Fair Trade movement. Detailed studies from coffee cooperatives in Costa Rica (Ronchi, 2002) and Mexico (Jaffee, 2007; Calo and Wise, 2005; Bacon, 2005) found that Fair Trade strengthened producer organisations and conclude that - in light of the coffee crisis of the early 1990s - Fair Trade can be said to have accomplished its goal of improving the returns to small producers and positively affecting their quality of life and the strength of the organisations that represent them locally, nationally and beyond. Other research stressed that FT initiatives substantially improved the well-being of small-scale farmers and their families, particularly due to better access to credit facilities and external funds, as well as through training and improved capabilities to enhance the quality of the product (Murray *et al.*, 2003). Fair Trade farmers are often more successful in improving their production systems, experience greater satisfaction in terms of prices obtained for their crop, improvements of monthly household food consumption and living conditions that result in a significant drop in child mortality (Becchetti and Costantino, 2006; see also Chapter 8 this volume).

A general difficulty with many impact studies is that no correction is made for differences in farm household characteristics. For instance, if larger or more progressive farmers are the ones that usually become engaged in Fair Trade, a major part of their welfare change might just be attributed to their initial characteristics. This so-called sample selection bias easily leads to an overestimation of the project outcomes (White and Bamberger, 2008). While descriptive stories about perceived changes in farmers' welfare and community organisation attributed to Fair Trade linkages are widely available (Milford, 2004; Murray *et al.*, 2003), this study is the first comparative quantitative assessment of the Fair Trade impact on farmers welfare and attitudes. In this introductory chapter, we provide an concise overview of the research approach and summarise the key finding derived from a comparative assessment of Fair Trade impact amongst coffee and bananas producers in different regions of Peru, Costa Rica, Ecuador, Mexico, Ghana and Kenya.

## 2. The purpose of Fair Trade

While Fair Trade was initiated with third world artisanal products in the early 1970s (sold initially through the so-called world shops), large-scale sales of coffee through supermarket and institutional channels started in 1988. The range of products has gradually been broadened to include fruits (particularly bananas), clothing, cosmetics, wines, honey, nuts and a whole range of other products. In 1997, the Fair Trade Labelling Organisation (FLO) was established for worldwide standard setting and certification purposes. Global Fair Trade sales have grown substantially over the past decades: in 2006 sales of Fair Trade labelled goods amounted to approximately €1.6 billion worldwide. Current certification covers 570 producer organisations in 57 developing countries that represent around 900,000 families of farmers and workers.[1]

The main guiding principles behind the concept of Fair Trade are: (1) creating better income opportunities for economically disadvantaged producers, (2) strengthening farmers' organisation and capacities, (3) payment of a fair price, (4) promoting gender equity, (5) improving working and living conditions and (6) enhancing environmental protection. In practice, this means that producers sell their production at a pre-defined and guaranteed (minimum) prices, receiving an additional premium for deliveries to Fair Trade market outlets. The latter premium is paid to the whole group of producers (either smallholder cooperatives or workers' organisations) and should be used for community purposes. Involvement of smallholders in Fair Trade supply chains – sometimes coupled with a shift to organic production methods – is supposed to provide valuable opportunities to enhance household income and producers' bargaining power. An important additional objective of Fair Trade chains is to reduce risk and improve credit access, thus enabling producers to engage in long-term investments. The latter aspect is considered of special relevance for poverty alleviation strategies focussing on changes in risk behaviour as a pre-condition for reducing asset-poverty (Zimmerman and Carter, 2003).

Fair Trade has been proposed as an alternative to traditional development aid, offering at the same time a challenge to global trade regimes that are controlled by large multinational corporation. Instead of creating a niche market, FT products are directed to mainstream consumers through a wide network of retail outlets. Some authors remain critical on the possibilities of FT to challenge or transform neo-liberal trade regimes (Fridell, 2007), while others point to the inherent tensions between market expansion while maintaining consumer support (Raynolds and Murray, 2007). Other discussions arise on most appropriate strategies for enabling further growth of FT towards broader market segments, based on further alliances with leading agro-food and retail companies, and including deliveries from midsize producers and plantations. For the latter strategic discussion, it might be highly helpful to better

[1] Raynolds and Long (2007) provide a concise overview of the historical and empirical dimensions of the rise and development of Fair Trade throughout the world.

understand how the different components of the FT business model in practice influence rural livelihood strategies amongst Southern producers and workers.

Recent discussion regarding knowledge generation and quality surveillance in the sector of the development cooperation tend to focus increasingly attention on the issue of FT impact assessment (White and Bamberger, 2008). Impact is explicitly considered as the net contribution of projects and programs to a series of well-defined parameters at individual, household and/or community level (including external effects for non-target groups). A sound and feasible system for impact assessment should contribute to three basic objectives:

a. learning and self-assessment of strong and weak points of Fair Trade programs in order to envisage possible structural improvements (that could eventually lead to operational adjustments in the design of Fair Trade initiatives);
b. assessment of intermediate and final results in order to review the effectiveness of interventions of Fair Trade initiatives and enhance the accountability of operations (towards donors and consumers);
c. policy and programming appraisal, trying to draw general lessons regarding the most effective exchange conditions and the type and sequence of appropriate supportive activities (including prospects for further FT upscaling).

The different contributions included in this volume tried to address in a balanced way these three objectives. Main emphasis is given to the effects for reducing poverty and strengthening livelihoods of local producer/worker and the derived implications for reinforcing local organisations and rural village economies.

## 3. Impact assessment approach

The current study has been commissioned by Solidaridad to gain insights in the field-level implications of Fair Trade, focussing attention on a wide range of possible impact factors.[2] The main objective of the study is to present an un-biased assessment of the welfare impact of farmers' engagement with Fair Trade. Key attention is given to differences between otherwise identical farm-households located in the same agro-ecological setting that can be attributed to their relationship with Fair Trade supply chains. The case studies almost exclusively focus on the impact at household and producer organisation level.

Program evaluations commonly distinguish between results on output, outcome and impact level. These results can be seen to be part of a chain: output leads to outcome and outcome leads to impact. Output results are defined as increased capacities of partner organisations to deliver outcomes at the level of the target group. Outcome results are defined as increased capacities of the target group to improve their living

[2] The study design maintained a strict methodological autonomy for the researchers and permits reliance on innovative methods for data collection and analysis.

conditions. Impact is defined as the (positive or negative) changes in living conditions of the target group, including both primary and long-term implications, direct and indirect effects as well as intended and unintended outcomes.[3]

Impact thus refers to differences in key socio-economic livelihood conditions and behavioural parameters that can be attributed to engagement in Fair Trade exchange. Current approaches for impact assessment focus on the micro (individual or household) level to identify the likely contributions to changes in living conditions and livelihood strategies of the target group (clients/beneficiaries) due to the support provided (White and Bamberger, 2008). In some cases, aggregation to village/regional level is pursued.

Research on impact assessment also addresses the so-called micro-macro interface, considering the role of the farmers' organisation (in charge of recollection, processing and export transactions) as the facilitating meso-level agency between the farmers and the market. Impact assessment of development interventions can be based on two broad approaches:

a. *before/after appraisal*: addressing changes in living conditions over a specified time period (e.g. comparing base line with ex-post survey);
b. *with/without appraisal*: addressing differences in behaviour and responses between the target group and a control group (composed of otherwise identical individuals). The development of the control group provides a counterfactual to the results reached by the target group.

The right combination of both approaches permits to assess the so-called '*difference-in-difference*', e.g. the before and after situation of both the target and the control group (see Box 1). This approach also provides fundamental insights in the relative success of supportive actions (i.e. investment or training projects; trade relationships), and excludes changes that are improperly related to wealth-biased client selection.

Impact studies focus attention on measuring farm household level impact of Fair Trade, making a simultaneous analysis of the changes in income and wealth between: (1) farmers involved in Fair Trade compared to their situation before the start of the program (before/after analysis), and (2) farmers involved in Fair Trade compared to other similar farmers delivering to the conventional market (with/without analysis). Such an analysis would require that field samples are collected regarding farmer's land use, production income and expenditures for two groups of farm-households (see Box 1): farmers involved in Fair Trade (treatment group) and other farmer's with similar intrinsic characteristics but not (yet) involved in Fair Trade (comparison group). Moreover, some recall information could be collected on the initial situation of both groups before the intervention started (base line). This also permits to identify which

[3] Impact analysis falls outside the scope of the formal monitoring and reporting cycle of most projects and thus needs to be assessed separately after some time of implementation of the program.

*Box 1. Impact assessment methodology.*

As base-line surveys that will allow to construct a 'first difference' estimator (A-E in Figure) are hardly available, we need to select a comparison group in the post-treatment state that closely resembles what would have been the situation of the Treatment Group if they would not have been treated (B).

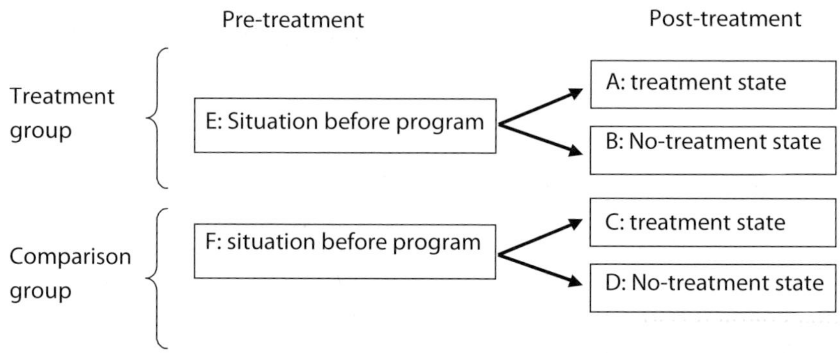


This can be done by using a so-called propensity score matching approach, that guarantees that relevant individual and group characteristics (like age, gender, farm size, education, years of membership) are maintained within the same range for both groups, so that individuals in the comparison group would have had similar chances of being treated than the ones in the treatment group. In terms of the Figure, the impact estimator is on the difference (A-D).

If base-line surveys for the pre-treatment situation are available, and include not only individuals in the treatment group but also individuals from the comparison group, this would allow an estimation of the impact of Fair Trade based on the changes in welfare between the treatment and the comparison group (equivalent to (A-E) – (D-F) in Figure 1). This so-called 'Difference-in-difference' approach permits to identify the real welfare improvements that can be attributed to Fair Trade involvement and corrects for the potential selection bias that frequently influences impact measurements.

type of farmers typically engage in Fair Trade and how they would have performed without the Fair Trade support (the so-called counterfactual).

The central issue on impact evaluation schemes resides on being able to answer the following question: 'What would have happened to a participant household if they would not have participated in the Fair Trade scheme?' This hypothetical situation is known as the counterfactual, and the way it is constructed is a key feature for correctly analysing the impact of a program or policy (Bourguignon, 1999). Problems arise since in cross-sectional studies we cannot observe both outcomes for the same individual at the same time. Just taking the mean outcome of non-participants as an approximation is likely to generate a 'selection bias', since participants and non-participants usually differ even in the absence of treatment.

We therefore relied on a 'matching approach' (Rubin, 1974; Rosenbaum and Rubin, 1983; Rubin and Thomas, 1996; Heckman *et al.*, 1997; Smith, 1997) as a solution for the selection problem. Its basic idea is to identify a group of non-participant who are similar to the participants in all relevant pre-treatment characteristics. Once that is accomplished, differences in outcomes of the control group and of participants can be fully attributed to the program.

Since identifying all relevant characteristics tends to be complicated, Rosenbaum and Rubin (1983) suggested to use so-called balancing scores, i.e. a function of relevant observed characteristics that gives a probability distribution that is independent of the participation in the program. A commonly used balancing score is the based on the probability of participating in the program as determined by a set of observable exogenous characteristics. Matching procedures based on this balancing score are known as Propensity Score Matching (PSM) and will be applied in the subsequent analysis of the Fair Trade (FT) impact (particularly in Chapters 2-5).

In order to implement the PSM estimation, data collection for the different case studies included not only a sample of farmers/workers participating in organisations with Fair Trade certification but also a sample of non-participant farmers/workers. An initial attempt to select organisations and farmers/workers with similar characteristics to the ones with FT certification was made in all cases.[4] After presenting the main characteristics and outcome variables for both groups, and comparing their means, we proceed with the estimation of the Propensity Score (p-score) by using a Probit model. Only variables that influence the participation decision, but not the outcome variables can be included in this model. The model should be build up based on economic theory, a sound knowledge of previous research, and information about the institutional settings.

The propensity score is estimated for each farmer in the complete sample by using the regression's predicted probability of having FT certification. With the distribution of the propensity scores we proceed to identify the regions of 'common-support'. These regions are set after eliminating the observations in the non-participant group with a p-score lower than the minimum p-score in the participant group, and the observations in the participant group with a p-score higher than the maximum p-score in the non-participant group. Further matching is only performed for observations that belong to this common-support.

[4] We used – when possible - the organisations member's registry to make an initial selection of farmers with similar crop areas. Wherever absent, snowball sampling methods were applied.

All matching estimators contrast the outcome of a treated individual with outcomes of comparison group members, and differ not only in the way the neighbourhood for each treated individual is defined but also with respect to the weights assigned to these neighbours. The most straightforward approach is the Nearest Neighbour matching estimator, where an individual from the comparison group is chosen as a matching partner for a treated individual that is closest in terms of propensity score (one-to-one matching). It is also suggested to use more than one nearest neighbour for each treated individual (the 2 or 3 closer ones for example) in order to reduce the variance of the estimator through reliance on more information in constructing the counterfactual for each individual. While these matching estimators use only a few observations from the comparison group for each treated individual, Kernel matching uses weighted averages of all individuals in the control group to construct the counterfactual outcome.[5]

## 4. Case studies

This study focuses on FT farming in 6 different countries: Peru, Costa Rica, Ecuador, Ghana, Kenya and Mexico. The sample of FT enterprises that were selected for the case studies responds to a number of general criteria. Each particular study therefore represents a typical case of the FT trajectory. We briefly outline the particular features of the selected case studies (see Table 1 for a full overview).[6]

The FT banana case in *Chira* valley, Northern Peru (Chapter 2) provides an ideal setting for studying the social, economic and environmental effects of FT banana production, including a sound comparison of conventional and organic production systems in a region where FT possesses an important market share. Moreover, the presence of different types of farmers' organisations in the same region enables to assess the institutional effects of FT compared to the counterfactual of non-FT farmers operating in similar circumstances.

The FT coffee study in Central Peru (Chapter 3) permits a thorough analysis of the socio-economic and organisational effects of FT within three different coffee cooperatives at different stages of involvement in FT deliveries (including a counterfactual of non-FT farmers in similar circumstances). Moreover, the study includes a detailed assessment of the FT premium effects, and addresses farmers' willingness to expand their coffee operations through hiring additional land.

[5] In general, the choice of a matching algorithm implies a trade-off between reduced variance of the estimator and an increased bias that results from including individuals from the comparison group that could be on average poorer matches. For that reason, our impact analysis of Fair Trade certification will present results for more than one matching algorithm.

[6] The case studies presented in Chapter 2-6 all apply matching procedures to control for selection bias. The production function comparison in Chapter 7 is based on an econometric test for non-pooling. The comparative studies included in Chapter 8 and 9 do not fully control for selection bias, but exogenous differences are acknowledged.

The impact assessment of FT banana production in Southern Costa Rica (Chapter 4) provides a unique opportunity to understand the operations of an associative enterprise as FT partner. Production in Coopetrabasur is managed under a common structure, where the cooperative is the owner of the land and the work is divided amongst members. Even while direct FT income effects are likely to be negligible, some other implications of FT on asset ownership and investments deserve major attention.

The analysis of FT coffee farming in Northern Costa Rica (Chapter 5) highlights the pitfalls of one of the early FT partners, Coopemontes de Oro R.L (part of Coocafe) in Guanacaste Province. Whereas earlier case studies confirm the positive effects related to the 'first-mover' advantage (Ronchi, 2002), more recent data indicate that - in the current dynamic setting of quality upgrading and higher coffee prices - the original comparative advantage can become seriously eroded. This study gives particular insights in the risks that FT certification might lead to certain (over)specialisation in coffee activities.

Particular attention is given to the impact of FT on the employees of VREL banana plantation in Ghana (Chapter 6), comparing – in addition to salaries, fringe benefits and working conditions – also workers' attitudes regarding job satisfaction, job security, corporate identification and sense of ownership. The latter aspects appear to be major distinguishing factors for workers in the FT plantation, even while concrete awareness of the meaning of FT is still relatively limited.

In the study on the impact of FT on farming in El Guabo cooperative in Ecuador (Chapter 7), specific attention is devoted to the differences between FT and non-FT farmers with respect to their production systems and willingness to investment. FT farmers reach considerable higher land and labour productivity under similar agro-ecological conditions, and thus there is still wide room for incorporating non-FT producers into the association as a first step towards improving yields and labour productivity (leading to better household incomes).

The comparative study of FT herbs (Kenya) and artisan handicraft products (Peru) enables to review some additional FT impact effects on less common indicators (see Chapter 8), like self esteem, life satisfaction, food consumption and dietary quality, child labour, infant morbidity, and education and schooling decisions. The study reveals that FT producers have a lower desired wage that is compensated by the superior provision of public or private goods and services. In addition, a positive and significant but non-linear effect of the duration of FT affiliation on the yield of the production activities is confirmed.

The final case study on FT coffee producers in Oaxaca, Mexico (Chapter 9) focuses on the production and income effects. In addition, FT and non-FT farmers are compared with respect to labour use, food security, migration tendencies and environmental practices. Important spill-over effects of FT to food consumption are registered, indicating that FT farmers are better able to satisfy their basic needs. It appears, however, that the guaranteed minimum FT price do not fully reach all producers and that it is losing a good deal of its value due to inflation. The author characterises Fair Trade as 'necessary, but not sufficient', indicating several required reforms in the FT system to enhance its impact.

The last two chapters included in this volume provide a more conceptual understanding of global FT impact at the levels of production, exchange and consumption. Chapter 10 discusses the implications of FT for global income distribution and the prospects for widening the FT movement through the incorporation of additional producers. Chapter 11 presents some ethical and moral imperatives of FT, arguing that governments should favour public standards that include FT aspects, thus enabling consumers to fulfil their moral duty towards fellow citizens.

All together, the case study included in this volume are expected to contribute further insights in the likely differences in FT impact between: (a) organisations with a different time-span of involvement in Fair Trade (e.g. focussing on possible learning effects during the Fair Trade life cycle and the prospects or limitations for their consolidation over time), and (b) differences in Fair Trade impact between specific types of rural grassroots organisations, focussing on a comparison between farmers' cooperatives, associative farm enterprises and farm workers in a plantation context.

Most of the field material collected for the different FT impact studies is based on a common sampling approach (outlined in section 3) and data collection methodology. The data analyses from the field studies in Peru and Costa Rica (presented in Chapter 2-6) rely on propensity score matching, while the studies on Ghana on Ecuador (Chapter 6 and 7) apply multiple regression techniques. The field studies from Kenya/Peru (Chapter 8) and Mexico (Chapter 9) are based on direct welfare differences but include some additional performance indicators. All studies mainly focus on individual farmers, except the Ghana study that concerns plantation workers.[7]

## 5. Direct welfare effects

The first and most well-known component of Fair Trade refers to the price guarantees offered to producers and the payment of a minimum price that is unaffected by fluctuations in the world price. International coffee prices were notably low in the early 1990s and between 2000 and 2005/06, but recently commodity prices have steadily gone up and world prices are now even higher than the FT minimum price. It should

[7] Implication of FT for the involvement of local wage labour and related salary payments are considered by looking at the division of tasks between family and hired (+ exchange) labour.

*Table 1. Overview of case studies.*

| Country | Enterprise | Establishment | Families | Sample size (N) |
|---|---|---|---|---|
| Peru (bananas) | | | | |
| FT | APVC | 2002 | 241 | 50 |
| Non-FT (organic) | APBOS | 2003 | 173 | 110 |
| Non-FT (conv.) | Indiv. producers | n.d. | >500 | 40 |
| Peru (coffee) | | | | |
| FT | CAC La Florida | 1966 | 1,250 | 60 |
| FT | CAC Pangoa | 1977 | 600 | 60 |
| FT | CAC Ubiriki | 1977 | 274 | 60 |
| Non-FT | CAC Tahuantinsuyo | 1975 | 233 | 60 |
| Non-FT | CAC Sangareni | 2004 | 293 | 60 |
| Non-FT | Ass. Productores Pichanaki | 2000 | 500 | 60 |
| Costa Rica (bananas) | | | | |
| FT | Coopetrabasur | 1980 | 70+100 | 50 |
| Non-FT | Finca San Pablo | 1968 | 200 | 50 |
| Costa Rica (coffee) | | | | |
| FT | Coopemontes de Oro R.L | 1984 | 286 | 50 |
| Non-FT | Café de Altura S.A | 2004 | 600 | 50 |
| Ghana (bananas) | | | | |
| FT | Volta River Estates | 1988 | 560 | 240 (50) |
| Non-FT | Golden Exotics | 2003 | 800 | 50 |
| Ecuador (bananas) | | | | |
| FT | El Guabo | 1998 | 400 | 57 |
| Non-FT | Independent farmers | n.d | > 500 | 63 |
| Kenya (herbs) | | | | |
| FT | Meru herbs | 1991 | 430 | 30+30 |
| Non-FT | OnlyFruit (outgrower) & Ng'uuru Gakirwe | n.d. | n.d. | 30+30 |
| Peru (artisanal) | | | | |
| FT | Minka (Juliaca) | 1979 | 60 groups | 80 |
| FT | Allpa (Chulucanas) | 1981 | 100 groups | 80 |
| Non-FT | Juliaca and Chulucanas | n.d. | n.d. | 80 |
| Mexico (coffee) | | | | |
| FT | Michiza Cooperative | 1986 | 1,100 | 26 |
| Non-FT | Unorganised & CNC Fraternal | n.d. | >5,000 | 25 |

Note: n.d. = no data available.

be noted that most of the field work for the case studies included in this volume refer to the 2006-07 harvest when international prices were relatively high.[8]

The procedure used to assess the direct FT welfare effects is based on a detailed reconstruction of several key socio-economic indicators of the farm-households, following five consecutive steps:

1. We start reviewing the implication of FT for the *production, yields and prices* of major agricultural activities, enabling the calculation of gross and net profit margins.
2. This is aggregated to household level income by including other non-farm and off-farm activities (including remittances), providing information on the level and composition of *total household income* and possible trade-offs or complementarities between FT production and other household activities.
3. Yearly *household expenditures* are calculated in a separate procedure, based on the standard procedures that are used in rural poverty studies (Deaton, 1997). This also permits disaggregation into several spending categories (e.g. consumption, transport, education, housing, health care, etc.) to identify possible differences in income use between FT and non-FT households.[9]
4. Next, attention is given to the available *capital resources* (fixed assets, value of cattle, household durables, savings) and possibilities for borrowing (credit access) that provide an indication of relative household wealth. Current and past investments for house upgrading or land improvements are specifically registered to account for changes in the wealth status.
5. Finally, farmers are asked to indicate their subjective appreciation of past and expected future *welfare perceptions* (e.g. whether they consider that their position improved, remained the same or has deteriorated).

It should be noted that the variability amongst the case studies does not always permit to draw general conclusions. However, some overall tendencies can be discerned that deserve full consideration.

### *5.1. Farm production, yields, prices and profit*

In most case, involvement in FT has a clear and discernable impact on the production efforts made by farmers to improve output and/or yield of their key crops. This is particularly evident for banana farms, whereas in some coffee farms the relative expansion came at the expense of reduced efforts devoted to other (food) crops, thus leading to a greater dependency on FT sales.

[8] The Mexican case study (in chapter 9) refers, however, to the 2002-03 harvest in a period where regular coffee prices were considerably lower, leading to stronger FT price and income effects.

[9] It should be noted that the level of household expenditures is frequently higher than the family income, due to omitted information on minor income-generating activities, informal transfers and irregular costs. This is a quite common feature in budget studies concerning peasant economies (see: McNetting, 1993). In the FT setting, individual expenses realised through (credit provision from) the FT premium fund also accounts for part of the difference between farm income and household expenditures.

On the other hand, FT involvement tends to increase input applications and strongly improved crop productivity (particularly in organic banana and coffee production in Peru; see Chapter 2 and 3). Guaranteed market outlets and stable prices appear to give a strong incentive to FT producers to engage in yield-enhancing investments. There are still major margins available for further productivity improvement e.g. through innovative precision-farming production and harvesting regimes (see Chapter 7) and by upgrading the quality of deliveries (see Chapter 8).

It is interesting to note, however, that most important net income and profit effects are generally found amongst organic FT producers. Even while they make substantial more costs for input use and the adaptation of their crop management systems (while price differences between FT and organic products are rather small), the positive pay-off for organic FT producers is quite considerable and compares favourable to the smaller (and sometimes negative) differences in net returns realised by conventional FT producers. This may be a clear indication that intensification of input use pays off, while FT producers that stay in traditional segments are facing major constraints.

### *5.2. Household income*

Fair Trade producers receive stable (and sometimes higher) prices with the primary aim to increase their farming returns and household income. The household income includes net returns both from the production and sales of FT crops as well as from other farming and non-farming activities. This criterion thus captures the overall implications of FT production, including the possible substitution effects with other household activities. Whether or not a positive effect of FT on net household income is registered mainly depends on (a) the differences between gross and net returns (considering the costs for FT production), (b) the land and labour requirements for FT production (i.e. the net factor returns), and (c) the possible substitution of resource use for engagement in other income-generating activities (and the implications for the degree of income diversification).

The majority of the case studies clearly suggest that higher net incomes from FT production can be reached particularly in the FT + Organic segment (see Chapter 2-3 and 8). Income differences in the regular segment are usually smaller or occasionally not significant (Bacon, 2005).

Figure 1 summarises the full income effects at farm-household level for FT and Non-FT farmers registered in each of the case studies. With the exceptions of (conventional) coffee production in Peru and Costa Rica (see Chapter 3 and 5), positive average net household income effects are registered. This implies that net FT returns generally more than compensate for changes in income generated from other activities (like food crops, off-farm work and non-farm activities). When this is not the case, this can be attributed to (a) reduced returns from food production or (b) less labour time available for off/non-farm activities. Several case studies indicate that - even while income from other crops declined - food consumption and dietary intake of

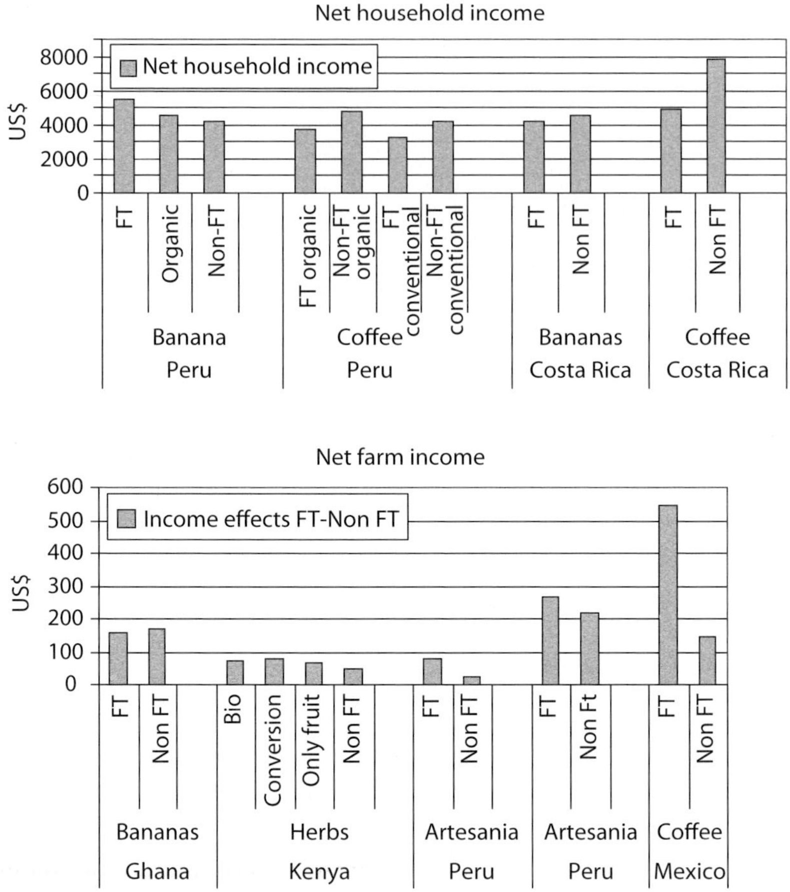


*Figure 1. Net income effects.*

FT households consistently improved, partly due to their larger purchasing power (see Chapter 8 and 9). Otherwise, also some positive spill-over effects from the FT crop to domestic food production are registered, based on improved input use (seeds, fertilisers) in other cropping activities funded by returns from FT production.

In addition to net household income, attention should be given to differences in factor productivity. When a higher production volume is reached with far more use of land, labour or capital resources, marginal factor returns may decrease. For a final judgement regarding the FT impact on household income, it is therefore important to account for differences in land and labour productivity. Many FT producers devote considerable more labour resources to crop management and quality maintenance activities, particularly when organic practices are used. This may lead to only small gains in terms of net daily labour rewards. The increased labour requirements can either be filled-in with family labour or hired (wage) labour. Interestingly, we observe in the case studies on bananas in Peru (Chapter 2) and on coffee in Mexico (Chapter 9) that FT production enhances the use of hired labour, thus occasioning additional local employment opportunities. This additional demand is, however, only leading to a slightly higher rural wage in the Peruvian case of organic bananas. At the same time, family labour use sometimes declined and is partly substituted by hired labour (thus increasing home leisure time). An opposite situation is found in (organic) coffee production in Peru and Costa Rica, where less hired labour is used (further discussed in Section 6).

A final aspect refers to the composition of household/family income. In most of the case studies, revenues derived from FT activities represents by far the major income component, with an average income share between 70 to 90 percent.[10] As shown most explicitly in the Costa Rican coffee case (Chapter 5), FT tends to enhance activity specialisation and thus reduced the degree of income diversification. This tendency is particularly observed in settings where cooperatives are able to sell a major share of their production to FT outlets. A noteworthy exception is found amongst employees of the banana plantations is Ghana (see Chapter 7) that derive less than half of their monetary income from wage earnings. This low but stable income component provides, however, the starting capital for other family-based operations in small-scale business or trade that generate important additional revenues. Moreover, employees of the FT plantation have considerable more time and resources available to invest in their own family plots, thus realising significantly higher food production both for sales and for self-consumption. Whereas the FT salary only represents a minor income share, it enables important income diversification activities that reduce vulnerability and stabilise household livelihoods.

### *5.3. Household expenditures*

Differences in household expenditures are by far the most important overall indicator of FT impact and are generally considered as key welfare indicator. Even when some (significant) positive net revenues or total income effects are registered, minor differences appear in total household expenditures: only in banana production higher expenditure for FT producers are found, while significant negative effects appear in the Costa Rican coffee case.[11]

More detailed analyses of the composition of household expenditures over different spending categories reveal, however, that FT producers show consistently higher relative expenditure shares devoted to long-term investments in household durables, house improvements and particularly education (even when – like in the Costa Rican coffee case – total FT expenditures are lower). This implies that FT farmers may not

[10] In the case study on herbs and artesian activities (Chapter 8) the share of FT in total household income is not explicitly accounted. The case study on coffee producers in Mexico (Chapter 9) reveals that coffee revenues represent less than 50% of family income.

[11] The difference between income and expenditures can be attributed to several unregistered revenue components (i.e. remittances, returns from informal exchange and omitted irregular incomes) or understated cost components (i.e. costs of family labour, home-produced organic inputs, certification costs, etc.).

appear directly as wealthier, but that they allocate their disposable income to other spending purposes that are likely to improve - in the medium and long run – their welfare and asset position.

### 5.4. Capital, wealth and credit

Another important aspect for impact analysis refers to observed changes in assets or capital stocks. This indicates whether (past) returns have been invested in capital accumulation, and if FT households could benefit from improved credit access. Both capital resources and savings contribute to better economic prospects for future investments in income-enhancing activities that reinforce the capacity of households to withstand adverse shocks.

Almost without exception, the case studies reveal substantial and significant positive effects for FT households with respect to credit access and asset value. The delivery contracts with FT market outlets appear to offer a suitable collateral for increased borrowing with financial institutions. Most investments in assets concern household durables, some acquisition of cattle, and – to a minor extent – investments in land improvements and the acquisition (by hire or purchase) of new land

### 5.5. Welfare perceptions

In line with the earlier discussion on income and expenditures, welfare perceptions of FT producers regarding changes experiences during the last five years and expected changes in the next five years reveal minor and mostly non-significant differences with non-FT producers. Only banana producers in Costa Rica are somewhat sceptical about the future (see Chapter 4), mainly due the critical current margin between production costs and prices.

It should be noted that the questions about past and future welfare perceptions capture the subjective overall feelings of FT/non-FT producers within similar local and macro-economic settings. They do consider, however, the implicit appreciation for community-wide social investment made from the FT premium that accrue – by definition – to all households, independently of their FT affiliation.

## 6. Changes in livelihoods

In addition to standard welfare measures (i.e. income, consumption expenditures and assets) it will be particularly important to detect other behavioural responses (i.e. changes in attitudes, empowerment, etc.) as well as changes at the level of farmers' organisation that may result from FT involvement. Although common problems related to attribution and complementarities should be acknowledged, the before outlined matching framework permits to make a largely unbiased assessment of the importance of these less-tangible benefits of Fair Trade.

The study of the overall Fair Trade impact therefore included five additional dimensions that deserve to be considered:

- *spill-over effects*: implications of Fair Trade engagements for other aspects of rural livelihood strategies (i.e. changes in other crops, adjustments in labour use within/outside the household); discussed in section 6.
- *attitudinal response*: impact of FT on behaviour and/or preferences (e.g. risk attitudes, willingness to invest; self esteem, happiness); section 6.
- *changes in intra-household decision-making procedures*: particularly concerning gender roles and inter-generational investments in sustainable land use practices; see section 7.
- *institutional effects*: impact of FT on the internal and external organisation (i.e. support received from the cooperative, changes in bargaining power, etc.); see section 8.
- *externalities*: implications of Fair Trade that might accrue to all households living in the region (e.g. Fair Trade premium use; general trends in prices or wages); see section 9.

Combining these aspects into an integrated approach permits to generate simultaneously insights in the effectiveness and constraints of targeting efficiency (i.e. inclusion of the poor and possible leakages to non-poor), as well as the broad socio-economic implications of FT at different scale levels (individuals, households, farmers' organisation, village/region).

### 6.1. Spill-over effects

Spill-over effects refer to the implications of Fair Trade engagement for other economic household activities. This aspect is frequently neglected in many FT studies, that focus almost exclusively their attention on the additional income received from FT sales. In practice, however, FT producers are usually engaged in a wide range of activities, including food production (for consumption and sales), (seasonal) off-farm wage employment and non-farm own-account activities (trading, processing, repair, etc.). It is likely that the expanded opportunities for FT sales also have implications for the restructuring of these other activities.

The case studies from banana producers (Chapter 2 and 4) indicate that substitution of activities in this sector is barely occurring, since other activities are rather scarce. In the coffee sector, however, farm households are usually involved in multiple activities. It is indeed observed that income derived from these other farming activities significantly decreased (see Chapter 3 and 5), while also the contribution from off-farm and non-farm activities became reduced. The slightly negative productivity effect for conventional FT coffee in Peru could possibly be attributed to reduced family labour efforts, indicating that part of the FT price effects is 'consumed' in the form of higher leisure.[12] Similar effects are registered in Costa Rica (see Chapter 5) as the result of the strongly increasing dependency of household income on returns from coffee production.

Full specialisation on the FT crop could increase the vulnerability of rural households to (climatic and market) shocks. Producers that are engaged with several different market outlets - since FT delivery contracts cannot always absorb the full harvest – can also take advantage of risk diversification. Also plantation workers benefit from spill-over effects, especially if their wage income is supplemented with food production on own plots and with income from trading and simple processing activities (see Chapter 6). Somewhat lean labour conditions enable the plantation workers to devote considerable time to these other activities, in such a way that the salary represents only half of family income (and a third of household expenditures). Nevertheless, the stable wage income provides the necessary guarantee for engagement in these other, more risky activities.

In a similar vein, most of the case studies confirm that household food expenditures have increased as a result of FT engagement, even when direct income effects were sometimes negligibly small or even absent. This is most clearly confirmed in the study from Kenya (see Chapter 8) that reveals significantly higher food intake and dietary quality amongst FT producers. In Mexico, improved food security was mainly guaranteed through higher own food production, since food bought with cash only accounts for a third of FT families' total household expenses, compared to more than half for the non-FT group (see Chapter 9).

### *6.2. Risk attitudes and behavioural responses*

Involvement in FT is believed to strengthen some of the behavioural attitudes that are considered critical for household poverty alleviation. In our farmers' field survey, questions were incorporated related to farmers' risk attitudes, time preferences and willingness to invest, giving indications on their entrepreneurial potential and capacities (see Chapter 2-5 and 7). In addition, the plantation workers survey involved a series of attitudinal questions regarding their feelings of job security, job satisfaction, corporate identification and sense of co-ownership (see Chapter 6).

With the only exception of some coffee farmers,[13] FT producers are generally found to be significantly less risk-averse. This implies, that the guaranteed sales to the FT market enable them to undertake other - sometimes risky - activities that can reinforce in the medium and long run their household economy. This is also confirmed when

[12] Note that higher leisure in a peasantry environment should be considered as a welfare-improving device, in line with the view of Chayanov that welfare is based on a combination of income and leisure (see: Ellis, 1986).

[13] Most likely, FT coffee farmers that become more specialised in coffee production exhibit a higher risk aversion. These farmers are, however, willing to invest in new land to further increase coffee production.

analysing differences between FT and Non-FT producers with respect to their longer time horizon and their higher willingness to invest. In both cases, the FT engagement provides a kind of 'financial floor' that permits farmers either to intensify their production systems or to diversify their household livelihood activities.

Similar effects are registered in the assessment of behavioural implications of FT for farmers self esteem and life satisfaction (see Chapter 8) that are significantly favoured by FT engagement. Also in this case, the subjective effects of belonging to the FT movement and the derived improved certainty regarding to market outlets may be considered as important non-tangible FT effects.

## 7. Gender and environment

Involvement in Fair Trade is frequently advocated because of its expected implications for greater gender empowerment and improved environmental care (see: Milford, 2004; Murray *et al.*, 2003; Ronchi, 2002). Empirical evidence on these effects is, however, rather scarce and largely descriptive. The common idea is that Fair Trade guarantees could provide opportunities for more involvement of women in the production and processing activities, whereas stable prices are generally considered as a positive incentive for realising long-term investment in ecosystem improvement and quality-enhancing production and management practices (Bacon *et al.*, 2008).

Regarding gender empowerment, the case studies from Peru and Costa Rica provide rather mixed evidence. In banana production, the contribution of females to household income seems to decline, whereas the role of the male household head in five key decision domains (i.e. purchase of food, purchase of housing durables, education of children, agricultural production plan and credit request) became reinforced. In coffee production, similar but somewhat less pronounced tendencies are registered. Only in organic coffee production, joint decision making became more common, related to the greater labour demands for maintenance activities that reinforce the bargaining position of female household members. It is likely that these limited effects of FT on changing gender roles can be largely attributed to the dominant male control on monetary income sources (coffee revenues and FT premium). Moreover, membership of the cooperatives is still strongly male-biased.

With respect to sustainable land use practices, FT shows positive effects on the use of organic inputs and some reduction in the reliance on chemical fertilisers. Even while changes in variable inputs use are frequently observed, investment in land-attached improvements (e.g. soil conservation structures, terraces, contour rows, drainage, etc.) still remain scarce. Apparently, the lump-sum required for realising these investments is still prohibitively high and the FT premium is hardly available for these activities. Otherwise, it is also possible that insecure land rights could have inhibited in-depth investments in land improvements (Fort, 2007).

The case study from Mexico (Chapter 9) indicates, however, that FT producers have far more incentives for getting involved in the coffee renovation towards organic production with shade trees, especially when an additional price premium is received. Wherever improvements for making production systems more sustainable rely on intensification of labour use (i.e. for mulching, composting, manual weeding, etc), FT can provide a positive contribution. In combination with the registered improved access to credit (necessary for purchasing substitutes for chemical fertilisers), the prospects for more sustainable practices applied in FT systems are likely to be high.[14] This is also confirmed in our comparison between FT and non-FT banana farmers in Ecuador (Chapter 7) that clearly point to the fact that a shift from chemical to organic fertilisation and *sigatoka* control measures has the greatest potential for improving local farming systems and rural livelihoods.

## 8. The role of farmers' organisation

The overall positive and significant effect of FT involvement on the strengthening of local farmers' organisations and trade unions is a very important result of the impact assessment. Whereas organisational consolidation of cooperatives and farmers' associations has been mentioned from the outset as one of the key FT objectives (see Section 2), empirical evidence is still largely descriptive (see: Murray *et al.*, 2003; Ronchi, 2002).

We applied a wide range of different indicators to analyse in depth the potential implications of FT on local organisations. In most of the cases (see Chapter 2-7), members' opinion regarding the enhanced bargaining power of their organisation was strongly and favourably influenced by their FT affiliation. Moreover, the satisfaction rates regarding service provision (technical assistance, trade, etc.) proved to be high (except for coffee in Costa Rica). Many farmers thus perceive their organisations as a vital link to the FT channel, and also consider the support received from their organisation as an important guarantee for upgrading the quality and reliability of their deliveries.

In a similar vein, Fair Trade in a plantation setting proved to have a positive effect on workers' feelings of job security, corporate identification and even reinforces their sense of co-ownership (see Chapter 6). This latter aspect deserves close consideration, since the principle of worker participation tends to be increasingly considered as one of the key distinguishing criteria for Fair Trade (Murray and Raynolds, 2007). Interestingly enough, the indicator developed to measure 'organisational identification' appears to be largely not significant for most of the cooperative and associative enterprises (with the positive exception of organic FT coffee producers in Peru). This may point to some

[14] Note that organic production using more labour use may eventually reduce returns to land and labour in the short run, particularly when complementary inputs (that provide necessary nutrients and organic matter) are not sufficiently available.

important deficiencies in terms of information provision, membership involvement in internal decision-making procedures, and renovation of genuine leadership that many of the cooperatives are currently facing. As also indicated by answers to questions regarding familiarity with Fair Trade, the general knowledge about the significance of Fair Trade and the information on the use of the FT premium funds is not always widely distributed amongst the members.

It was originally envisaged that cooperatives with a longer trajectory of FT involvement are likely to be better off compared to recently affiliated FT producers. This so called 'life cycle' effect would indicate the advantages of prolonged FT participation. Empirical evidence points, however, in a somewhat different direction. Some of the early FT coffee cooperatives from Costa Rica seem to suffer from limited incentives for improving their production and organisation systems and might have lost their initial advantage (see Chapter 5). Otherwise, the detailed comparison of three cooperatives with a different number of years of FT deliveries in Peru reveals that FT cooperatives with a longer time period of affiliation possess significantly more assets and animal stock and have better access to credit, whereas more recently involved cooperatives still suffer from credit constraints and risk-averse behaviour (see Chapter 3). But this does not imply that coffee yields, net returns and profits are necessary higher in the 'older' cooperatives. Their established position may even give rise to certain neglect of production innovations and further engagement with conventional market channels. Finally, a positive initial but clearly non-linear life cycle effect – with declining marginal return over a longer time span – is confirmed in the study of FT artisan cooperatives in Peru (see Chapter 8). This is mainly attributed to strong learning effects in the early stage of FT affiliation that reinforce bargaining power.

## 9. Regional externalities

Most impact studies limit their attention to the farm-households that have been directly involved in Fair Trade deliveries. This implies that positive or negative implications for other farmers living in the same region are largely neglected. As indicated by Maseland and de Vaal (see Chapter 10, this volume), distributive implications of Fair Trade for other households deserve serious consideration. We therefore assessed the so-called spatial externalities of FT for non-FT producers.

Theory predicts that Fair Trade may cause a negative demand externality for producers outside FT cooperatives. Focussing on poorer farmers that still have a large scope for productivity improvement might therefore be an appropriate strategy for improving farm-household welfare without affecting other (non-FT) farmers. This requires, however, that additional benefits from FT are mainly invested in quality upgrading and not simply used for horizontal area expansion. This is indeed the strategy observed in the case studies from Ecuador (banana farmers shifting towards precision farming to increase yields) and Peru (coffee farmers investing a major share of the FT premium in credit and technical assistance).

Important positive spatial externalities from FT are registered in the Northern Peruvian region of *Valle de Chira*, where the strong expansion of (mainly organic) FT production leads to a general rise in market prices for non-FT bananas (see Chapter 2). Given the particular geographic properties of this area, it is unknown whether similar externality effects are to be expected elsewhere as well. In areas where FT production has reached a substantial market share (roughly beyond 30%), options for exercising local market power clearly become apparent. Otherwise, the Costa Rican coffee case study (see Chapter 5) indicates that full dependence on the FT channel may easily result in a monopsonic market structure that reduces incentives for activity diversification and quality upgrading.

In addition to price externalities, FT may also have a significant impact on the contract conditions for wage labour. This is clearly confirmed in the case of the Ghanaian banana plantation (See Chapter 6), where the collective labour arrangement signed with the FT firm VREL proved to provide the regional floor conditions for hiring wage labour. Basically, stipulations on salaries, working conditions and fringe benefits are incorporated by the Labour Union into the contract with other private plantations one year after they have been signed by the FT firm. This indicates that FT plantations and cooperatives might be able to exercise regional market power to influence general market conditions.

A particular type of externality is related to the FT Premium. According to FLO regulations, this premium accrues to the whole community and should therefore be invested in collective goods (like schooling, health care services, water and electricity, road infrastructure, etc.). In practice, many FT farmers express preference for using the FT premium to enhance their individual household welfare. Some intermediate solutions are therefore found by allocating the FT premium into programs for microcredit, school fees, health insurance, input provision and technical assistance activities (mostly limited to FT farmers).[15] As indicated in several of the case studies (see Chapter 2, 3, 5 and 9), the FT premium can represent a substantial amount of money that could also benefits the wider community, but in practice the rather 'isolated' management of the premium resources – without establishing effective interfaces with other community-oriented programs operated by local NGOs, voluntary groups (like funeral associations or savings and credit unions) as well as churches strongly limits the possibilities for reaching the desired multiplier effects.

Finally, we should acknowledge that the presented impact studies hardly considered possible implications of FT for changes in the value distribution throughout the supply chain. Since this was not part of the primary design of the study, capturing such dynamic effects requires a more thorough value chain approach (see: Ruben *et al.*, 2006, 2007; Gereffi and Korzeniewicz, 1994). Few studies are available that compare

[15] Occasionally, the FT premium is maintained on a bank account and used for short-term loans. This is particularly the case when the local FT committee faces constraints in reaching mutual consent for allocating the premium to collective investments.

value added distribution in FT supply chains. Ruben and van Eyk (2007) reviewed the input-output structure for four typical tropical fruit and vegetables chains in order to detect the distribution of value added amongst chain partners. On average, the stage located within developing countries captures between 9 and 32 percent of the f.o.b. (free on board) value, while the value share received by the growers ranges from 4 to 14 percent of the total retail price.[16] This indicates that the 'struggle on the margin' still opens scope for further bargaining, particularly since current tendencies towards vertical supply chain integration and upcoming new outgrower schemes tend to shift a larger share of the quality surveillance costs towards primary producers.

## 10. Summary

In an effort to synthesise the key findings of the different case studies - while recognising the diversified picture that emerges from reality – we present a concise overview of the most important FT impact effects (see Table 2).

Some important caveats of these results need to be acknowledged. First, a major limitation to observe long-term changes in FT impact is the notable absence of base-line studies.[17] Even while we applied careful matching, it remained sometimes difficult to select farmers in similar agro-ecological conditions and to include some FT cooperatives that have been subject to long-term targeted assistance, due to the absence of suitable comparative non-FT enterprises located in a similar production environment.

Second, most data was collected at household level, thus partly ignoring welfare effects derived from community-level activities. Institutional data regarding FT premium allocation was scarcely available (requests to FLO were denied with arguments of confidentiality). In most cases, we were able to reconstruct FT premium use over the last few years, also including questions regarding farmers' preferences for FT premium allocations. This provides useful insights in some current trade-offs between individual and collective decision-making. Also the costs for (organic, FLO, ISO and EurepGAP) certifications that are usually covered by the cooperatives are not fully considered.[18]

[16] International transport accounts for 11 to 21 percent of the retail price and thus captures a significant part of the value in the chain. The tax share in the supply chain is highly variable and ranges between 7 and 24 percent of the retail value. Importers' margins range from 8 till 26 percent. Finally, retailers capture between 34 to 46 percent of the consumer price (Ruben and Van Eyk, 2007).

[17] We originally conceived the option to build upon earlier field studies and repeat visits to the same - or similar - farmers, but this proved to be rather impossible due to insufficient registration of farmers' coordinates (e.g. hardly any names or GPS coordinates of producers were available).

[18] A detailed cost-benefit analysis of FLO certification is not readily available. At current (2007) prices, organic certification certainly pays off, whereas FT certification costs are sometimes considered prohibitively high, particularly for cooperatives with a large number of smallholder producers. See: Jaffee (2007) and Fridell (2007) for other critical remarks regarding current FT certification systems.

*Table 2. Summary findings of FT impact.*

| Indicator | FT | Non-FT | Remarks |
|---|---|---|---|
| Production and income effects | | | |
| • Crop production | + | - | particularly in bananas |
| • Crop yield | ++ | - | major effect in organic production |
| • Crop price | + | n.s. | higher price mainly for organic crops |
| • Other crops | - | + | more specialisation (esp. in coffee) |
| • Non/off-farm income | - | + | FT demands more on-farm labour use |
| Household expenditures | | | |
| • Net Household Income | + | - | except in conventional coffee |
| • Household Expenditures | n.s. | n.s. | |
| • Past/future perceptions | n.s. | n.s. | |
| Wealth and investments | | | |
| • Durable assets | + | - | mainly household durables |
| • Credit access | ++ | - | |
| • Land investments | + | - | mostly hire/lease, sometimes purchase |
| • Housing investments | + | - | |
| • Educational investments | + | - | even when total FT income is lower |
| Organisational reinforcement | | | |
| • Organisational force | + | - | decreasing with older cooperatives |
| • Organisational satisfaction | ++ | - | except when FT is only buyer (CR case) |
| • Organisational identification | n.s. | n.s. | positive in organic FT coops (Peru) |
| Gender and environment | | | |
| • Sustainable input use | + | - | particularly in organic systems |
| • Soil conservation investment | n.s. | n.s. | |
| • Female-based decisions | -/+ | n.s. | mostly negative (except organic coffee) |
| Regional externalities | | | |
| • Prices | + | +/- | particularly for (organic) bananas |
| • Wages | + | + | occasionally higher wage labour demand |
| • FT premium | n.s. | n.s. | accrues to all households |
| Risk behaviour | | | |
| • Risk acceptance | + | - | n.s. for FT coffee producers |
| • Willingness to invest | + | - | |

Note: + = general significant positive effect; ++ strong positive effect; - = general significant negative effect; +/- = mainly positive effects, but some negative outcomes; -/+ = mainly negative effects, but some positive outcomes; n.s. = not significant.

Finally, the impact analysis for the coffee and banana cases involves some major differences in terms of internal organisation (i.e. cooperatives/associations vs. plantation-type production) and related livelihood strategies for farmers and workers. Some FT banana plantations are involved in a process towards strengthening of co-ownership. This motivated to include a specific appraisal of ownership feelings of FT plantation workers and the organisational strength of FT cooperatives as key dimensions of the empowerment process. Within the sector of agrarian cooperatives, major differences in terms of the degree of collective action and shared innovation are registered. This makes it complicated to identify whether and how FT is tailored in line with the idiosyncrasy of local organisations. In general terms, there is little doubt that FT has reinforced the organisational potential of farmers and workers. Otherwise, evidence regarding the dynamics of organisational renewal and innovation is scarce (the case of Asoguabo presented in Chapter 7 is a positive example), and general consciousness about the significance of Fair Trade is fairly limited. This points to the fact that further deepening of FT might be required in order to be able to create and capture not only static, but particularly dynamic welfare effects.

## 11. Outlook and future challenges

The different impact analysis studies included in this volume all focus primarily at the micro-economic level of producer/worker households and their organisations. These insights can be, however, relevant starting points for further discussions about the perspectives of Fair Trade for reducing rural poverty and transforming global trade regimes.

Acknowledging the FT household-level advantages and constraints provides insights in the realistic dimensions and transfer mechanisms that are in force within FT supply chains. Even while important effects on asset accumulation, credit use, investments, expenditure patterns and organisational force are registered, the direct tangible net income effects remain fairly modest.[19] Externality effects on local prices and wages - reinforced through the FT premium use - that offer FT benefit to non-FT producers deserve far more attention. In addition, most significant changes are observed in several attitudinal aspects (i.e. improved risk behaviour, larger time-horizon and higher willingness to invest) that point to entrepreneurial responses to improved income certainty. Spill-over and outreach effects thus tend to dominate direct income effects. This may indicate that long-term delivery contract and the assurance of stable and large-scale market outlets are far more important FT features than the price advantage. Even while such messages might be more difficult to communicate towards large segments of consumers, it is more in line with FT reality than the simple transfer of an extra price margin.

In the current discussions on the future development potential of FT major attention is given to horizontal growth for improving market outlets and sales volumes. This seems fully justified, given the still limited share of FT sales in total commodity trade (i.e. FT coffee represents about 1.2% of the European market). With this small market

[19] Note that this limited direct income effect is partly due to relative high market prices during the period of field research, that reduce the influence of the FT price advantage.

size, many FT cooperatives can currently only sell part of their production directly to FT outlets (Renard, 2005). Consequently, the FLO price advantage and social premium transferred to producers represent in 2004 together roughly US$ 50 million in a total FT market valued at US$ 1.6 billion (based on: Raynolds and Long, 2007), thus offering a small, albeit important 3% extra value. Even while large annual FT growth rates are registered (up to 30-40% in terms of volume and value), the total marketed volume still remains small and further expansion depends on the involvement of large-scale retail networks and possibly mainstreaming of key elements of the FT approach towards international corporations.

This is a highly debated issue within the FT movement, where proponents of horizontal expansion and growth (i.e. involving more producers and finding additional market outlets) and other groups that advocate instead for deepening Fair Trade (i.e. FT as an alternative business model challenging the power structures of global capitalism; see Fridell, 2007) represent contesting viewpoints. Considering this debate against the background of the results from our impact analysis, the different positions might be less contradictory. Reaching scale in FT purchases at local level is found to be of fundamental importance for generating lasting behavioural and organisational effects. Moreover, sizable upwards trends in prices and wages can be realised once Fair Trade becomes a competitive regional player (i.e. capturing up to 30% or more of total regional production). It is therefore highly important for reinforcing its structural impact that Fair Trade reaches a stable and recognisable regional market share. On the other hand, full dependence only on single FT outlets is also not to be preferred, since this may reduce incentives for upgrading and affect their bargaining power position.

Other emancipatory aspects of the FT – related to its impact on gender empowerment, sustainable environmental management and organisational strength – still deserve key attention in shaping alternative business models. We found only scarce evidence of female empowerment in FT organisations and limited changes in household decision making procedures of FT farm-households. Attitudinal changes require better linkages between farm (production) and household (consumption) decisions. With respect to environmental implications, FT has most impact on (short-term) sustainable input use, but still remains short in stimulating (long-term) in-depth investments in soil quality and quality upgrading investments. This implies that due attention should be given to effective strategies for reinforcing positive gender and environment changes that are considered critical to guarantee the translation of Fair Trade into household welfare

The institutional strengthening of local organisations is one of the main results of the FT system. Farmers and plantation workers benefit from improved service provision, technical assistance, market outlet assurance and better access to credit facilities that lead to higher certainty and less risk-avoiding behaviour. This insurance function of FT that triggers local investments and asset accumulation might indeed be more relevant than the direct income-generation effects, and provides important prospects for durable poverty reduction (Lybbert *et al.*, 2004; Zimmerman and Carter, 2003).

The FT premium could further support this process if it is allowed to use premium funds for joint investment programs (in farmers' cooperatives) or for the transition to co-ownership regimes (in plantations). The parallel structure of premium committees is not always favourable for strengthening farmers organisation, and better alliances with other community networks (i.e. credit unions, village committees, school parents groups, etc) can contribute to large multiplier effects.

Finally, even while this study did not focus explicitly on the character of the supply chain relationships and the procedures for value added distribution throughout the supply chain, many FT farmers express a high esteem of their local organisation but limited influence on downstream linkages with other supply chain agents. Current certification systems are strongly focussed on upstream linkages with producers' organisations and provide little incentives for strengthening downstream cooperation (i.e. co-ownership and profit sharing in processing and distribution networks). When FT mainstreaming is further explored, it is likely that attention is broadened from common bargaining issues between FT producers and traders/importers towards strategies based on long-term business partnerships with shared strategic principles and common values (Kolk, 2005; Fowler, 2000). This may also imply that the current emphasis on producer/product certification needs to be broadened towards a strategy of full supply chain certification. Ultimately, the challenge then shifts to questions regarding how Fair Trade standards can become a public good that is considered of fundamental value for improving worldwide welfare distribution.

## References


Bacon, C.M., V.E. Mendez, S.R. Gliessman, D. Goodman and J.A. Fox (2008). *Confronting the Coffee Crisis: Fair Trade, Sustainable Livelihoods and Ecosystems in Mexico and Central America.* Cambridge Mass.: MIT Press.

Bacon, C. (2005). Confronting the Coffee Crisis: Can Fair Trade, Organic, and Specialty Coffees Reduce Small-Scale Farmers Vulnerability in Northern Nicaragua? *World Development* 33: 497-511.

Bourguignon, F. (1999). *The Mystery of the Vanishing Benefits.* World Bank Research Paper No. 2153. Washington: The World Bank.

Becchetti, L and M. Constantino (2006) *Fair Trade on Marginalized Producers: an Impact Analysis on Kenyan Farmers.* Rome: University of Rome. Working paper CEIS 220 / ECINEQ2006.

Calo, M. and T.A. Wise (2005). *Revaluing Peasant Coffee Production: Organic and Fair Trade Markets in Mexico.* Global Development and Environment Institute, Medford MA: Tufts University

Deaton, A. (1997). *The Analysis of Household Surveys: a Microeconomic Approach to Development Policy.* Baltimore/London: The Johns Hopkins University Press.

Ellis, F. (1986). *Peasant Economics: Farm Households and Agrarian Development.* Cambridge UK: Cambridge University Press.

Fort, R. (2007). *Property Rights after Market Liberalization Reforms: Land Titling and Investments in Rural Peru.* Wageningen: Wageningen Academic Publishers.

Fowler, A. (2000). Partnerships: Negotiating Relationships: a Resource for Non-governmental Development Organizations. Oxford: INTRAC.

Fridell, G. (2007). *Fair Trade Coffee: the Prospects and Pitfalls of Market-driven Social Justice.* Toronto: University of Toronto Press.

Gereffi, G. and Korzeniewicz, M. (1994). *Commodity Chains and Global Capitalism.* Westport, Conn: Preager.

Heckman, J., H. Ichimura and P. Todd (1997). Matching as an Econometric Evaluation Estimator: Evidence from Evaluating a Job Training Programme. *Review of Economic Studies* 64: 605-654.

Jaffee, D. (2007). *Brewing Justice: Fair Trade Coffee, Sustainability and Survival.* Berkeley: University of California Press.

Kolk, A. (2005). Corporate Social Responsibility in the Coffee Sector: the Dynamics of MNC Responses and Code Development. *European Management Journal* 23: 228-236.

Lybbert, T.J., C.B. Barett, S. Desta and D.L. Coppock (2004). Stochastic Wealth Dynamics and Risk Management among a Poor Population. *Economic Journal* 114: 750-777.

McNetting, R. (1993). *Smallholders, Householders: Farm Families and the Ecology of Intensive Sustainable Agriculture.* Stanford: Stanford University Press.

Milford, A. (2004). *Coffee, Co-operatives and Competition: The Impact of Fair Trade.* Bergen: Chr. Michelsen Institute.

Murray D., L. Raynolds and P. Taylor (2003). *One Cup at a time: Poverty Alleviation and Fair Trade Coffee in Latin America.* Colorado State University: Fair Trade Research Group.

Murray, D.L. and L.R. Raynolds (2007). Globalization and it Antinomies: Negotiating a Fair Trade Movement. In: L.T. Raynolds, D.L. Murray and J. Wilkinson (Eds.) *Fair Trade: The Challenges of Transforming Globalization,* London: Routledge, pp. 3-14.

Raynolds, L.T. and M.A. Long (2007). Fair/Alternative Trade: Historical and Empirical Dimensions. In: L.T. Raynolds, D.L. Murray and J. Wilkinson (Eds.) *Fair Trade: The Challenges of Transforming Globalization*, London: Routledge, pp. 15-32.

Renard, M-C (2005). Quality Certification, Regulation and Power in Fair Trade. *Journal of Rural Studies* 21: 419-431.

Ronchi, L. (2002). *The impact of Fair Trade on Producers and their Organizations: a Case Study with COOCAFE in Costa Rica.* Poverty Research Unit Working paper No 11. Brighton: University of Sussex.

Rosenbaum, P. and D. Rubin (1983). The Central Role of the Propensity Score in Observational Studies for Causal Effects. *Biometrika* 70: 41-50.

Ruben, R., M. Van Boekel, A. Van Tilburg and J. Trienekens, Eds. (2007). *Tropical food chains: Governance regimes for quality management.* Wageningen: Wageningen Academic Publishers.

Ruben, R. and K. Van Eyk (2007). The Dynamics of the Global Fruit and Vegetable Chains: Export-oriented Agriculture as a pro-poor Strategy? *Faith & Economics* 50: 42-63.

Ruben, R., M. Slingerland and H. Nijhoff (2006). *International Agro-food Chains and Networks as Instruments for Development.* Dordrecht: Kluwer-Springer Verlag.

Rubin, D. and N. Thomas (1996). Matching Using Estimated Propensity Scores: Relating Theory to Practice. *Biometrics* 52: 249-264.

Rubin, D. (1974). Estimating Causal Effects to Treatments in Randomised and Non-randomised Studies. *Journal of Educational Psychology* 66: 688-701.

Shreck, A. (2005). Resistance, Redistribution, and Power in the Fair Trade Banana Initiative. *Agriculture and Human Values* 22: 17-29.

Smith, H. (1997). Matching with Multiple Controls to Estimate Treatment Effects in Observational Studies. *Sociological Methodology* 27: 325-353.

White, H. and M. Bamberger (2008). Impact Evaluation in Official Development Agencies. Special Issue on Impact Evaluation. *IDS Bulletin* 39: 1-11.

Zimmerman, F.J. and M.R. Carter (2003). Asset Smoothing, Consumption Smoothing and the Reproduction of Inequality under Risk and Subsistence Constraints. *Journal of Development Economics* 71: 233-260.

# Chapter 2

## The impact of Fair Trade on banana producers in Northern Peru

*Ricardo Fort and Ruerd Ruben*

### 1. Introduction

Even though the principal objective of Fair Trade (FT) labelling is to provide small producers with new opportunities to improve their livelihoods, few studies can be found that analyse the effects of participating in this supply chain for the final beneficiaries. The basic question of '*what would have being the situation of the producers involved in FT if they had not participated*' is of key relevance and fundamental importance to evaluate the real impact of FT. The principal objective of this chapter is to answer this question by using information from a sample of FT banana producers in the north coast of Peru and comparing them with Non-FT producers with similar characteristics.

The expected effects that are likely to appear as a consequence of FT involvement can be of different sorts. First, the higher price that FT farmers usually get for their products will most likely increase their monetary income derived from the production of the FT commodity, even in the short run (Hayes, 2006). A change in relative prices, as well as the price stability that is part of the FT arrangement, can also create a specialisation effect with farmers concentrating more efforts on the production of the FT good and moving away from others (Fridell, 2004; Page and Slater, 2003). This behaviour will be more likely to appear when farmers have a favourable perception about FT benefits and a reliable relationship with their farmer's association.

Second, the investment made from the FT premium that is received by the farmer's association can generate different types of economic and social impacts on individual producers, depending on how the premium money is used (Socias Salva and Doblas, 2005). Provision of agricultural inputs, investments in large infrastructures, improvements in schools, provision of loans, are some of the commonly made expenditures with this premium. It is important to note that some of these investments (i.e. loans) can benefit only FT farmers, while other types of premium use (i.e. schools) also benefit other farmers living in the same area.

Third, if we combine these two principal effects of FT for smallholder producers, it is expected to observe also some changes in terms of household welfare after several years of FT involvement. Households' consumption expenditures, the value of durable goods and agricultural assets and animal stocks are likely to experience improvement. Finally, getting and maintaining the FT certification implies - amongst other things - using environmentally safe production techniques and a participatory process for decision making, which is expected to generate some changes in production process and in the perception of their organisation (Suranovic, 2002; Hamilton, 2001).

This study focuses attention on farm household level impact of Fair Trade participation, making a simultaneous analysis of the changes in income and wealth between farmers involved in Fair Trade compared to other similar farmers delivering to the conventional market (so-called with/without analysis).[1] Such an analysis requires that field data are collected regarding farmers land use, production income, assets and expenditures for two groups of households: farmers involved in Fair Trade (treatment group) and other farmers with similar intrinsic characteristics but not (yet) involved in Fair Trade (comparison or control group). Moreover, some information was collected on the changes in welfare, credit use and organisation during the last 3-5 years to assess differences in their situation before the intervention started. This also permits to identify which type of farmers typically engage in Fair Trade and how they might have performed without the Fair Trade support (the so-called counterfactual).

The remainder of this chapter is structured as follows: In section 2 we provide a short overview of the context in which certified FT banana production has emerged and is organised in the northern Piura region of Peru. Hereafter, we discuss in section 3 the criteria for the selection of the treatment and control groups for analysing the different expected impact effects mentioned before, as well as the sampling strategy used for choosing farm-households within each group. Section 4 presents the characteristics of farmers in each group and highlights the main differences found between them. In Section 5 we outline the propensity score matching technique applied to 'balance' the overall sample of farmers to be compared, and in Section 6 we analyse the difference between treatment and control groups for selected impact indicators. Section 7 explores the perception of farmers about their benefits from the use of the FT premium, and finally we present the conclusions for this study on Section 8.

## 2. Regional context: banana production in Chira Valley, Piura

Banana production for exports from Piura started in the beginning of the 1990's with the arrival of a few international traders to the region. First attempts to deliver the product to the USA and European markets failed because of quality problems and bad coordination between the different agents in the chain. Given the highly appropriate

[1] Due to the absence of a good base-line study concerning the situation before farmers engaged in Fair Trade, a real 'difference-in-difference' analysis of the changes in welfare before and after FT is not possible.

conditions of the Chira Valley to develop organic production,[2] the Agricultural Ministry started in 1999 a program to promote the production and export chain for organic banana from the region (Inurritegui, 2006). The program promoted producer's association and provided them with technical assistance as well as credit for the purchase of organic fertilisers and packing equipment.

As a result, several trading enterprises started to work in the Valley since the year 2000, increasing the volume of organic banana exports in more than 30 times its initial level in less than 5 years. Currently, there are only three export firms operating in the Valle: (1) *Biocosta*, that started in 2002 and provides products for *T.Port* in Germany; (2) *COPDEBAN/DOLE*, that started in 2001 and provides organic bananas to the US market; and (3) *Grupo Hualtaco*, that started in 2002 (previously called *Biorganika*) and concentrates more than 80 percent of their sales on organic Fair Trade bananas to the European market.

By the time this study, there were around 14 organisations of producers selling banana for exports to these traders. Most of them were associated to one of two Networks in the valley: (1) the *Central Piurana de Bananeros* Organicos (CEPIBO), functioning since 2004 with five member organisations; and (2) the *Red de Pequeños Productores de Banano Organico Comercio Justo* (REPEBAN), which started in 2005 with six member organisations. One of the oldest producers association in the valley - which does not belong to any of these networks - is the *Asociación de Productores de Banano Orgánico del Valle del Chira* (APVCH), established in 2001 by a group of farmers that are members of the Peasant Community of Querecotillo and Salitral. The Community exists since 1820 and is located in the Department of Piura, Province of Sullana, Districts of Querecotillo and Salitral. It currently counts with more than 6,000 peasants as affiliated members. Land is formally owned by the Community as a whole (title officially registered), but it is distributed equally among its members, each receiving around 1.5 hectares.

APVCH has a strong relationship with the *Grupo Hualtaco* with whom they worked since its formalisation, and the latter assisted them in obtaining their Organic and FT certifications. APVCH counts at this moment with 241 associates, 95% of them are organically certified since 2002, and the rest obtained certification since 2006. FT sales started also since 2002 and have being steadily increasing since then. This producers association was selected as the treatment group to evaluate the impact of FT, given the relatively longer period that their members have being able to benefit from Fair Trade engagement.

[2] The climatic conditions of the Chira Valley impede the development of Black Sigatoka which is one of the principal plagues affecting banana production. Therefore, the region offers ideal conditions for organic production.

## 3. Selection of banana producers for impact evaluation

While producers of the *Asosiación de Productores de Banano Orgánico del Valle del Chira* (APVCH) were selected as the treatment group, we decided to select two different control groups for this study. Given the idiosyncrasy of farmers belonging to the Peasant Community, and their structural difference with other farmers in the region who acquired land trough the Agrarian Reform, both control groups will be composed by Community farmers. The first group consists of farmers participating since the year 2003 in the *Asociacion de Productores de Banano Organico de Salitral* (APBOS), located in the District of Salitral.[3] This association, currently counts with 173 members who obtained FT certification at the beginning of 2007 but have not yet made any sales under this trademark.[4]

The second control group is composed by banana producers that belong to the Community, but are not associated in any organisation (consequently, they do not have FT) and do not have organic production of banana. This category of farmers can be considered as traditional banana producers. The main difference with the other groups is that these farmers are not integrated to the export chain and sell only to local intermediaries.

We collected information for 50 producers of APVCH, 110 producers of APBOS (= Control 1) and 40 non-associated producers of conventional banana (= Control 2), for a total number of 200 surveys. For the selection of APVCH and APBOS farmers we made use of the *Padron de Miembros* (List of all members) of these organisations, containing information on total farm size and the size of their banana plantation. Sample selection for control group 1 was done in two steps. First we randomly selected farmers from the APVCH group. Hereafter, we restricted the universe of farmers from APBOS to the ones with total farm size and size of their banana plantations within the range of the APVCH sample, and then we made a random sampling from this group. This procedure helps to obtain a better matching afterwards, and the matching helps to reduce the potential selection bias.

For the selection of non-associated conventional farmers (= control 2) we implemented another strategy. After finishing a questionnaire with a farmer from APVCH, the surveyor asked him to recommend two neighbouring farmers that are non-organic banana producers, but do not belong to any association and sell their product to local intermediaries. The surveyors then visited each of them and used some 'filter' questions before starting the interview. These initial questions provided confirmation

[3] APBOS is one of the Associations members of the CEPIBO network.

[4] We originally wanted to select from this group a sample of farmers with organic banana production and another sample with conventional banana production. However, this distinction could not be implemented in practice as there were only a few producers within the association that did not have organic certification or where not in transitional period to become organic producers. Moreover, we registered that even producers with parcels in transition to become organic are selling some percentage of their production as if they were already organic producers.

on the required farmer' characteristics (i.e. community member, non-organic banana producer, do not belong to any association, sale to local intermediaries). Field supervisors checked the questionnaires every night to ensure that farmers from Control-2 indeed match the required characteristics.

## 4. Characteristics of banana producers

The questionnaire format used for the field data collection is composed of ten sections that permit thorough and concise information gathering on farm-household characteristics, wealth and investments, perceptions on and degree of satisfaction with Fair Trade, gender participation and risk attitudes. Based on the survey questions, we constructed a set of indicators and indices that allow for comparison between the FT and non-FT producers. The survey included major information regarding the following issues:

a. household composition (e.g. family size, age, gender and education);
b. farm size and agricultural production;
c. economic indicators (income level and composition, expenditures, loans and savings);
d. assets and wealth (house, cattle, machinery, including investments in sustainable practices);
e. membership of local organisations;
f. farmers' perceptions regarding the past and future welfare impact of Fair Trade;
g. strength and bargaining power of farmers' organisations (force index);
h. degree of organisational identification (and satisfaction with the services provided);
i. changing gender incidence in household decisions;
j. use of environmental practices and organic inputs;
k. attitudes regarding risk.

Annex B provides a full overview of the indicators used in the survey questionnaire. Figure 1 gives an illustration of the main data categories and their mutual interactions.

The comparison of households between the three groups reveals some significant differences that need to be taken into account for an un-biased impact analysis (see Table 1). First, the household heads of the APVCH group have on average three years less of schooling than their counterpart in the APBOS group. Second, parcels in the Fair Trade APVCH group are located further away from the district's capital than the ones in the other two groups. Consequently, the travel time to the market and to their parcels is substantially longer. Third, the mean area of banana plantation in the APVCH group is larger than the average area for conventional farmers.

These variables - as well as some other variables that might affect expected outcomes from FT or influencing the probability of getting the FT certification - have to be taken

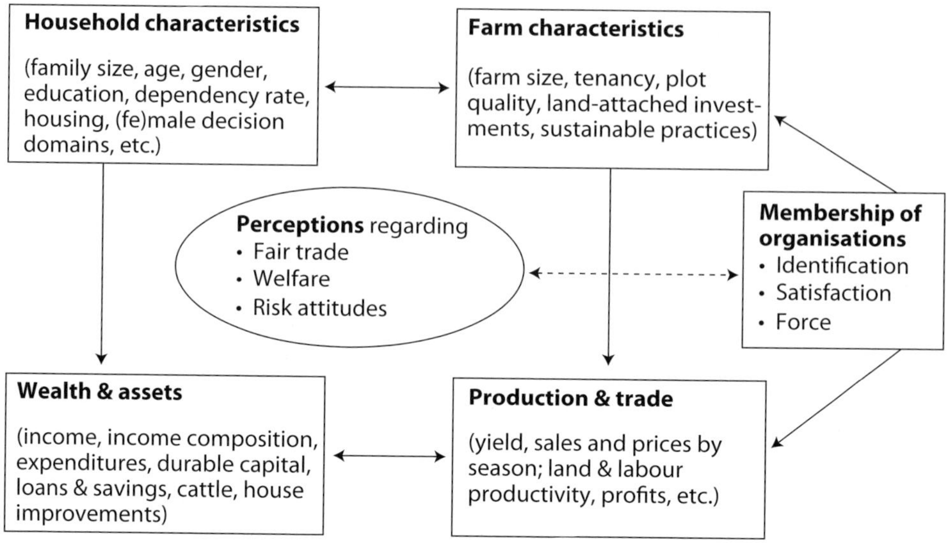


*Figure 1. Questionnaire design.*

into account in order to construct a good counterfactual for measuring the impact on FT producers. The survey design permits to identify the direct and indirect welfare effects of FT involvement at household level (both in terms of income and wealth, and considering income composition), including the complementary livelihood implications for other family activities (i.e. off-farm employment, investments in education, improvements in other cropping and non-farm activities). In addition, local/regional spill-over effects forthcoming from Fair Trade involvement on floor-level prices and wages for other farmers can be traced. Specific attention is given to the specification of attitudinal FT implications, particularly in terms of risk attitudes (willingness to invest), trust and organisational identification, the adoption of environmentally-friendly practices and changes in the gender role division.

## 5. Matching procedures for measuring the Fair Trade impact

The central issue on impact evaluation schemes requires answering the following question: 'What would have happened to a participant household if they would not have participated in the Fair Trade scheme?' This hypothetical situation is known as the counterfactual, and the way it is constructed is a key feature for correctly analysing the impact of a program or policy (Bourguignon, 1999). Problems arise since in cross-sectional studies we cannot observe both outcomes for the same individual at the same time. Just taking the mean outcome of non-participants as an approximation is likely to generate a 'selection bias', since participants and non-participants usually differ even in the absence of treatment.

*Table 1. Sample characteristics.*

| | Fair Trade | APBOS | Conventional | FT vs. APBOS | FT vs. Conventional |
|---|---|---|---|---|---|
| Variables | Mean | | | Significance / t-test ( p>\|t\| ) [2] | |
| **Household characteristics** | | | | | |
| Age head of household (years) | 55.4 | 53.9 | 56.5 | 0.56 | 0.71 |
| Education head of household (years) | 4.7 | 7.8 | 5.8 | 0.00 *** | 0.26 |
| Family size (number) | 4.1 | 4.1 | 3.6 | 0.99 | 0.16 |
| Migration (number) | 1.6 | 1.4 | 1.3 | 0.36 | 0.39 |
| Local residence (years living in community) | 29.5 | 27.7 | 33.3 | 0.50 | 0.22 |
| **Land** | | | | | |
| Area banana (Ha.) | 1.0 | 0.9 | 0.7 | 0.29 | 0.01 ** |
| Area other crops (Ha.) | 0.0 | 0.2 | 0.1 | 0.17 | 0.44 |
| Total productive area (Ha.) | 1.1 | 1.1 | 0.8 | 0.70 | 0.03 ** |
| **Accessibility** | | | | | |
| Time from parcel to capital (minutes) | 24.0 | 12.5 | 13.1 | 0.00 *** | 0.00 *** |
| Time from house to parcel (minutes) | 21.1 | 13.7 | 15.0 | 0.00 *** | 0.04 ** |
| Time from house to capital (minutes) | 8.7 | 3.6 | 3.9 | 0.00 *** | 0.02 ** |
| **Income** | | | | | |
| Salary income (soles) | 3,058 | 3,804 | 3,243 | 0.48 | 0.90 |
| Non-salary income (soles) | 938 | 1,898 | 2,121 | 0.19 | 0.22 |
| Gross income banana (soles) | 12,817 | 9,232 | 7,875 | 0.00 *** | 0.00 *** |
| Gross income other crops (soles) | 453 | 749 | 539 | 0.46 | 0.78 |
| Total gross income (soles) | 17,266 | 15,683 | 13,778 | 0.34 | 0.13 |
| Total net income (soles) | 15,572 | 13,026 | 11,752 | 0.09 * | 0.08 * |
| Profit banana production (soles) | 11,339 | 6,910 | 6,039 | 0.00 *** | 0.00 *** |
| Banana production (kg) | 27,924 | 20,509 | 21,449 | 0.00 *** | 0.08 * |
| Banana productivity (kg/Ha) | 27,712 | 23,492 | 32,132 | 0.02 ** | 0.14 |
| Price banana-high season (soles) | 0.5 | 0.4 | 0.3 | 0.17 | 0.00 *** |
| Price banana-low season (soles) | 0.5 | 0.5 | 0.4 | 0.97 | 0.01 ** |
| **Wealth** | | | | | |
| Yearly household expenditures (soles) | 10,061 | 10,893 | 7,225 | 0.36 | 0.01 ** |
| Value household durables (soles) | 1,892 | 1,653 | 1,276 | 0.59 | 0.25 |

*Table 1. Continued*

| Variables | Fair Trade | APBOS | Conventional | FT vs. APBOS | FT vs. Conventional |
|---|---|---|---|---|---|
| | Mean | | | Significance / t-test ( p>\| t \| ) [2] | |
| Value agricultural assets (soles) | 89.6 | 480.9 | 90.4 | 0.41 | 0.98 |
| Value of animals stock (soles) | 647 | 466 | 546 | 0.27 | 0.67 |
| Credit access (yes/no) | 0.6 | 0.4 | 0.3 | 0.04 ** | 0.00 *** |
| Amount of credit (soles) | 2,177 | 2,355 | 585 | 0.83 | 0.02 ** |
| Value of savings (soles) | 102 | 28 | 278 | 0.14 | 0.23 |
| Value household assets since 2000 (soles) | 1,527 | 1,344 | 949 | 0.66 | 0.23 |
| Value household assets until 1999 (soles) | 365 | 309 | 327 | 0.59 | 0.80 |
| Value agricultural assets since 2000 (soles) | 80.3 | 474 | 67 | 0.41 | 0.52 |
| Value agricultural assets until 1999 (soles) | 9.3 | 7.1 | 23.1 | 0.72 | 0.23 |
| **Investments** | | | | | |
| Made land-attached investment (yes/no) | 0.1 | 0.2 | 0.1 | 0.67 | 0.19 |
| Value of land-attached investments (soles) | 54.9 | 72.5 | 3.2 | 0.66 | 0.12 |
| Made land-attached investments (yes/no) | 0.1 | 0.1 | 0.1 | 0.80 | 0.63 |
| Made house improvement investments (yes/no) | 0.4 | 0.5 | 0.2 | 0.37 | 0.06 * |
| Investment in new bananas (soles) | 90.9 | 147.0 | 120.3 | 0.57 | 0.72 |
| Family labour jornales in banana (amount) | 201.5 | 290.9 | 120.6 | 0.39 | 0.00 *** |
| Hired labour jornales in banana (amount) | 30.5 | 20.8 | 6.3 | 0.38 | 0.08 * |
| Value of hired jornal (amount) | 13.6 | 13.0 | 12.8 | 0.50 | 0.44 |
| **Perceptions and participation[1]** | | | | | |
| Economic perception last 5 years (scale 1-3) | 1.7 | 1.8 | 2.0 | 0.42 | 0.11 |
| Economic perception next 5 years (scale 1-3) | 1.7 | 2.4 | 1.7 | 0.57 | 0.65 |
| Satisfaction with price (scale 1-10) | 4.4 | 5.1 | | 0.07 * | |
| Satisfaction with technical assistance (scale 1-10) | 7.1 | 6.2 | | 0.01 ** | |

*Table 1. Continued*

| Variables | Fair Trade | APBOS | Conventional | FT vs. APBOS | FT vs. Conventional |
|---|---|---|---|---|---|
| | Mean | | | Significance / t-test ( p>\| t \| ) [2] | |
| Satisfaction with trade (scale 1-10) | 6.8 | 6.1 | | 0.06 * | |
| Identification index (scale 1-10) | 3.8 | 3.6 | | 0.10 * | |
| Force index (scale 1-5) | 3.8 | 3.6 | | 0.00 *** | |
| Member of organisations (amount) | 3.9 | 3.9 | 2.7 | 0.98 | 0.00 *** |
| Number of organisations before 2000 | 2.1 | 2.2 | 2.1 | 0.65 | 0.79 |
| Number of organisations after 2000 | 1.8 | 1.7 | 0.5 | 0.72 | 0.00 *** |
| Willingness to buy land (soles) | 42,833 | 22,553 | 23,306 | 0.01 ** | 0.12 |
| Willingness to rent land (soles) | 4,004 | 2,370 | 1,761 | 0.02 ** | 0.04 ** |
| **Gender and environment** | | | | | |
| Number of decisions head of household | 1.7 | 1.3 | 1.1 | 0.23 | 0.13 |
| Number of decisions spouse | 0.5 | 0.4 | 0.4 | 0.52 | 0.38 |
| Number of joint decisions | 2.6 | 3.0 | 3.4 | 0.24 | 0.07 * |
| Number of environmental practices | 1.5 | 1.6 | 1.2 | 0.29 | 0.20 |
| Organic fertiliser used in banana (%) | 0.2 | 0.2 | 0.1 | 0.97 | 0.48 |
| Chemical fertiliser used in banana (%) | 0.3 | 0.2 | 0.3 | 0.69 | 0.60 |
| Organic fertiliser used in other crops (%) | 0.5 | 0.7 | 0.3 | 0.00 *** | 0.00 *** |
| Chemical fertiliser used in other crops (%) | 0.0 | 0.0 | 0.5 | 0.43 | 0.00 *** |
| **Risk attitude** | | | | | |
| Risk attitude (1 = high, 7 = low) | 3.9 | 4.4 | 4.8 | 0.04 * | 0.01 ** |
| Number of valid observations | 48 | 103 | 36 | | |

[1] Variable definitions:
- Economic perceptions: 1 = better off, 2 = same, 3 = worse off.
- Satisfaction scale: 1 = little satisfied to 7 = highly satisfied.
- Identification and force index: 1 = fully disagree to 5 = fully agree.

[2] Significant differences: *** sign at 99%; ** sign at 95%; * sign at 90%.

We relied on a 'matching approach' (Rubin, 1974; Rosenbaum and Rubin, 1983; Rubin and Thomas, 1996; Heckman *et al.*, 1997; Smith, 1997) as possible solution for the selection problem. Its basic idea is to find within a group of non-participants those individuals who are similar to the participants in all relevant pre-treatment characteristics *X*. Once that is accomplished, differences in outcomes of this adequate control group and of participants can be attributed to the program. Since conditioning on all relevant covariates might be limited in case of having a high dimensional vector *X*, Rosenbaum and Rubin (1983) suggest the use of so-called balancing scores *b(X)*, i.e. functions of the relevant observed covariates X such that the conditional distribution of *X* given by *b(X)* is independent of assignment into treatment. A commonly used balancing score in the literature is the based on the probability of participating in the program given observed characteristics *X*. Matching procedures based on this balancing score are known as Propensity Score Matching (PSM) and will be applied for our subsequent analysis of the Fair Trade (FT) impacts (Caliendo and Kopeing, 2005).

In order to implement the PSM estimation, data collection for the different case studies included not only a sample of farmers participating in organisations with Fair Trade certification but also a sample of non-participant farmers. After presenting the main characteristics and outcome variables for both groups, and comparing their means, we proceed with the estimation of the Propensity Score (p-score) by using a Probit model. Only real exogenous variables that influence the participation decision but are not influenced by FT participation should be included in this model. The propensity score is estimated for each farmer in the complete sample by using the regression's predicted probability of having FT certification. With the distribution of the propensity scores we proceed to identify the regions of 'common-support'. These regions are set after eliminating the observations in the non-participant group with a p-score lower than the minimum p-score in the participant group, and the observations in the participant group with a p-score higher than the maximum p-score in the non-participant group. The matching estimation is performed only for observations on this common-support. In order to 'balance' the sample of FT farmers with the samples of the two control groups we estimate the probability of having FT certification based on a set of exogenous characteristics and pre-treatment variables (see Table 2).

For the comparison between FT producers and members of APBOS we find a significant difference in terms of the level of education of the household head and the distance of the parcel to the district's capital. This later difference is maintained when comparing them with the sample of conventional farmers who also present a significantly smaller size of their banana parcels and a higher value of agricultural assets before the year 2000. More importantly, this model presents an overall explanatory power (according to the Pseudo $R^2$ reported) of around 21% for the comparison with APBOS and 27% for the sample of conventional farmers.

*Table 2. Likelihood of FT participation (Probit regression).*

| Variables | FT-Organic (APBOS) | | | FT-Conventional | | |
|---|---|---|---|---|---|---|
| | Coeff. | SE | Sign | Coeff. | SE | Sign |
| Age head of household | -0.015 | (0.014) | | 0.012 | (0.0189) | |
| Education head of household | -0.096 | (0.035) | ** | -0.020 | (0.049) | |
| Family size | 0.049 | (0.081) | | 0.153 | (0.123) | |
| Banana area | 0.085 | (0.242) | | 0.921 | (0.362) | ** |
| Area other crops | -0.594 | (0.599) | | -0.755 | (0.923) | |
| Time parcel to capital | 0.040 | (0.011) | *** | 0.049 | (0.016) | ** |
| Value agricultural assets until 1999 | 0.002 | (0.004) | | -0.007 | (0.003) | ** |
| Organisations before year 2000 | -0.055 | (0.146) | | 0.156 | (0.204) | |
| Years residing in the locality | 0.000 | (0.012) | | -0.030 | (0.018) | |
| Constant | 0.128 | (0.880) | | -1.898 | (1.281) | |
| | Number of Obs= 150 | | | Number of Obs = 84 | | |
| | LR $chi^2(9) = 38.95$ | | | LR $chi^2(9) = 31.43$ | | |
| | Prob > $chi^2 = 0.000$ | | | Prob > $chi^2 = 0.0002$ | | |
| | Pseudo $R^2 = 0.2071$ | | | Pseudo $R^2 = 0.2739$ | | |

Note: Standard errors in parentheses. * significant at 10%; ** significant at 5%; *** significant at 1%.

Based on the results of these regressions we proceed by estimating the propensity score (p-score = predicted probability of having FT certification) for each comparison (FT-Organic/APBOS; FT-Conventional) and identifying the regions of 'common-support'. These regions are set after eliminating some observations in the control group (1) with a p-score lower than the minimum p-score in the treatment group, or (2) taking out observations in the treatment group with a p-score higher than the maximum p-score in the control group (see Annex A). The matching estimation is performed for both comparisons on common-support observations.

Matching estimators contrast the outcome of a treated individual with outcomes of comparison group members, and differ not only in the way the neighbourhood for each treated individual is defined but also with respect to the weights assigned to these neighbours. We used three different matching algorithms to check the robustness of the results to the method applied:

a. Kernel matching is a non-parametric matching estimator that uses weighted averages of all individuals in the control group to construct the counterfactual outcome.
b. One-to-One matching (with replacement) chooses for each treatment observation the observation in the control group that is closest in terms of propensity score.
c. Nearest Neighbour matching (3) uses a weighted average of the three closest neighbours in terms of propensity scores for each treatment observation.

Given the small size of our sample (in particular of the control groups) and the strong restrictions placed on the common-support, we will mainly rely on the results from the Kernel matching in discussing our findings. Because the principal idea of the propensity score matching technique is to balance the treatment and control samples by using the propensity scores derived from these regressions, we carry out two methods to assess the reliability and robustness of our approach. Annex Table A2 shows the results of the same Probit regressions but this time only considering the observations that are used for the matching. We also present a plot of the distribution of the estimated propensity scores before and after the matching is done (see Annex Figures A1 and A2). Overall variability is largely reduced and the distributions of the propensity scores reveal now a more balanced sample.

## 6. Results

Only few studies have been made concerning the FT impact for bananas, whereas many studies are available on coffee. We present the first comprehensive results of the comparisons between (a) FT banana and non-FT banana farmers both involved in organic production (see Table 3) and (b) FT banana farmers with conventional non-FT banana farmers (Table 4). These results provide a new insight in the real welfare and attitudinal implications of FT involvement, compared to farmers that have otherwise identical intrinsic characteristics.

In terms of the comparison between FT banana producers and organic non-FT producers from APBOS (see Table 3), we observe a significant difference on net household income which is mainly driven by a higher productivity in banana production. It is interesting to note that the difference in profits is obtained despite the similarity of banana prices for farmers in both organisations (prices for organic banana and organic-FT banana are very close). The net income and the profits for FT producers are significantly higher, and this is almost exclusively due to bananas (income derived from other crops is low and not significantly different).

Although we do not find significant differences in total household expenditures, FT farmers present a higher value of household assets and also receive more credit than the controls. The value of household assets acquired since the year 2000 is significantly higher than the one for the controls, which may imply that FT farmers invested a large proportion of their extra earnings on these improvements. Another impact of FT in terms of household wealth can be derived from the perception of higher land values. The price that an average FT household is willing to pay for an additional parcel with the same characteristics as his own plot (i.e. willingness to buy) is almost double the price for an average farmer from APBOS. In other areas, FT producers are also more identified with their organisation (higher Identification index) and more convinced of their good bargaining capacity (Force index). Finally, FT banana farmers are less risk-averse compared to APBOS producers, indicating their willingness to engage in higher return activities

Broadly similar results are obtained when comparing FT producers with Conventional farmers (see Table 4), but this time the higher income in banana production is mainly driven by the price difference rather than banana productivity. Moreover, FT farmers make substantially more land-attached investments. Conventional farmers are more affected by local market conditions during the high-season when excess supply drives banana prices down. Despite this price difference, it is very important to notice that the introduction of the FT market for banana producers in the valley seems to have an important effect on local farm-gate prices for conventional banana. As many key informants in the valley suggested, local retailers who buy conventional banana for markets in the region and in Lima appear to have being forced to increase prices in order to maintain their providers working with them. As we can observe in Figure 2, the price for conventional banana in the valley (cents per kg) has being increasing together with the amount of organic and FT banana exports (in thousands of tons). This suggests that other (non-FT) farmers also received the benefits of the higher average banana price, thus leading to important externalities of FT for the whole region.

Total household expenditures are also significantly higher for FT farmers when compared to the non-FT group, reflecting an overall welfare effect of FT. Important new differences emerge in terms of the larger number of jornales used for banana production, and the increased use of organic fertilisers while reducing reliance on chemical fertiliser. FT farmers do not only use more family labour for this activity but also employ more wage labour from outside the household. This fact, together with the increased willingness to bear risk, seems to indicate that FT farmers are

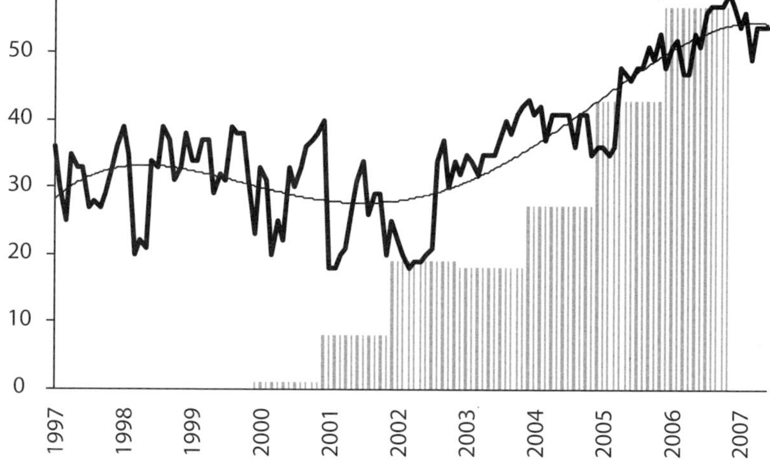


*Figure 2. Banana exports and price of conventional banana in Piura.*
*Source: based on Sisagri database-Ministry of Agriculture and Prompex database.*

*Table 3. FT vs. non-FT organic bananas (APBOS).*

| Variable | Kernel | | | One to one | | | Near neighbour(3) | | |
|---|---|---|---|---|---|---|---|---|---|
| | Difference | S.E. | t-stat | Difference | S.E. | t-stat | Difference | S.E. | t-stat |
| **Income** | | | | | | | | | |
| Salary income | 711 | 1,001 | 0.71 | 1,094 | 1,335 | 0.82 | 1,204 | 1,169 | 1.03 |
| Non-salary income | 16 | 667 | 0.02 | -1,463 | 996 | -1.47 | 16 | 659 | 0.02 |
| Gross income banana | 2,864 | 1,593 | 1.80* | 4,015 | 1,626 | 2.47** | 2,777 | 1,639 | 1.69* |
| Gross income other crops | 9 | 321 | 0.03 | -128 | 518 | -0.25 | -85 | 512 | -0.17 |
| Total gross income | 3,600 | 1,802 | 2.00** | 3,518 | 2,146 | 1.64* | 3,771 | 2,128 | 1.77* |
| Total net income | 4,252 | 1,582 | 2.69*** | 3,928 | 1,890 | 2.08** | 4,432 | 1,953 | 2.27** |
| Profit banana production | 3,559 | 1,375 | 2.59** | 4,440 | 1,444 | 3.08*** | 3,464 | 1,413 | 2.45** |
| Banana production (kg) | 6,007 | 3,251 | 1.85* | 8,339 | 3,670 | 2.27** | 5,685 | 3,420 | 1.66 |
| Banana productivity (kg/Ha) | 5,338 | 2,123 | 2.51** | 4,615 | 2,961 | 1.56* | 5,489 | 2,629 | 2.09** |
| Price banana-high season | 0.00 | 0.01 | 0.50 | 0.01 | 0.01 | 0.51 | 0.01 | 0.01 | 0.52 |
| Price banana-low season | 0.00 | 0.01 | 0.47 | 0.01 | 0.01 | 0.60 | 0.00 | 0.01 | 0.26 |
| **Wealth** | | | | | | | | | |
| Household expenditures | -101 | 1,091 | -0.09 | 1,414 | 1,294 | 1.09 | 115 | 1,196 | 0.10 |
| Value household durables | 1,062 | 407 | 2.61** | 680 | 592 | 1.15 | 1,109 | 472 | 2.35** |
| Value agricultural assets | -225 | 137 | -1.64 | -198 | 248 | -0.80 | -137 | 245 | -0.56 |
| Value of animals stock | -297 | 185 | -1.61 | -340 | 280 | -1.21 | -376 | 244 | -1.54 |
| Credit Access | 0.29 | 0.10 | 2.89*** | 0.29 | 0.14 | 2.07** | 0.28 | 0.13 | 2.16** |
| Amount of credit | 1,225 | 645 | 1.90* | 1,355 | 647 | 2.09** | 1,374 | 633 | 2.17** |
| Value of savings | -350 | 262 | -1.34 | -202 | 214 | -0.95 | -208 | 281 | -0.74 |
| Value household assets since 2000 | 817 | 397 | 2.06** | 380 | 564 | 0.67 | 872 | 432 | 2.02** |
| Value agricultural assets since 2000 | -223 | 146 | -1.53 | -200 | 232 | -0.86 | -136 | 240 | -0.57 |
| **Investments** | | | | | | | | | |
| Have land-attached investment | -0.02 | 0.09 | -0.26 | -0.02 | 0.13 | -0.18 | -0.06 | 0.12 | -0.46 |
| Value of land-attached investments | -11 | 43 | -0.26 | -7 | 58 | -0.11 | -35 | 58 | -0.60 |
| Made new land-attached investment | -0.01 | 0.07 | -0.13 | 0.00 | 0.10 | 0.00 | -0.04 | 0.08 | -0.48 |
| Made house improvements | -0.07 | 0.11 | -0.61 | -0.07 | 0.14 | -0.51 | -0.06 | 0.13 | -0.42 |
| Investment in new bananas | 5 | 12 | 0.42 | 4 | 16 | 0.23 | 10 | 13 | 0.80 |

*Table 3. FT vs. non-FT organic bananas (APBOS).*

| Variable | Kernel | | | One to one | | | Near neighbour(3) | | |
|---|---|---|---|---|---|---|---|---|---|
| | Difference | S.E. | t-stat | Difference | S.E. | t-stat | Difference | S.E. | t-stat |
| Family labour jornales in banana | -136 | 120 | -1.13 | -112 | 98 | -1.14 | -106 | 119 | -0.89 |
| Hired labour jornales in banana | 13 | 17 | 0.74 | 11 | 18 | 0.62 | 18 | 16 | 1.13 |
| Value of hired jornal | 2 | 1 | 1.25 | 2 | 1 | 1.24 | 2 | 1 | 1.72* |
| **Perceptions and participation** | | | | | | | | | |
| Economic perception-1 | 0.11 | 0.21 | 0.51 | -0.07 | 0.25 | -0.28 | 0.08 | 0.22 | 0.35 |
| Economic perception-2 | -2.30 | 2.95 | -0.78 | 0.31 | 2.07 | 0.15 | -1.04 | 2.27 | -0.46 |
| Satisfaction price | -0.61 | 0.50 | -1.20 | -0.21 | 0.59 | -0.36 | -0.67 | 0.55 | -1.21 |
| Satisfaction technical assistance | 0.81 | 0.52 | 1.56 | 0.50 | 0.62 | 0.80 | 0.66 | 0.53 | 1.24 |
| Satisfaction trade | 0.79 | 0.48 | 1.63* | 0.88 | 0.61 | 1.45 | 0.86 | 0.58 | 1.48 |
| Identification index | 0.25 | 0.15 | 1.66* | 0.21 | 0.19 | 1.09 | 0.23 | 0.17 | 1.35 |
| Force index | 0.24 | 0.10 | 2.49** | 0.21 | 0.12 | 1.75* | 0.24 | 0.11 | 2.13** |
| Number organisations | 0.30 | 0.26 | 1.16 | 0.31 | 0.27 | 1.13 | 0.33 | 0.24 | 1.34 |
| Number of organisations after 2000 | 0.26 | 0.22 | 1.16 | 0.19 | 0.26 | 0.74 | 0.31 | 0.25 | 1.25 |
| Willingness to buy | 20,004 | 11,211 | 1.78* | 24,405 | 11,978 | 2.04** | 20,976 | 11,121 | 1.89* |
| Willingness to rent | 1,853 | 1,123 | 1.65* | 1,662 | 1,133 | 1.47 | 1,690 | 1,100 | 1.54 |
| **Gender and environment** | | | | | | | | | |
| Number decisions head household | 0.27 | 0.44 | 0.61 | 0.21 | 0.48 | 0.45 | 0.40 | 0.41 | 0.96 |
| Number decisions spouse | 0.15 | 0.19 | 0.77 | 0.21 | 0.19 | 1.10 | 0.24 | 0.18 | 1.35 |
| Number decisions both | -0.24 | 0.47 | -0.50 | -0.21 | 0.57 | -0.37 | -0.48 | 0.57 | -0.84 |
| Number environmental practices | -0.27 | 0.17 | -1.61* | -0.29 | 0.21 | -1.38 | -0.27 | 0.18 | -1.53 |
| Organic fertiliser in banana | 0.00 | 0.01 | 0.32 | 0.01*** | 0.01 | 0.55 | 0.01 | 0.01 | 0.96 |
| Chemical fertiliser in banana | 0.00 | 0.02 | 0.24 | -0.01 | 0.03 | -0.22 | 0.00 | 0.02 | -0.16 |
| Organic fertiliser in other crops | -0.20 | 0.06 | -3.36*** | -0.23 | 0.07 | -3.25*** | -0.23 | 0.07 | -3.23*** |
| Chemical fertiliser in other crops | -0.01 | 0.03 | -0.59 | 0.02 | 0.03 | 0.72 | 0.00 | 0.03 | -0.17 |
| **Risk attitude** | | | | | | | | | |
| Risk attitude | -0.69 | 0.34 | -2.05** | -0.54 | 0.46 | -1.17 | -0.65 | 0.36 | -1.80* |

Note: t-stat >2.66 = *** sign. at 99%; T-stat >2.00 = ** sign. at 95%; T-stat > 1.67 = * sign. at 90%.

*Table 4. Fair Trade vs. conventional bananas.*

| Variable | Kernel | | | One to one | | | Near neighbour(3) | | |
|---|---|---|---|---|---|---|---|---|---|
| | Difference | S.E. | t-stat | Difference | S.E. | t-stat | Difference | S.E. | t-stat |
| **Income** | | | | | | | | | |
| Salary income | 555 | 1,708 | 0.33 | 603 | 1,835 | 0.33 | 1,542 | 1,647 | 0.94 |
| Non-salary income | -1,896 | 2,361 | -0.80 | -379 | 2,669 | -0.14 | -1,896 | 2,550 | -0.74 |
| Gross income banana | 3,357 | 2,059 | 1.63* | 4,944 | 2,596 | 1.90* | 3,885 | 2,364 | 1.64* |
| Gross income other crops | -8 | 386 | -0.02 | 91 | 404 | 0.22 | -33 | 371 | -0.09 |
| Total gross income | 2,008 | 3,272 | 0.61 | 5,259 | 3,358 | 1.57 | 2,427 | 3,167 | 0.77 |
| Total net income | 2,801 | 2,968 | 0.94 | 5,573 | 3,426 | 1.63* | 3,452 | 3,104 | 1.11 |
| Profit banana production | 4,243 | 1,942 | 2.18** | 5,355 | 2,929 | 1.83* | 5,020 | 2,357 | 2.13** |
| Banana production (kg) | 3,733 | 4,570 | 0.82 | 7,045 | 5,830 | 1.21 | 4,662 | 6,189 | 0.75 |
| Banana productivity (kg/Ha) | 3,609 | 5,336 | 0.68 | 3,343 | 5,124 | 0.65 | 5,267 | 5,245 | 1.00 |
| Price banana-high season | 0.14 | 0.02 | 6.67*** | 0.14 | 0.03 | 5.55*** | 0.14 | 0.02 | 6.08*** |
| Price banana-low season | 0.02 | 0.01 | 1.78** | 0.03 | 0.01 | 1.96* | 0.02 | 0.02 | 1.61* |
| **Wealth** | | | | | | | | | |
| Household expenditures | 3,392 | 1,551 | 2.19** | 3,470 | 1,231 | 2.82*** | 3,021 | 1,297 | 2.33*** |
| Value household durables | 891 | 599 | 1.49 | 912 | 667 | 1.37 | 1,068 | 595 | 1.79* |
| Value agricultural assets | 35 | 33 | 1.05 | -5 | 37 | -0.13 | 22 | 30 | 0.74 |
| Value of animals stock | 183 | 301 | 0.61 | 169 | 328 | 0.52 | 204 | 314 | 0.65 |
| Credit access | 0.30 | 0.18 | 1.70* | 0.38 | 0.19 | 2.06** | 0.32 | 0.19 | 1.75* |
| Amount of credit | 1,198 | 516 | 2.32** | 1,994 | 722 | 2.76*** | 1,882 | 690 | 2.73*** |
| Value of savings | 64 | 125 | 0.51 | 85 | 99 | 0.86 | 99 | 124 | 0.79 |
| Value household assets since 2000 | 588 | 530 | 1.11 | 588 | 644 | 0.91 | 748 | 503 | 1.49 |
| Value agricultural assets since 2000 | 24 | 30 | 0.82 | -12 | 31 | -0.40 | 14 | 27 | 0.51 |
| **Investments** | | | | | | | | | |
| Have land-attached investment | 0.08 | 0.06 | 1.33 | 0.10 | 0.05 | 2.01** | 0.09 | 0.06 | 1.69* |
| Value of land-attached invest | 7 | 6 | 1.21 | 20 | 14 | 1.47 | 19 | 14 | 1.42 |
| Made land-attached investment | 0.02 | 0.03 | 0.61 | 0.05 | 0.04 | 1.23 | 0.04 | 0.04 | 1.19 |
| Made house improvement | 0.16 | 0.18 | 0.87 | -0.05 | 0.20 | -0.25 | 0.09 | 0.19 | 0.50 |
| Investment in new bananas | -36 | 34 | -1.07 | -34 | 27 | -1.25 | -8 | 36 | -0.23 |
| Family labour jornales in banana | 97 | 35 | 2.76*** | 76 | 29 | 2.63** | 82 | 27 | 3.05*** |

*Table 4. Fair Trade vs. conventional bananas.*

| | Kernel | | | One to one | | | Near neighbour(3) | | |
|---|---|---|---|---|---|---|---|---|---|
| Variable | Difference | S.E. | t-stat | Difference | S.E. | t-stat | Difference | S.E. | t-stat |
| Hired labour jornales in banana | 23 | 13 | 1.79* | 30 | 13 | 2.25** | 30 | 12 | 2.37** |
| Value of hired jornal | -4 | 4 | -0.87 | -5 | 4 | -1.47 | 0 | 3 | -0.10 |
| **Perception and participation** | | | | | | | | | |
| Economic perception1 | -0.33 | 0.31 | -1.04 | -0.77 | 0.41 | -1.89* | -0.36 | 0.31 | -1.18 |
| Economic perception2 | -0.11 | 0.31 | -0.35 | -0.36 | 0.37 | -0.97 | -0.03 | 0.29 | -0.12 |
| Number organisations | 1.32 | 0.33 | 3.99*** | 1.33 | 0.33 | 4.04*** | 1.31 | 0.30 | 4.40*** |
| Number of organisations after 2000 | 1.30 | 0.31 | 4.24*** | 1.21 | 0.30 | 4.03*** | 1.28 | 0.27 | 4.70*** |
| Willingness to buy | -3,410 | 26,876 | -0.13 | -1,205 | 21,570 | -0.06 | -7,419 | 21,841 | -0.34 |
| Willingness to rent | 1,620 | 1,606 | 1.01 | 1,665 | 1,329 | 1.25 | 1,219 | 1,248 | 0.98 |
| **Gender and environment** | | | | | | | | | |
| Number decisions head household | 0.91 | 0.45 | 2.00** | 0.64 | 0.52 | 1.24 | 0.81 | 0.50 | 1.62 |
| Number decisions spouse | -0.13 | 0.43 | -0.29 | 0.36 | 0.53 | 0.68 | -0.06 | 0.47 | -0.13 |
| Number decisions both | -1.01 | 0.72 | -1.41 | -1.21 | 0.84 | -1.43 | -0.96 | 0.78 | -1.23 |
| Number environmental practices | 0.12 | 0.41 | 0.29 | 0.56 | 0.50 | 1.14 | 0.06 | 0.40 | 0.15 |
| Organic fertiliser in banana | 0.04 | 0.02 | 2.11** | 0.04 | 0.02 | 1.94* | 0.04 | 0.02 | 2.19** |
| Chemical fertiliser in banana | -0.07 | 0.09 | -0.86 | -0.06 | 0.07 | -0.75 | -0.07 | 0.07 | -0.89 |
| Organic fertiliser in other crops | 0.14 | 0.11 | 1.25 | 0.26 | 0.14 | 1.83* | 0.10 | 0.13 | 0.74 |
| Chemical fertiliser in other crops | -0.38 | 0.12 | -3.26*** | -0.48 | 0.14 | -3.39*** | -0.37 | 0.13 | -2.87*** |
| **Risk attitude** | | | | | | | | | |
| Risk attitude | -1.06 | 0.58 | -1.83* | -1.20 | 0.57 | -2.11** | -1.31 | 0.59 | -2.21** |

Note: t-stat >2.66 = *** sign. at 99%; t-stat >2.00 = ** sign. at 95%; t-stat >1.67 = * sign. at 90%.

concentrating their effort on banana production instead of pursuing more income diversification activities that could reduce their risk exposure (but also decrease their expected income). Other effects related to better access to credit, higher risk acceptance and stronger engagement with local farmers' organisations are equally confirmed. Interestingly, also some significant implications for intra-household decision-making procedures are observed: in families involved in (conventional) FT the male household head has a stronger influence in critical household decisions, whereas less decisions are taken jointly by the spouses. This points towards a reduced role of women in farm household decision procedures.

## 7. The FT premium

Another important benefit from FT certification can be derived from the use of the FT premium. We incorporated a section in the survey to recover the perception of farmers about the benefits they get from the use of the premium. All sampled farmers from APVCH declared to be familiar with the existence of the FT premium and 92% considered that their households received some direct benefit from its use.

Farmers where also asked to identify all the different categories in which they got some benefit and also to put a value of that benefit for the last year. All of them mentioned the distribution of agricultural inputs as an important and valuable benefit, followed by the improvement of education services and access to credit. The use of the premium for the development of infrastructure was only mentioned as a benefit by 9% of the sampled farmers, but the value they placed on it was very large compared to other items.

Adding up the perceived value of benefits for each household derived from the use of the FT premium gives on average amount almost three thousand soles per household, representing around one fifth of their yearly net income.

*Table 5. FT Premium use.*

| Variable | % who benefit from | Mean value (soles) |
|---|---|---|
| Technical assistance | 37% | 84 |
| Education | 46% | 155 |
| Credit | 46% | 334 |
| Health services | 13% | 83 |
| Infrastructure | 9% | 1,146 |
| Agricultural inputs | 100% | 1,083 |
| Food basket | 39% | 23 |
| Total value | | 2,906 |

## 8. Discussion and conclusions

This study provides one of the first detailed analyses of the impact of FT banana certification at the household level. With a careful selection of treatment and control farmers (through their associations) and the use of a propensity score matching technique, we were able to construct an appropriate counterfactual for the situation of FT farmers prior to their involvement in this supply chain. Due to the fact that all sales of FT banana in the Chira Valley also have an organic certification, and to be able to distinguish the effects of FT involvement from the effects of participating in the organic market, we compared the outcomes of organic farmers which belong to a FT association with the outcomes of two different types of farmers: (a) organic farmers which belong to an association recently FT certified (APBOS), and (b) conventional farmers in the same area which do not belong to any association.

In both cases the net income derived from banana production is higher for FT producers. While this difference is exclusively based on higher productivity levels in the comparison with organic non-FT farmers, it is mainly derived from a better price than the one conventional farmers get. Higher productivity levels for FT farmers might be obtained in part because the FT premium is used in technical assistance, better delivery of agricultural inputs, and more credit availability. Their better attitude towards risk could also explain FT farmer's concentration in banana production. In particular, a higher use of family and hired labour for this activity appears to be compensating for the chemical fertilisers that conventional farmers use intensively.

A clear difference in terms of household wealth appears for the comparison with conventional farmers. Household expenditures for FT producers are around 40% higher than the ones of conventional farmers. Even though this effect is not present when comparing expenditures with organic non-FT farmers, some other indicators, like the value of durable assets and the value of land, also reveal a welfare effect derived from FT. These results provide clear evidence of the impact of FT involvement on income and overall welfare indicators for banana farmers in the Chira Valley. These improvements are not only achieved via the better price obtained for FT sales but also because of higher productivity levels obtained as a results of FT premium investment. Moreover, the introduction of the FT market for banana producers in the Valley seems to have had an important effect on local farm-gate prices for conventional bananas. Local retailers that buy conventional banana for markets in the region and in Lima appear to have being forced to increase prices in order to maintain their providers working with them.

A similar type of externality could be expected in terms of the FT premium use if this will be invested more on infrastructure development and improvements of public services. So far, however, the use of the premium is mostly oriented to improve the working conditions of FT members. Even though this use might be needed at the beginning for FT farmers to take-off, community development investments in the near future can produce important externalities for a broader and more sustainable progress. Given the reduced size of the international market for FT products, it would be important to take advantage of the current FT opportunities to help built the grounds for other development prospects in the region.

## References


Bourguignon, F. (1999). *The Mystery of the Vanishing Benefits.* World Bank Research Paper No. 2153. Washington: The World Bank.

Caliendo, M. and S. Kopeing (2005). *Some Practical Guidance for the Implementation of Propensity Score Matching.* Discussion Paper Series N.1588. Bonn, IZA.

Fridell, G. (2004). The Fair Trade Network in Historical Perspective. *Canadian Journal of Development Studies* 25: 411-428.

Hamilton, C. (2001). The Case for Fair Trade. *Journal of Australian Political Economy* 48: 60-72.

Hayes, M. (2006). On the Efficiency of Fair Trade. *Review of Social Economy* 64: 447-468.

Heckman, J., H. Ichimura and P. Todd (1997). Matching as an Econometric Evaluation Estimator: Evidence from Evaluating a Job Training Programme. *Review of Economic Studies* 64: 605-654.

Inurritegui, M. (2006). Es Importante el Capital Social para que el Pequeño Agricultor se beneficie del Comercio Exterior?: estudio de caso sobre la cadena de exportación del banano orgánico en el valle del Chira, Piura. In: *Perú: el Problema Agrario en Debate*; SEPIA XI. Trujillo, SEPIA.

Page, S. and R. Slater (2003). Small Producer Participation in Global Food Systems: Policy Opportunities and Constraints. *Development Policy Review* 21: 641-654.

Rosenbaum, P. and D. Rubin (1983). The Central Role of the Propensity Score in Observational Studies for Causal Effects. *Biometrika* 70: 41-50.

Rubin, D. (1974). Estimating Causal Effects to Treatments in Randomised and Nonrandomised Studies. *Journal of Educational Psychology* 66: 688-701.

Rubin, D. and N. Thomas (1996). Matching Using Estimated Propensity Scores: Relating Theory to Practice. *Biometrics* 52: 249-264.

Smith, H. (1997). Matching with Multiple Controls to Estimate Treatment Effects in Observational Studies. *Sociological Methodology* 27: 325-353.

Socias Salva, A. and N. Doblas (2005). El Comercio Justo: Implicaciones Economicas y Solidarias. (Fair Trade: Implications on the Economy and Solidarity. With English summary). *CIRIEC Espana, Revista de Economia Publica, Social y Cooperativa* 51: 7-24.

Suranovic, S. (2002). International Labour and Environmental Standards Agreements: Is This Fair Trade? *World Economy* 25: 231-245.

## Annex A. Tables

*Table A1. Number of observations on/off common support.*

| | ON-CS | OFF-CS | Total |
|---|---|---|---|
| Fair Trade | 42 | 6 | 48 |
| APBOS (Organic) | 97 | 6 | 103 |
| Fair Trade | 39 | 9 | 48 |
| Conventional | 30 | 6 | 36 |

*Table A2. Probit model after matching.*

| Variables | FT-APBOS | | FT-Conventional | |
|---|---|---|---|---|
| Age head of household | -0.011 | (0.019) | 0.012 | (0.024) |
| Education head of household | -0.051 | (0.047) | -0.005 | (0.063) |
| Family size | 0.025 | (0.123) | 0.179 | (0.154) |
| Area banana | -0.072 | (0.310) | 0.052 | (0.516) |
| Area other crops | -0.998 | (0.860) | -1.143 | (1.020) |
| Time parcel capital | -0.007 | (0.018) | 0.033 | (0.024) |
| Value agricultural assets until 1999 | 0.027 | (0.026) | -0.003 | (0.006) |
| Organisations before year 2000 | 0.000 | (0.232) | -0.037 | (0.246) |
| Years that household reside in locality | 0.008 | (0.015) | -0.017 | (0.023) |
| Constant | 1.148 | (1.257) | -0.471 | (1.772) |
| | Number of obs = 66 | | Number of obs = 51 | |
| | LR $chi^2(9) = 5.09$ | | LR $chi^2(9) = 5.42$ | |
| | Prob > $chi^2 = 0.826$ | | Prob > $chi^2 = 0.7962$ | |
| | Pseudo $R^2 = 0.0589$ | | Pseudo $R^2 = 0.0974$ | |

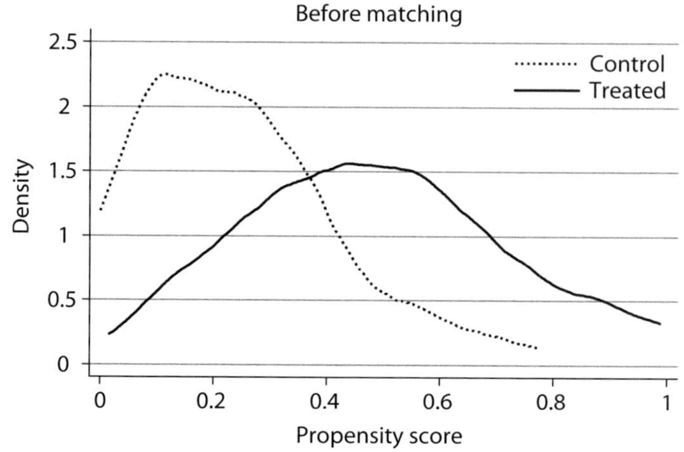


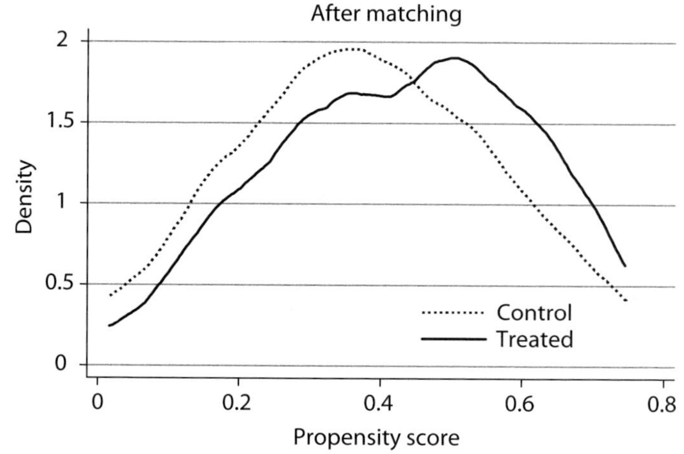


*Figure A1. Fair Trade vs. organic (APBOS) bananas: distribution of propensity scores.*

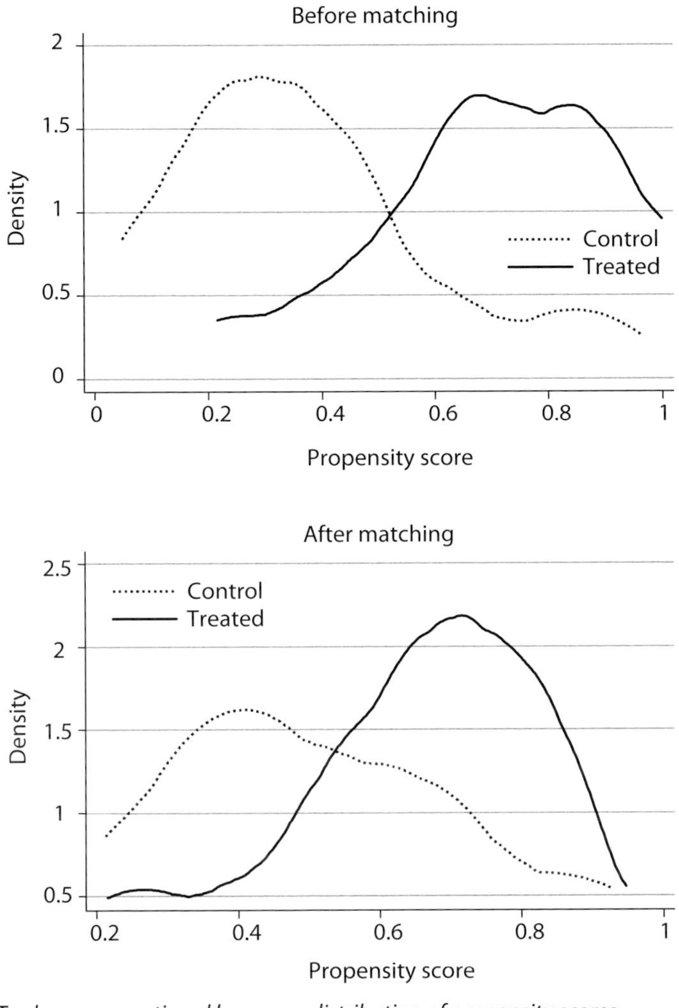


*Figure A2. Fair Trade vs. conventional bananas: distribution of propensity scores.*

## Annex B. Description of variables used.

| # | Variables | Description of variables | Units |
|---|---|---|---|
| **Household characteristics** | | | |
| 1 | Age head of household | Age of head of the household | year |
| 2 | Education head of household | Years of education of head of household | year |
| 3 | Family size | Number of members in household | Nº |
| 4 | migration | Number of members of household that migrated | Nº |
| 5 | years live in locality | Years that family live in locality | year |
| **Land** | | | |
| 6 | Area banana (Ha.) | Total area under banana production | Ha |
| 7 | Area other crops | Total area producing other crops | Ha |
| **Accessibility** | | | |
| 8 | Time from parcel to capital | Travel time | minutes |
| 9 | Time from house to parcel | Travel time | minutes |
| 10 | Time from house to capital | Travel time | minutes |
| **Income** | | | |
| 11 | Salary income | Income from wage work outside own farm or other activities | S/ |
| 12 | Non-salary income | Own business income (self employment) | S/ |
| 13 | Gross income banana | Total production * price received | S/ |
| 14 | Gross income other crops | Total production * price received | S/ |
| 15 | Total gross income | = 11+12+13+14 | S/ |
| 16 | Total net income | = 15 -/- Total production costs | S/ |
| 17 | Profit banana production | = 13 -/- Total banana production cost | S/ |
| 18 | Banana production | Volume | Kg |
| 19 | Banana productivity | = 18 / 6 | Kg/Ha |
| 20 | Price banana-high season | Price received | S/ |
| 21 | Price banana-low season | Price received | S/ |
| **Wealth** | | | |
| 22 | Household expenditures | Yearly expenditures (all categories) | S/ |
| 23 | Value household durables | Stock of household durables | S/ |
| 24 | Value agricultural assets | Stock of farm assets | S/ |
| 25 | Value of animals stock | Stock of animals | S/ |
| 26 | Credit access | Credit access in the last 3 years | Yes/No |
| 27 | Amount of credit | Amount of credit received during last 3 years | S/ |
| 28 | Value of savings | Value | S/ |
| 29 | Value household assets since 2000 | Value | S/ |
| 30 | Value household assets until 1999 | Value | S/ |
| 31 | Value agricultural assets since 2000 | Value | S/ |
| 32 | Value agricultural assets until 1999 | Value | S/ |

| | | | |
|---|---|---|---|
| **Investments** | | | |
| 33 | Have land-attached investment | Realised land-attached investment | Yes/No |
| 34 | Value of land-attached invest | Value | S/ |
| 35 | Made land-attached investment | Since year 2000 | Yes/No |
| 36 | Made house improvement | In the last 5 years | Yes/No |
| 37 | Investment in new bananas | Investments made in banana renovation/ expansion | S/ |
| 38 | Family labour jornales in banana | Family labour use | Nº |
| 39 | Hired labour jornales in banana | Hired labour use | Nº |
| 40 | Value of hired jornal | Salary per journal | S/ |
| **Perceptions and participation** | | | |
| 41 | Economic perception1 | Last 5 years. 1='Better off'; 2='Same'; 3='Worse off' | 1-3 |
| 42 | Economic perception2 | Next 5 years. 1='Better off'; 2='Same'; 3='Worse off' | 1-3 |
| 43 | Satisfaction price | 1='little satisfied' – 10 = 'very satisfied' | 1-10 |
| 44 | Satisfaction technical assistance | 1='little satisfied' – 10 = 'very satisfied' | 1-10 |
| 45 | Satisfaction trade | 1='little satisfied' – 10 = 'very satisfied' | 1-10 |
| 46 | Identification index | 1='totally disagree' - 5 = 'totally agreed' | 1-5 |
| 47 | Force index | 1='totally disagree' - 5 = 'totally agreed' | 1-5 |
| 48 | Number organisations | Membership of community organisations | Nº |
| 49 | Number of organisations before 2000 | Membership of community organisations before 2000 | Nº |
| 50 | Number of organisations after 2000 | Membership of community organisations after 2000 | Nº |
| 51 | Willingness to buy | Perceived land selling price | S/ |
| 52 | Willingness to rent | Perceived land rental price | S/ |
| **Gender and environment** | | | |
| 53 | Number decisions head of household | Key household decisions made by head of household | Nº |
| 54 | Number decisions spouse | Key household decisions made by spouse | Nº |
| 55 | Number decisions both | Key household decisions made together | Nº |
| 56 | Number environmental practices | Amount on land conservation practices applied | Nº |
| 57 | Organic fertiliser in banana | Expenditures in organic fertiliser/total expenditures | % |
| 58 | Chemical fertiliser in banana | Expenditures in chemical fertiliser/total expenditures | % |
| 59 | Organic fertiliser in other crops | Expenditures in organic fertiliser/total expenditures | % |
| 60 | Chemical fertiliser in other crops | Expenditures in chemical fertiliser/total expenditures | % |
| **Risk attitude** | | | |
| 61 | Risk attitude | 1='Risk lover' - 7 = 'Risk adverse' | 1-7 |

# Chapter 3

## The impact of Fair Trade certification on coffee producers in Peru

*Ricardo Fort and Ruerd Ruben*

### 1. Introduction

The effects of Fair Trade (FT) certification on coffee producers and organisations have been analysed in several recent studies. Detailed studies from coffee cooperatives in Costa Rica (Ronchi, 2002), Nicaragua (Bacon, 2005) and Mexico (Jaffee, 2007; Calo and Wise, 2005; Milford, 2004) found that FT strengthened producer organisations and conclude that - in light of the coffee crisis of the early 1990s - FT can be said to have accomplished its goal of improving the returns to small producers and positively affecting their quality of life and the strength of the organisations that represent them locally, nationally and beyond. Other research stressed that Fair Trade initiatives substantially improved the well-being of small-scale coffee farmers and their families, particularly due to better access to credit facilities and external funds, as well as through training and improved capabilities to enhance the quality of the product (Conroy, 2005; Murray *et al.*, 2003). FT farmers were also more successful in diversifying their production, experienced greater satisfaction in terms of prices obtained for their crop, improvements in terms of monthly household food consumption and living conditions that resulted in a significant drop in child mortality (Becchetti and Costantino, 2006).

The European Fair Trade Association (EFTA) provides an overview of FT impact studies that were realised since 2000, but none of these studies count with ample field work or a rigorous comparison with otherwise similar non-FT producers. Most of them emphasise the positive effects on producer's organisations – focusing on the process of capitalisation from the FT premium payments for example – while little attention is given to the individual and household-level implications (Taylor, 2005; Raynolds *et al.*, 2004). Other studies refer to the effects on prices and productivity and the role of FT for improving competitiveness (Becchetti and Constantino, 2006). Some major constraints that are identified refer to difficulties of involving farmers in marketing decisions and the importance of public consciousness-raising for enhancing the size of the FT market.

A general limitation with many impact studies is that no correction is made for differences in farm household characteristics when comparing FT farmers with other groups. For instance, if smaller and poorer farmers are the ones that usually become engaged in FT, farmers with similar characteristics would have to be used as comparison in order to get an unbiased measure of FT impact. The principal objective of this chapter is to evaluate this impact by using information on a sample of FT coffee producers in the central region of Peru and comparing them with non-FT producers with similar characteristics.

The remainder of this chapter is structured as follows: In section 2 we give an overview of the regional context where the study has taken place. Hereafter, we discuss in section 3 the criteria for the selection of the treatment and control groups, as well as the sampling strategy used for choosing farmers within each group. Section 4 presents the characteristics of farmers, dividing them not only by treatment and control but also according to their principal production mode (organic or conventional producers), highlighting the main differences found between these producers. In Section 5 we use a propensity score matching technique to 'balance' the sample of farmers to be compared in each group, and then we analyse the difference between treatment and controls for the selected outcome indicators. Section 6 explores the perception of farmers about their benefits from the use of the FT premium, and finally we present the conclusions of the study in Section 7.

## 2. Regional context and selection of coffee producers for impact evaluation

To evaluate the impact of FT on coffee producers we have selected three organisations located in the *Selva Central* of Peru, in two provinces of the department of Junín. Since the second half of the $19^{th}$ century, this area was one of the biggest hacienda economies in the country, with coffee plantations covering vast amounts of land. With the process of land reform in the 1960's, these provinces started to develop a cooperative model for the commercialisation of coffee. As farms were still managed individually, the agrarian structure of the region can be characterised by the predominance of small- and medium-size land holdings. While many of these cooperatives were dissolved during the 1990's (the so-called 'Parcellation'), some of them manage to survive the structural reforms of that time, and some other have being recently reactivated. Currently, there are around 10 farmers organisations active in the Provinces of Chanchamayo and Satipo of the department of Junín.

The three FT cooperatives are labelled FT1 (Ubiriki Coop), FT2 (Pangoa Coop) and FT3 (La Florida Coop), according to the year of FT certification (see Table A1 in the Annex). Another important characteristic to take into account is that all of them have at least half of their associates under organic coffee production. In terms of location, FT1 and FT3 both belong to the Province of Chanchamayo, and their members are relatively close to each other. Members of FT2, however, are located in the Province of Satipo which is farther away from principal markets and with less accessible roads.

Based on the characteristics of the FT organisations under study and relying on the personal interviews with their representatives, we decided to select members of three other organisations presented in Table A1 as the control group. Most of them are younger organisations and have just recently started organic production and sales. C3 (Tahuantisuyo Coop) is the only one with FT certification since last year, but their FT sales were relatively small and they have not being able to spend the FT premium yet given a judicial problem. The other two have just started their FT application process at the time of the survey. In terms of location, C3 and C1 (Pichanaki Coop) are located in the Province of Chanchamayo, while C2 (Sangareni Coop) members are placed in the Province of Satipo.

We could count with databases containing information on total farm sizes, size of coffee plantations, and year of organic certification (or transition) for all members of these organisations. Using this basic information, we initially selected 60 coffee producers of each organisation, 30 organic and 30 non-organic, for a total sample of 360 surveys. Sampling based on areas was done first for the FT organisations, and after that we selected producers on the same area range for the control groups. This setup of the sample may allow us not only to estimates impacts of FT vs. non-FT, but also a separate comparison for organic and conventional farmers, as well as potential differences between 'recent' and 'mature' FT farmers.

## 3. Characteristics of coffee producers

We decided to first separate coffee farmers in our sample by the type of production mode that they undertake into organic and conventional producers.[1] Table A2 in the Annex shows the distribution of the sample by type of production and treatment status. Due to reclassification after the field survey, surveys formats with incomplete information on important variables and others that were considered as outliers and as such removed from the analysis,[2] the original balance between treatment and control observations in both groups was slightly modified.

Table 1 shows some basic characteristics and pre-treatment variables for both groups of farmers and its comparison between treatment and controls. Table A3 in the Annex provides the full list of descriptive statistics, including the potential outcome variables.

[1] Even though this differentiation was considered since the beginning of the sampling procedure, with the use of the information in the '*Padrones de productores*' (producers list) the classification had to be readjusted given that some farmers had coffee parcels under both production systems. In those cases, we classified organic farmers as the ones with at least half of their total coffee area under this type or production.

[2] Most observations considered as outliers were farmers with productivity levels completely out of the possible range, and within the control group, some farmers that reported selling some coffee with the FT label outside their cooperative.

*Table 1. Characteristics of coffee producers by group.*

| | Organic | | | | | Conventional | | | | |
|---|---|---|---|---|---|---|---|---|---|---|
| | Fair Trade | | Control | | t-test | Fair Trade | | Control | | t-test |
| | N | Mean | N | Mean | (p>\|t\|) | N | Mean | N | Mean | (p>\|t\|) |
| **Household characteristics** | | | | | | | | | | |
| Age head of household | 91 | 47.3 | 63 | 41.9 | 0.01** | 75 | 48.6 | 91 | 43.6 | 0.01** |
| Education head of household | 91 | 6.4 | 63 | 7.6 | 0.03** | 75 | 6.4 | 91 | 6.0 | 0.48 |
| Family size | 91 | 4.6 | 63 | 4.7 | 0.72 | 75 | 4.6 | 91 | 4.8 | 0.57 |
| Residence | 91 | 24.3 | 63 | 13.7 | 0.00*** | 75 | 22.1 | 91 | 16.8 | 0.01** |
| **Land** | | | | | | | | | | |
| Area coffee (Ha) | 91 | 5.6 | 61 | 7.8 | 0.00*** | 74 | 5.7 | 90 | 6.4 | 0.22 |
| Area other crops | 91 | 0.3 | 63 | 0.5 | 0.48 | 75 | 0.4 | 91 | 0.3 | 0.70 |
| Total productive area | 91 | 5.9 | 63 | 8.1 | 0.00*** | 75 | 6.0 | 91 | 6.7 | 0.26 |
| **Accessibility** | | | | | | | | | | |
| Time from parcel to capital | 91 | 103.8 | 60 | 131.7 | 0.00*** | 74 | 109.5 | 90 | 122.1 | 0.25 |
| Time from house to parcel | 91 | 24.5 | 61 | 23.7 | 0.91 | 74 | 21.0 | 90 | 20.6 | 0.94 |
| Time from house to capital | 90 | 98.7 | 62 | 108.7 | 0.40 | 75 | 101.1 | 91 | 114.7 | 0.26 |
| **Initial wealth** | | | | | | | | | | |
| Value household assets until 1999 | 91 | 321 | 63 | 159 | 0.56 | 75 | 295 | 91 | 208 | 0.73 |
| Value agricultural assets until 1999 | 91 | 658 | 63 | 1,268 | 0.39 | 75 | 288 | 91 | 891 | 0.17 |
| **Participation** | | | | | | | | | | |
| Number of organisations before 2000 | 91 | 1.3 | 63 | 0.6 | 0.00*** | 75 | 1.2 | 91 | 1.0 | 0.04** |

Note: * significant at 10%; ** significant at 5%; *** significant at 1%.

Fair Trade farmers in both groups have on average an older and less educated head of the households, are already living longer in their localities, have parcels further away from the district's capital, and were participating in more organisations than producers in the control group. Most importantly, land holdings of FT farmers are smaller on average than the ones for farmers in the control group, in particular for organic producers. These variables, as well as other variables that might be affecting the expected outcomes from FT or influencing the probability of getting the FT certification, have to be taken into account in order to construct a good counterfactual for measuring the impact on FT producers. The matching for getting un-biased groups of FT and non-FT farm-households can only rely on characteristics that – as such – are not influenced by participation in Fair Trade (Heckman *et al.*, 1997).

## 4. Matching producers to analyse the impact of Fair Trade

In order to 'balance' the sample of FT farmers with the sample of the controls, we estimate the probability of having FT certification for the organic and conventional groups, based on a set of exogenous characteristics[3] and pre-treatment variables (see Table 2).

The probability model for organic farmers reveals a significant effect in terms of the years of residence in the locality, the number of organisations in which members of the households were participating before the year 2000, and in the size of their coffee plantation. Only this later effect is maintained for conventional farmers, that also show a significant difference regarding the head of household's age. The first model presents an overall explanatory power (according to the Pseudo $R^2$ reported) of 27%, while this measure is only of 10% for the model of conventional farmers. Even though the explanatory power of the last model might be considered limited, the inclusion of other variables that could also influence the participation decision and the outcome variables did not improve this measure.

*Table 2. Factors influencing likelihood of FT participation (Probit regression).*

| | Organic | S.E. | Sign | Conventional | S.E. | Sign |
|---|---|---|---|---|---|---|
| Age head of household | 0.003 | (0.013) | | 0.021 | (0.012) | * |
| Education head of household | -0.007 | (0.041) | | 0.055 | (0.035) | |
| Family size | 0.005 | (0.060) | | -0.045 | (0.046) | |
| Area coffee | -0.128 | (0.037) | *** | -0.053 | (0.027) | ** |
| Area other crops | 0.110 | (0.093) | | 0.028 | (0.092) | |
| Time parcel capital | -0.002 | (0.002) | | 0.000 | (0.002) | |
| Value agricultural assets until 1999 | 0.000 | (0.000) | | 0.000 | (0.000) | |
| Organisations before year 2000 | 0.447 | (0.168) | *** | 0.182 | (0.133) | |
| Years that household reside in locality | 0.038 | (0.013) | *** | 0.013 | (0.010) | |
| Constant | 0.065 | (0.833) | | -1.350 | (0.724) | * |
| | Number of obs = 151 | | | Number of obs = 164 | | |
| | LR $chi^2(9)$ = 54.98 | | | LR $chi^2(9)$ = 21.4 | | |
| | Prob > $chi^2$ = 0.0000 | | | Prob > $chi^2$ = 0.011 | | |
| | Pseudo $R^2$ = 0.2709 | | | Pseudo $R^2$ = 0.0948 | | |

Note: Standard errors in parentheses.
* significant at 10%; ** significant at 5%; *** significant at 1%.

[3] In principle, the current size of land holdings could be considered as a variable potentially affected by FT involvement. However, land markets in this region are very underdeveloped so that the chances of buying or selling land appear to be limited. Moreover, similar results for the Probit model were obtained when using the initial size of land holdings of the head of household.

Based on the results of these regressions we proceed by estimating the propensity score (p-score - predicted probability of having FT certification) for each group (organic and conventional) and identifying the regions of 'common-support' (Caliendo and Kopeing, 2005; Rosebaum and Rubin, 1983). These regions are set after eliminating the observations in the control group with a p-score lower than the minimum p-score in the treatment group, and the observations in the treatment group with a p-score higher than the maximum p-score in the control group. The numbers of observations on and off the common support are presented in Table A2 in the Annex. The matching estimation is performed for both groups only on common-support observations.

We initially use three different matching algorithms in order to check the robustness of the results to the method applied:

a. Kernel matching is a non-parametric matching estimator that uses weighted averages of all individuals in the control group to construct the counterfactual outcome.
b. One-to-one matching (with replacement) chooses for each treatment observation the observation in the control group that is closest in terms of propensity score.
c. Nearest Neighbour matching (3) uses a weighted average of the 3 closest neighbours in terms of propensity scores for each treatment observation.

Given the small size of our sample (in particular of the sample in the control groups) and the strong restrictions placed on the common-support, we will use the results from the Kernel matching to discuss our findings. Because the principal idea of the propensity score matching technique is to balance the treatment and control samples by using the propensity scores derived from these regressions, we carry out two methods to assess the reliability of our model. In the Annex Table A4 we show the results of the same Probit regressions but this time only considering the observations that are used for the matching. Annex Figures A1 and A2 plot the distribution of the estimated propensity scores before and after the matching is done.[4] Overall variability is largely reduced: there are no significant differences anymore between the two groups, and the distribution of the propensity scores reveals a more balanced sample composition that is appropriate for subsequent comparisons.

## 5. Results

Based on the before described matching procedure, we made a detailed comparison between (a) organic FT and non-FT producers (see Table 3) and (b) conventional FT and non-FT producers (see Table 4). Each comparison analyses significant differences in the defined performance indicators. In addition, attention is given to one specific variable, namely the influence of the duration of FT involvement (see Annex Tables A5 and A6).

[4] Observations included for these graphs are the ones within the identified region of common-support and then used for the calculation of the one-to-one matching estimator.

As we can observe in Table 3, there is no significant difference in income generating activity between FT and non-FT organic coffee producers. Even though FT farmers seem to have higher levels of coffee productivity and receive better average prices, these differences are not strong enough to represent a clear effect. The lack of a price difference can be explained by two factors. First, the market prices for organic FT coffee and just organic (non-FT) coffee are not so different, particularly in the year that the survey was undertaken. Second, not all production from organic farmers in FT cooperatives is sold as organic FT. Moreover, as FT sales are normally limited to small amounts, the system of cooperatives like Pangoa (FT2) and Ubiriki (FT1) is to gather all organic coffee from its members and pay them an average price of the different markets where it is sold (normally as organic FT and organic non-FT, but sometimes also as conventional FT or non-FT). La Florida (FT3), on the contrary, claims to keep a record of the coffee from each producer and the market where it was sold, so that each of them receives that market price. In Table A3 in the Annex we can see that while only 65 out of 91 producers in the organic FT sample were selling some production as organic FT, 60 out of 63 producers in the control sample were selling some production as organic. Furthermore, when we look at the matching estimation of the price weighted average (average price received by a farmer weighted by the amount of coffee sold in each market) by cooperative, we notice that farmers from La Florida appear to be the ones that are driving this price difference down because of the small amount of FT sales for our sampled farmers in this cooperative.

In order to see if some of the observed effects (or the lack of them) can be explained by a longer period of FT participation, we also performed a separate matching estimation for farmers in each FT cooperative. Using the same propensity scores from the Probit estimation for each group, we proceed to match with a one-to-one method the observations for each treated cooperative with the closest observation in any cooperative of the control sample. The matching results for some key variables are presented in the annex (Annex Table A5 and A6).

In terms of potential wealth effects, even though we did not find a significant difference in the level of household expenditures, FT farmers present higher levels of animal stocks and have accumulated more agricultural assets in past years. As we can observe in the matching comparison by cooperative according to the time period of FT involvement (Annex Table A5 and A6), the almost negative effect on household's consumption level as well as the significantly smaller amounts of credit received by FT farmers can be mostly attributed to the performance of farmers in Pangoa and Ubiriki, the two 'youngest' FT cooperatives of the sample. Accumulation of animal stocks and the lack of participation on credit markets are two activities often related to risk-adverse attitudes. Our results show that FT farmers in this group do in fact present higher levels of risk aversion than their counterparts. However, we will have expected a change in attitudes towards a more risk taking perspective as a consequence of the potential income stabilisation and sustainability provided by FT. A closer look to this effect by cooperative (see Annex) indicates that the significance

*Table 3. Comparison FT vs. non-FT organic coffee farmers.*

| Variable | Ps-match kernel | | | Ps-match one-to-one | | | Ps-match neighbour(3) | | |
|---|---|---|---|---|---|---|---|---|---|
| | Difference | S.E. | T-stat | Difference | S.E. | T-stat | Difference | S.E. | T-stat |
| **Income** | | | | | | | | | |
| Salary income | 649 | 396 | 1.64* | 738 | 566 | 1.30 | 569 | 515 | 1.11 |
| Non-salary income | -13 | 483 | -0.03 | -544 | 667 | -0.82 | -180 | 409 | -0.44 |
| Gross income coffee | -211 | 1,979 | -0.11 | -1,565 | 3,091 | -0.51 | -1,343 | 2,660 | -0.50 |
| Gross income other crops | 561 | 481 | 0.01 | 149 | 764 | 0.20 | -84 | 697 | -0.12 |
| Total gross income | 359 | 2,332 | 0.15 | -1,209 | 3,449 | -0.35 | -1,099 | 2,991 | -0.37 |
| Total net income | 1,707 | 1,594 | 1.07 | 1,813 | 2,218 | 0.82 | 784 | 1,540 | 0.51 |
| Profit coffee production | 878 | 1,792 | 0.49 | 750 | 2,444 | 0.31 | -14 | 1,870 | -0.01 |
| Price average | 0.20 | 0.16 | 1.26 | 0.17 | 0.19 | 0.88 | 0.14 | 0.20 | 0.72 |
| Price weighted average | 0.18 | 0.23 | 0.77 | 0.13 | 0.22 | 0.58 | 0.07 | 0.22 | 0.31 |
| Production gross coffee | 698 | 1,355 | 0.51 | -15.9 | 2,058 | -0.01 | -18.6 | 1,546 | -0.01 |
| Production processed coffee | 181 | 503 | 0.36 | -24.3 | 597 | -0.04 | 2.7 | 550 | 0.00 |
| Productivity gross coffee | 394 | 369 | 1.07 | 275 | 337 | 0.81 | 387 | 318 | 1.22 |
| **Wealth** | | | | | | | | | |
| Household expenditures | -1,395 | 1,196 | -1.17 | -2,540 | 1,566 | -1.62 | -1,906 | 1433 | -1.33 |
| Value household durables | 5.1 | 574 | 0.01 | -150 | 562 | -0.27 | -527 | 586 | -0.90 |
| Value agricultural assets | 2,001 | 941 | 2.13** | 1,713 | 1,490 | 1.15 | 1,712 | 964 | 1.78* |
| Value of animals stock | 290 | 171 | 1.70* | 271 | 137 | 1.98* | 342 | 116 | 2.95*** |
| Credit access | -0.21 | 0.15 | -1.38 | -0.16 | 0.15 | -1.07 | -0.23 | 0.14 | -1.64* |
| Amount of credit | -2,621 | 746 | -3.51*** | -2,738 | 1,516 | -1.81* | -2,928 | 1,066 | -2.75*** |
| Value of savings | 750 | 684 | 1.10 | 639 | 804 | 0.79 | 797 | 664 | 1.20 |
| Value household assets since 2000 | -225 | 456 | -0.49 | -189 | 514 | -0.37 | -616 | 545 | -1.13 |
| Value agricultural assets since 2000 | 1,880 | 863 | 2.18** | 1,444 | 904 | 1.60* | 1,756 | 735 | 2.39** |
| **Investments** | | | | | | | | | |
| Have land-attached investment | -0.08 | 0.19 | -0.45 | -0.26 | 0.32 | -0.81 | -0.27 | 0.27 | -1.00 |
| Value of land-attached invest | 58.8 | 225 | 0.26 | 137 | 203 | 0.68 | 88.6 | 185 | 0.48 |
| Made land-attached investment | 0.18 | 0.19 | 0.95 | 0.04 | 0.45 | 0.09 | -0.12 | 0.43 | -0.27 |

| | | | | | | | | | |
|---|---|---|---|---|---|---|---|---|---|
| Made house improvement | -0.08 | 0.11 | -0.74 | -0.16 | 0.15 | -1.10 | -0.19 | 0.13 | -1.47 |
| Investment in new coffee plants | -315 | 331 | -0.95 | -725 | 470 | -1.54 | -566 | 476 | -1.19 |
| Family labour jornales in coffee | -1.32 | 14.09 | -0.09 | 4.07 | 14.53 | 0.28 | -3.73 | 15.89 | -0.23 |
| Hired labour jornales in coffee | -2,164 | 1,376 | -1.57* | -3,734 | 1,865 | -2.00** | -2,082 | 1,477 | -1.41 |
| Value of hired jornal | -1.27 | 1.68 | -0.75 | -1.51 | 1.72 | -0.88 | -1.14 | 1.68 | -0.67 |
| **Perception and participation** | | | | | | | | | |
| Economic perception1 | -0.23 | 0.17 | -1.37 | -0.16 | 0.24 | -0.69 | -0.15 | 0.21 | -0.69 |
| Economic perception2 | -0.30 | 0.09 | -3.20*** | -0.36 | 0.17 | -2.19** | -0.19 | 0.12 | -1.57* |
| Satisfaction price | 2.43 | 0.43 | 5.62*** | 2.41 | 0.81 | 2.96*** | 1.68 | 0.75 | 2.25** |
| Satisfaction technical assistance | 2.08 | 0.43 | 4.86*** | 2.16 | 0.64 | 3.40*** | 1.68 | 0.51 | 2.56** |
| Satisfaction trade | 2.08 | 0.57 | 3.62*** | 2.12 | 0.89 | 2.37** | 1.29 | 0.76 | 2.56** |
| Identification index | 0.41 | 0.18 | 2.26** | 0.38 | 0.21 | 1.84* | 0.28 | 0.20 | 1.35 |
| Force index | 0.51 | 0.18 | 2.92*** | 0.45 | 0.23 | 1.99* | 0.40 | 0.19 | 2.09** |
| Number organisations | -0.25 | 0.25 | -0.99 | -0.27 | 0.40 | -0.68 | -0.35 | 0.32 | -1.09 |
| Number of organisations after 2000 | -0.17 | 0.16 | -1.07 | -0.14 | 0.28 | -0.48 | -0.38 | 0.27 | -1.43 |
| Willingness to buy plot 1 | 1,768 | 8,406 | 0.21 | 5,914 | 11,847 | 0.50 | -1,107 | 9,521 | -0.12 |
| Willingness to buy plot 2 | 1,724 | 2,422 | 0.71 | 1,304 | 3,412 | 0.38 | -115 | 2,668 | -0.04 |
| Willingness to rent plot 1 | 3,337 | 1,421 | 2.35** | 3,288 | 1,577 | 2.08** | 2,775 | 1,326 | 2.09 |
| Willingness to rent plot 2 | 54.6 | 782 | 0.07 | -145 | 1,384 | -0.10 | -648 | 1,090 | -0.59 |
| **Gender and environment** | | | | | | | | | |
| Number decisions head household | -0.78 | 0.47 | -1.65* | -0.50 | 0.61 | -0.82 | -0.42 | 0.74 | -0.57 |
| Number decisions spouse | 0.03 | 0.15 | 0.24 | 0.00 | 0.21 | 0.00 | -0.05 | 0.15 | -0.36 |
| Number decisions both | 0.75 | 0.51 | 1.47 | 0.50 | 0.82 | 0.61 | 0.49 | 0.60 | 0.82 |
| Number environmental practices | -0.41 | 0.37 | -1.09 | -0.61 | 0.34 | -1.81 | -0.71 | 0.55 | -1.28 |
| Organic fertiliser in coffee | 0.04 | 0.02 | 2.15** | 0.04 | 0.02 | 1.81* | 0.04 | 0.02 | 1.86* |
| Other fertiliser in coffee | 0.00 | 0.00 | 1.06 | 0.00 | 0.00 | 1.29 | 0.00 | 0.00 | 1.50 |
| Organic fertiliser in other crops | 0.00 | 0.02 | -0.12 | -0.02 | 0.04 | -0.62 | -0.01 | 0.02 | -0.72 |
| Chemical fertiliser in other crops | 0.00 | 0.00 | 1.02 | 0.00 | 0.00 | 0.95 | 0.00 | 0.00 | 1.00 |
| Other fertiliser in other crops | 0.00 | 0.00 | -0.98 | 0.00 | 0.00 | 0.00 | 0.00 | 0.00 | -0.99 |
| **Risk attitude** | | | | | | | | | |
| Risk attitude | 0.46 | 0.23 | 1.97* | 0.36 | 0.29 | 1.24 | 0.58 | 0.28 | 2.09** |

Note: * significant at 10%; ** significant at 5%; *** significant at 1%.

*Table 4. Comparison FT vs. non-FT conventional coffee farmers.*

| | Ps-match kernel | | | Ps-match one-to-one | | | Ps-match Neighbour(3) | | |
|---|---|---|---|---|---|---|---|---|---|
| | Difference | S.E. | T-stat | Difference | S.E. | T-stat | Difference | S.E. | T-stat |
| **Income** | | | | | | | | | |
| Salary income | -795 | 572 | -1.39 | -1,301 | 698 | -1.86* | -794 | 670 | -1.18 |
| Non-salary income | -799 | 1206 | -0.66 | -570 | 1,236 | -0.46 | -799 | 1,050 | -0.76 |
| Gross income coffee | -1,778 | 2346 | -0.76 | -876 | 3,426 | -0.26 | -1,196 | 2,947 | -0.41 |
| Gross income other crops | -766 | 524 | -1.46 | -433 | 524 | -0.83 | -639 | 377 | -1.69* |
| Total gross income | -4,172 | 2280 | -1.83* | -3,238 | 3,556 | -0.91 | -3,433 | 3,106 | -1.11 |
| Total net income | -3,531 | 1978 | -1.79* | -3,254 | 2,388 | -1.36 | -2,677 | 2,229 | -1.20 |
| Profit coffee production | -1,661 | 1545 | -1.08 | -1,106 | 2,079 | -0.53 | -1,033 | 1,565 | -0.66 |
| Price average | 0.05 | 0.09 | 0.53 | 0.01 | 0.12 | 0.04 | 0.02 | 0.11 | 0.15 |
| Price weighted average | -0.03 | 0.14 | -0.22 | -0.13 | 0.19 | -0.68 | -0.11 | 0.14 | -0.73 |
| Production gross coffee | -1,467 | 1246 | -1.18 | -831 | 1,534 | -0.54 | -1,266 | 1,365 | -0.93 |
| Production processed coffee | -344 | 431 | -0.80 | -165 | 510 | -0.32 | -222 | 533 | -0.42 |
| Productivity gross coffee | -327 | 161 | -2.03** | -277 | 211 | -1.32 | -320 | 184 | -1.74* |
| **Wealth** | | | | | | | | | |
| Household expenditures | 138 | 690 | 0.20 | 367 | 1,108 | 0.33 | -435 | 1,086 | -0.40 |
| Value household durables | 988 | 794 | 1.25 | 844 | 945 | 0.89 | 1,266 | 1,067 | 1.19 |
| Value agricultural assets | 1,486 | 1078 | 1.38 | 1,604 | 991 | 1.62 | 1,510 | 865 | 1.74* |
| Value of animals stock | 669 | 314 | 2.13** | 681 | 327 | 2.08** | 678 | 341 | 1.99* |
| Credit access | 0.13 | 0.10 | 1.33 | 0.18 | 0.10 | 1.72* | 0.17 | 0.08 | 2.15** |
| Amount of credit | -609 | 857 | -0.71 | 333 | 1,032 | 0.32 | -690 | 1,485 | -0.46 |
| Value of savings | 1.06 | 301 | 0.00 | 334 | 532 | 0.63 | -99 | 404 | -0.24 |
| Value household assets since 2000 | 885 | 1039 | 0.85 | 954 | 900 | 1.06 | 1,286 | 670 | 1.92* |
| Value agricultural assets since 2000 | 1,412 | 827 | 1.71 | 1,517 | 777 | 1.95* | 1,444 | 985 | 1.47 |
| **Investments** | | | | | | | | | |
| Have land-attached investment | 0.07 | 0.06 | 1.09 | 0.04 | 0.07 | 0.57 | 0.05 | 0.08 | 0.59 |
| Value of land-attached invest | -139 | 480 | -0.29 | 279 | 497 | 0.56 | -69 | 413 | -0.17 |
| Made land-attached investment | 0.19 | 0.10 | 1.85* | 0.17 | 0.12 | 1.42 | 0.13 | 0.10 | 1.40 |
| Made house improvement | 0.15 | 0.07 | 2.11** | 0.21 | 0.10 | 2.14** | 0.09 | 0.07 | 1.36 |

| | | | | | | | | | |
|---|---|---|---|---|---|---|---|---|---|
| Investment in new coffee plants | -191 | 173 | -1.10 | -78 | 227 | -0.34 | -247 | 166 | -1.49 |
| Family labour jornales in coffee | 25 | 15 | 1.66 | 1.8 | 21 | 0.09 | 26 | 18 | 1.44 |
| Hired labour jornales in coffee | 218 | 1,305 | 0.17 | 219 | 1,710 | 0.13 | 290 | 1,668 | 0.17 |
| Value of hired jornal | -1.66 | 0.89 | -1.86* | -0.93 | 1.17 | -0.79 | -1.61 | 1.02 | -1.59 |
| **Perception and participation** | | | | | | | | | |
| Economic perception1 | -0.10 | 0.14 | -0.76 | -0.14 | 0.20 | -0.70 | -0.10 | 0.16 | -0.60 |
| Economic perception2 | 0.05 | 0.13 | 0.37 | 0.08 | 0.14 | 0.61 | 0.02 | 0.14 | 0.17 |
| Satisfaction price | 0.42 | 0.46 | 0.92 | 0.24 | 0.42 | 0.56 | 0.28 | 0.48 | 0.59 |
| Satisfaction technical assistance | 0.32 | 0.45 | 0.71 | -0.10 | 0.56 | -0.17 | 0.14 | 0.47 | 0.30 |
| Satisfaction trade | 0.50 | 0.39 | 1.29 | 0.22 | 0.48 | 0.46 | 0.33 | 0.45 | 0.74 |
| Identification index | 0.15 | 0.12 | 1.22 | 0.25 | 0.19 | 1.36 | 0.19 | 0.19 | 1.03 |
| Force index | 0.24 | 0.13 | 1.93* | 0.28 | 0.18 | 1.54 | 0.28 | 0.15 | 1.90* |
| Number organisations | 0.23 | 0.17 | 1.35 | 0.11 | 0.23 | 0.47 | 0.28 | 0.20 | 1.41 |
| Number of organisations after 2000 | 0.24 | 0.14 | 1.67* | 0.14 | 0.14 | 0.97 | 0.29 | 0.16 | 1.83* |
| Willingness to buy plot 1 | 108 | 3,508 | 0.03 | 1,765 | 4,100 | 0.43 | 581 | 4,254 | 0.14 |
| Willingness to buy plot 2 | -323 | 2,589 | -0.12 | -704 | 2,993 | -0.24 | -1,089 | 2,496 | -0.44 |
| Willingness to rent plot 1 | 1,119 | 1,628 | 0.69 | 1,603 | 1,570 | 1.02 | 1,060 | 1,978 | 0.54 |
| Willingness to rent plot 2 | -1,028 | 1,249 | -0.82 | -1,033 | 1,380 | -0.75 | -1,025 | 1,148 | -0.89 |
| **Gender and environment** | | | | | | | | | |
| Number decisions head household | 0.75 | 0.41 | 1.84* | 0.60 | 0.39 | 1.54 | 0.56 | 0.35 | 1.65* |
| Number decisions spouse | 0.07 | 0.09 | 0.77 | 0.10 | 0.11 | 0.92 | 0.08 | 0.11 | 0.75 |
| Number decisions both | -0.81 | 0.38 | -2.14** | -0.69 | 0.38 | -1.81* | -0.64 | 0.46 | -1.40 |
| Number environmental practices | -0.17 | 0.17 | -0.97 | -0.15 | 0.19 | -0.80 | -0.13 | 0.19 | -0.68 |
| Organic fertiliser in coffee | 0.02 | 0.02 | 0.74 | 0.01 | 0.02 | 0.65 | 0.02 | 0.02 | 1.08 |
| Other fertiliser in coffee | -0.01 | 0.02 | -0.65 | -0.01 | 0.02 | -0.33 | -0.02 | 0.02 | -0.76 |
| Organic fertiliser in other crops | 0.00 | 0.01 | 0.49 | 0.00 | 0.01 | -0.02 | 0.01 | 0.01 | 0.69 |
| Chemical fertiliser in other crops | 0.02 | 0.01 | 1.46 | 0.02 | 0.01 | 1.40 | 0.02 | 0.01 | 1.89* |
| Other fertiliser in other crops | -0.01 | 0.00 | -1.70* | 0.00 | 0.01 | -0.30 | 0.00 | 0.00 | -1.15 |
| **Risk attitude** | | | | | | | | | |
| Risk attitude | 0.26 | 0.17 | 1.55 | 0.27 | 0.26 | 1.04 | 0.26 | 0.22 | 1.22 |

Note: * significant at 10%; ** significant at 5%; *** significant at 1%.

of this unexpected effect is almost entirely driven by farmers in Ubiriki's cooperative, i.e. the ones that have just being involved in FT sales.

A very important effect of FT can be observed in terms of farmer's perception about their future wellbeing and the level of satisfaction with the services provided by their cooperative. FT farmers are not only more satisfied than their counterparts in terms of prices, technical assistance and trade management, but they also feel more identified with their cooperatives and are more convinced of its bargaining power. Although we do not observe significant differences in perceptions about the sales value of land, FT farmers perceived their land as having a higher renting value. This finding is consistent with a very limited regional market for land sales but an active one in terms of land rentals. Finally, despite the fact that all producers in this group have an organic certification, we find that FT farmers use a higher percentage of organic fertilisers for coffee production than farmers in non-FT cooperatives. This difference might be attributed to a better service provided by FT cooperatives in terms of technical assistance and provision or agricultural inputs.

The results of the matching estimation for the group of conventional farmers reveal a negative effect of FT on total gross and net income, even though the difference is only significant when performing the Kernel estimation. This negative effect seems to be driven by a significantly lower coffee productivity of FT producers as compared to conventional non-FT farmers. The lack of a significant price difference can be explained in part for the same reason stated for farmers in the organic group. Only 31 out of 75 producers in the FT conventional group were selling some part of their coffee production to the FT market. Even more, the average amount sold to this market is just half of what they sold as non-FT conventional coffee. Apart from that, the year the survey was undertaken coincided with a year of adverse weather conditions for coffee growers in the region what in turn increased local prices for conventional coffee and thus reduced the gap with the price paid at the FT market.

Surprisingly, when we look at the matching estimation by cooperative we find that the output of the sample of producers from La Florida is the one that can explain the low level of profit in coffee production because of their difference in prices and production levels. This finding can have two possible explanations. First, the directory of La Florida is trying to move all their members towards organic farming and because of that many farmers of our sample of conventional FT producers are in fact in the transition process towards becoming organic. Adjusting to the new technique might be then reducing their productivity levels. Second, the cooperative management cares more about organic farmers than conventional ones and as such they benefit less from their services in terms of technical assistance and commercial trading. This explanation is also consistent with the lack of a significant difference in the satisfaction indexes of FT farmers in terms of prices, technical assistance and trading. They only differ from non-FT farmers in their perception about the strength and bargaining power of their organisation.

A similar pattern to the one found for organic producers can be observed in terms of wealth effects. FT farmers have a higher stock of animals and have invested more in agricultural assets in the last years. However, there are no significant differences now in access to credit and the amounts received. Moreover, FT farmers have pursued more house improvements and land-attached investments in the last years than their counterparts in non-FT cooperatives.

## 6. Impact of the FT premium

Even though the Fair Trade premium is supposed to be one of the most important benefits from the FT certification, farmer's answers about its use reveal some limitations regarding its distribution. Table 5 provides information on farmers perceptions regarding the benefits derived from the FT premium.

More than 10% of the total number of farmers interviewed within the FT cooperatives did not have any knowledge about the existence of the FT premium. This percentage doubles for farmers interviewed in Pangoa. Moreover, the number of farmers that claimed to have received any benefit from the use of the premium is less than one fourth of the total sample. The percentage of beneficiary farmers increases for the cooperatives with a longer FT certification. Another important finding is that organic farmers appear to be the ones who benefit the most from the use of the premium. Out of the 31 farmers who benefit in la Florida, 21 where organic farmers, and 8 out of 10 in Pangoa where of the same category.

Farmers who claimed to have received any benefit where then asked to identify all the different categories in which they got some benefit and to place a value to that benefit for the last year. In general, technical assistance and credit access are the categories where most farmers perceived a benefit. Adding up the perceived value of benefits for each household we have calculated that the use of the FT premium gives on average three thousand soles per beneficiated household. The perceived total value for farmers in La Florida is twice as high as the value for farmers in Pangoa (see Table 6).

*Table 5. Farmer's perception about the FT premium.*

| | La Florida | Pangoa | Ubiriki | Total |
|---|---|---|---|---|
| Do not know | 4 | 13 | 5 | 22 |
| Know | 56 | 47 | 55 | 158 |
| % know | 93% | 78% | 92% | 88% |
| No benefit perceived | 25 | 37 | 54 | 116 |
| Any benefit perceived | 31 | 10 | 1 | 42 |
| % Any benefit | 52% | 17% | 2% | 23% |

*Table 6. Perception of benefits from FT premium.*

| | La Florida | | Pangoa | | Total | |
|---|---|---|---|---|---|---|
| | % benefit | Avg. Value | % benefit | Avg. Value | % benefit | Avg. Value |
| Technical assistance | 65% | 172 | 60% | 89 | 64% | 148 |
| Education | 32% | 18 | 20% | 605 | 29% | 157 |
| Credit | 68% | 2,745 | 60% | 915 | 64% | 2,244 |
| Health services | 32% | 37 | 40% | 119 | 33% | 56 |
| Infrastructure | 29% | 535 | 10% | 40 | 26% | 405 |
| Total value (soles) | | 3,508 | | 1,768 | | 3,010 |

## 7. Discussion and conclusions

This study presents important empirical evidence to understand the effects of FT certification on coffee farmers in the central region of Peru. A detailed selection of treatment and control coffee cooperatives and the use of a propensity score matching technique allowed us to constructed a good counterfactual for the situation of FT farmers prior to their involvement in this supply chain. Given the importance of organic farming in the region and in the chosen cooperatives, we decided to analyse the impact of FT separately for organic and conventional farmers within these cooperatives. Moreover, the three FT cooperatives selected have different time spans with the FT certification what also made possible to explore the importance of this fact on the perceived benefits.

For both groups of farmers (organic and conventional) our results did not show any significant effect of FT involvement in terms of higher household income. Productivity levels for organic FT farmers seem to be slightly higher than their counterparts but no significant difference could be found, although a negative and significant difference was obtained for FT conventional farmers. However, the lack of a real price difference between FT and non-FT producers in both groups seems to be the main limitation for observing higher benefits. The still reduced market for FT sales in the region and the high local prices for conventional and organic coffee paid the year of the survey as a consequence of a production shortage can at least in part explain this fact.

Even though there is no significant difference in household expenditures for FT producers in either the organic or conventional groups, both of them present higher levels of animal stocks and an increment in their value of agricultural assets in the last years. In terms of their general wellbeing, farmers in older FT cooperatives appear to be better-off than the ones in cooperatives with a recent FT involvement. Additionally, FT farmers in the conventional group have also managed to invest more in house improvements and land-attached infrastructure than their counterparts. The improvements made in relation to coffee production might reveal an effect of FT in terms of providing more stable income to farmers and thus moving them towards a more specialised activity. However, the maintenance of higher animal stocks can be exposing a still present reluctance to full specialisation and the preference of a more diversified portfolio.

The lack of many expected effects from FT can at least partially be attributed to the deficient distribution and use of the FT premium as perceived by our sample of farmers. The fact that only 23% of the total number of interviewed FT producers claim to get any benefit from the use of this premium is a clear indication. Cooperative's directories might have to find new ways for a more effective distribution of the premium between their members so that its use can help boosting productivity levels and allow a sustainable increase of their welfare.

## References

Becchetti, L. and M. Constantino (2006). *Fair Trade on Marginalized Producers: an Impact Analysis on Kenyan Farmers.* Rome: University of Rome. Working paper CEIS 220/ECINEQ2006.

Bacon, C. (2005). Confronting the Coffee Crisis: Can Fair Trade, Organic, and Specialty Coffees Reduce Small-Scale Farmer Vulnerability in Northern Nicaragua? *World Development* 33: 497-511.

Caliendo, M. and S. Kopeing (2005). *Some Practical Guidance for the Implementation of Propensity Score Matching.* Discussion Paper Series N.1588. Bonn, IZA.

Calo, M. and T.A. Wise (2005). *Revaluing Peasant Coffee Production: Organic and Fair Trade Markets in Mexico.* Global Development and Environment Institute, Medford MA: Tufts University.

Conroy, M.E. (2005). *Certification Systems as Tools for Natural Asset Building: Potential, Experiences to Date, and Critical Challenges.* Political Economy Research Institute, University of Massachusetts: Amherst. Working paper series no. 100.

Heckman, J., H. Ichimura and P. Todd (1997). Matching as an Econometric Evaluation Estimator: Evidence from Evaluating a Job Training Programme. *Review of Economic Studies* 64: 605-654.

Jaffee, D. (2007). *Brewing Justice: Fair Trade Coffee, Sustainability and Survival.* Berkeley: University of California Press.

Milford, A. (2004). *Coffee, Co-operatives and Competition: The Impact of Fair Trade.* Bergen: Chr. Michelsen Institute.

Murray D., L. Raynolds and P. Taylor (2003). *One Cup at a time: Poverty Alleviation and Fair Trade coffee in Latin America.* Colorado State University: Fair Trade Research Group.

Raynolds, L.T., D. Murray and P.L. Taylor (2004). Fair Trade Coffee: Building Producer Capacity via Global Networks. *Journal of International Development* 16: 1109-1121.

Ronchi, L. (2002). *The Impact of Fair Trade on Producers and their Organisations: a Case Study with Coocafe in Costa Rica.* Policy Research Unit. Sussex: University of Sussex.

Rosenbaum, P. and D. Rubin (1983). The Central Role of the Propensity Score in Observational Studies for Causal Effects. *Biometrika* 70: 41-50.

Taylor, P.L. (2005). In the Market but Not of It: Fair Trade Coffee and Forest Stewardship Council Certification as Market-Based Social Change. *World Development* 33: 129-147.

# Annex

*Table A1. Coffee cooperatives in Junin (sample characteristics).*

| | Cooperativa Agraria La Florida | Coop. Agraria Cafetalera Pangoa Ltda. | Coop.Agraria Cafetelera Sostenible Valle Ubiriki | C.A.C Tahuantisuyo | Cooperativa Agraria Sangareni | Asociacion Central de productores de Café de Pichanaki |
|---|---|---|---|---|---|---|
| Group | FT3 | FT2 | FT1 | C3 | C2 | C1 |
| Foundation year | 1966 | 1977 | 1977 | 1975 [a] | 2004 | 2000 |
| Year organic certification | 1996 | 2003 | 2004 | 2005 | 2005 | 2005 |
| Year FT certification | 1986 | 2003 | 2006 | 2006 | - | - |
| Median of farmer's land (Ha) [b] | 4.0 | 5.5 | 5.0 | 6.7 | 6.0 | 6.8 |
| Estimated total production [c] | 8334 QQ | 8845 QQ | 3137 QQ | 4450 QQ | 3942 QQ | 10665 QQ |
| Percentage of sales conventional output | 30% | 50% | 29% | 10% | 74% | 53% |
| Percent of sales organic output | 70% | 50% | 71% | 90% | 26% | 47% |
| FT premium received ($) | No information | 42,000 | 15,685[a] | - | - | - |
| Number of initial members | 50 | 50 | 73 | 50 | 32 | 904 |
| Number of current members | 1200 | 591 | 273 | 280 | 293 | 250 |
| Initial membership fare (S/.) | 300 | 100 | 200 | 100 | 100 | 0 |
| Annual membership quota (S/.) | No information | 90 | One quintal of Coffee | 120 | Not decided yet | 255 |

[a] Firm did no yet use FT premium
[b] Data has been taken from surveys' sample.
[c] QQ (quintals) = approx. 46-50 kg.

*Table A2. Observations on/off common support.*

| | Observations organic | | | Observations conventional | | |
|---|---|---|---|---|---|---|
| | Treatment | Control | Total | Treatment | Control | Total |
| Initially collected | 97 | 81 | 178 | 82 | 99 | 181 |
| Incomplete/outliers | 6 | 18 | 24 | 7 | 8 | 15 |
| Final sample | 91 | 63 | 154 | 75 | 91 | 166 |
| Off common support | 17 | 7 | 24 | 2 | 3 | 5 |
| On common support | 74 | 53 | 127 | 72 | 87 | 159 |

*Table A3. Descriptive statistics.*

| Output Variables | Organic | | | | | Conventional | | | | |
|---|---|---|---|---|---|---|---|---|---|---|
| | Fair Trade | | Control | | t-test | Fair Trade | | Control | | t-test |
| | N | Mean | N | Mean | (p>\|t\|) | N | Mean | N | Mean | (p>\|t\|) |
| **Income** | | | | | | | | | | |
| Salary income (S/.) | 91 | 1,064 | 63 | 551 | 0.20 | 75 | 710 | 91 | 1,106 | 0.24 |
| Non-salary income | 91 | 1,403 | 63 | 1,211 | 0.76 | 75 | 1,311 | 91 | 1,842 | 0.47 |
| Gross income coffee | 91 | 12,216 | 63 | 20,119 | 0.00*** | 75 | 11,239 | 91 | 13,929 | 0.18 |
| Gross income other crops | 91 | 926 | 63 | 875 | 0.88 | 75 | 1,223 | 91 | 1,452 | 0.57 |
| Total gross income | 91 | 15,620 | 63 | 22,888 | 0.00*** | 75 | 14,498 | 91 | 18,392 | 0.08* |
| Total net income | 91 | 10,507 | 63 | 13,671 | 0.06* | 75 | 9,399 | 91 | 11,947 | 0.11 |
| **Production** | | | | | | | | | | |
| Profit coffee production | 91 | 7,786 | 63 | 11,463 | 0.01** | 75 | 6,649 | 91 | 8,522 | 0.16 |
| Production gross coffee (kg) | 91 | 7,269 | 62 | 12,033 | 0.00*** | 75 | 6,498 | 91 | 8,701 | 0.05** |
| Production processed coffee | 91 | 2,681 | 63 | 3,599 | 0.07* | 75 | 2,113 | 91 | 2,618 | 0.17 |
| Production organic coffee FT | 65 | 2,272 | | | | 3 | 1,800 | | | |
| Production organic coffee non-FT | 35 | 1,946 | 60 | 3,372 | 0.03** | 3 | 1,880 | 2 | 1,325 | 0.75 |
| Production conventional coffee FT | 13 | 494 | | | | 31 | 959 | | | |
| Production conventional coffee non-FT | 23 | 703 | 15 | 1,325 | 0.05** | 60 | 1,867 | 91 | 2,524 | 0.09* |
| Productivity gross coffee (kg/Ha) | 91 | 1,584 | 62 | 1,715 | 0.69 | 75 | 1,207 | 91 | 1,577 | 0.01** |
| Productivity processed coffee | 91 | 545 | 63 | 525 | 0.78 | 75 | 396 | 91 | 478 | 0.05** |
| Productivity organic coffee FT | 65 | 458 | | | | 3 | 193 | | | |
| Productivity organic coffee non-FT | 35 | 384 | 60 | 490 | 0.15 | 3 | 248 | 2 | 360.4 | 0.62 |
| Productivity conventional coffee FT | 13 | 87 | | | | 31 | 333 | 0 | 458.8 | 0.00*** |
| Productivity conventional coffee non-FT | 23 | 186 | 15 | 212.6 | 0.62 | 60 | 333 | 91 | 458.8 | 0.05* |
| Price average (S/. x kg) | 91 | 5.38 | 63 | 5.52 | 0.55 | 75 | 5.39 | 91 | 5.35 | 0.71 |
| Price weighted average | 91 | 5.25 | 63 | 5.42 | 0.45 | 75 | 5.15 | 91 | 5.23 | 0.53 |
| Price organic coffee FT | 65 | 5.71 | | | | 3 | 6.23 | | | |
| Price organic coffee non-FT | 35 | 5.11 | 60 | 5.57 | 0.07* | 3 | 5.80 | 2 | 5.40 | 0.07* |
| Price conventional coffee FT | 13 | 5.69 | | | | 31 | 5.64 | 0 | | |
| Price conventional coffee non-FT | 23 | 5.29 | 15 | 5.25 | 0.82 | 60 | 5.23 | 91 | 5.35 | 0.24 |

| Output Variables | Organic | | | | | Conventional | | | | |
|---|---|---|---|---|---|---|---|---|---|---|
| | Fair Trade | | Control | | t-test | Fair Trade | | Control | | t-test |
| | N | Mean | N | Mean | (p>\|t\|) | N | Mean | N | Mean | (p>\|t\|) |
| **Wealth** | | | | | | | | | | |
| Household expenditures | 90 | 7,415 | 61 | 8,216 | 0.37 | 73 | 7,141 | 89 | 6,934 | 0.79 |
| Value household durables | 91 | 1,370 | 63 | 1,569 | 0.74 | 75 | 2,085 | 91 | 1,493 | 0.49 |
| Value agricultural assets | 91 | 3,122 | 63 | 3,196 | 0.95 | 75 | 2,720 | 91 | 2,004 | 0.41 |
| Value of animals stock | 91 | 697 | 63 | 404 | 0.04** | 75 | 1,126 | 91 | 456 | 0.01** |
| Credit access | 91 | 0.43 | 63 | 0.32 | 0.17 | 75 | 0.45 | 91 | 0.33 | 0.10* |
| Amount of credit | 91 | 876 | 63 | 2,550 | 0.00*** | 75 | 1,603 | 91 | 3,303 | 0.28 |
| Value of savings | 91 | 1,091 | 63 | 886 | 0.76 | 75 | 661 | 91 | 738 | 0.78 |
| Value household assets since 2000 | 91 | 1,049 | 63 | 1,410 | 0.50 | 75 | 1,791 | 91 | 1,285 | 0.54 |
| Value agricultural assets since 2000 | 91 | 2,464 | 63 | 1,928 | 0.57 | 75 | 2,433 | 91 | 1,113 | 0.07* |
| **Investments** | | | | | | | | | | |
| Have land-attached investment | 91 | 1.14 | 63 | 1.08 | 0.47 | 75 | 1.03 | 91 | 0.97 | 0.35 |
| Value of land-attached invest | 91 | 952 | 63 | 1,268 | 0.33 | 75 | 1,025 | 91 | 899 | 0.67 |
| Made land-attached investment | 91 | 1.0 | 63 | 0.9 | 0.39 | 75 | 0.89 | 91 | 0.74 | 0.07* |
| Made house improvement | 91 | 0.2 | 63 | 0.3 | 0.86 | 75 | 0.35 | 91 | 0.26 | 0.25 |
| Investment in new coffee | 91 | 371 | 63 | 375 | 0.98 | 75 | 252 | 91 | 620 | 0.10* |
| Family labour jornales in coffee | 91 | 94 | 63 | 105 | 0.27 | 75 | 121 | 91 | 105.4 | 0.19 |
| Hired labour jornales in coffee | 91 | 4,052 | 63 | 7,542 | 0.00*** | 75 | 5,058 | 91 | 5,287 | 0.82 |
| Value of hired jornal | 91 | 5.5 | 63 | 9.4 | 0.00*** | 75 | 4.7 | 91 | 7.9 | 0.00*** |
| **Perception and participation** | | | | | | | | | | |
| Economic perception1 | 91 | 1.6 | 62 | 1.8 | 0.03** | 75 | 1.7 | 91 | 1.9 | 0.15 |
| Economic perception2 | 91 | 1.3 | 63 | 1.3 | 0.32 | 75 | 1.5 | 91 | 1.4 | 0.43 |
| Satisfaction price | 91 | 7.6 | 62 | 5.9 | 0.00*** | 75 | 6.3 | 91 | 5.9 | 0.26 |
| Satisfaction technical assistance | 91 | 7.4 | 62 | 5.8 | 0.00*** | 75 | 6.1 | 91 | 5.8 | 0.33 |
| Satisfaction trade | 91 | 7.6 | 62 | 6.1 | 0.00*** | 75 | 6.6 | 91 | 6.0 | 0.10 |
| Identification index | 91 | 4.0 | 62 | 3.8 | 0.07* | 75 | 3.5 | 91 | 3.4 | 0.45 |
| Force index | 91 | 3.9 | 62 | 3.6 | 0.01** | 75 | 3.5 | 91 | 3.3 | 0.17 |
| Number organisations | 91 | 2.8 | 63 | 2.6 | 0.14 | 75 | 2.8 | 91 | 2.5 | 0.11 |

| Output Variables | Organic | | | | | Conventional | | | | |
|---|---|---|---|---|---|---|---|---|---|---|
| | Fair Trade | | Control | | t-test | Fair Trade | | Control | | t-test |
| | N | Mean | N | Mean | (p>\|t\|) | N | Mean | N | Mean | (p>\|t\|) |
| Number of organisations after 2000 | 91 | 1.5 | 63 | 1.9 | 0.01** | 75 | 1.5 | 91 | 1.5 | 0.91 |
| Willingness to buy plot 1 | 91 | 26,254 | 63 | 24,762 | 0.72 | 75 | 22,987 | 91 | 22,384 | 0.86 |
| Willingness to buy plot 2 | 91 | 4,786 | 63 | 5,095 | 0.88 | 75 | 4,807 | 91 | 4,409 | 0.83 |
| Willingness to rent plot 1 | 91 | 7,745 | 63 | 6,570 | 0.47 | 75 | 7,054 | 91 | 5,665 | 0.23 |
| Willingness to rent plot 2 | 91 | 1,062 | 63 | 1,639 | 0.44 | 75 | 1,136 | 91 | 1,676 | 0.43 |
| **Gender and environment** | | | | | | | | | | |
| Number decisions head of households | 91 | 1.3 | 63 | 1.5 | 0.48 | 75 | 2.4 | 91 | 1.8 | 0.06* |
| Number decisions spouse | 91 | 0.3 | 63 | 0.3 | 0.99 | 75 | 0.2 | 91 | 0.2 | 0.52 |
| Number decisions both | 91 | 3.4 | 63 | 3.1 | 0.37 | 75 | 2.3 | 91 | 3 | 0.05* |
| Number environmental practices | 91 | 1.2 | 63 | 1.4 | 0.13 | 75 | 1.1 | 91 | 1.1 | 0.73 |
| Organic fertiliser in coffee | 91 | 0.03 | 63 | 0.004 | 0.11 | 75 | 0.03 | 91 | 0.01 | 0.22 |
| Chemical fertiliser in coffee | 91 | 0.00 | 63 | 0.00 | | 75 | 0.00 | 91 | 0.00 | 0.70 |
| Organic fertiliser in other crops | 91 | 0.04 | 63 | 0.03 | 0.64 | 75 | 0.03 | 91 | 0.02 | 0.23 |
| Chemical fertiliser in other crops | 91 | 0.00 | 62 | 0.00 | 0.41 | 74 | 0.00 | 91 | 0.01 | 0.07* |
| **Risk attitude** | | | | | | | | | | |
| Risk attitude | 91 | 4.7 | 62 | 4.2 | 0.01** | 75 | 4.5 | 91 | 4.2 | 0.17 |

Note: * significant at 10%; ** significant at 5%; *** significant at 1%.

*Table A4. Probit estimation after matching.*

| | Organic | | Conventional | |
|---|---|---|---|---|
| Age head of household | 0.006 | (0.015) | -0.001 | (0.015) |
| Education head of household | 0.031 | (0.050) | 0.017 | (0.041) |
| Family size | 0.067 | (0.074) | -0.067 | (0.053) |
| Area coffee | -0.053 | (0.051) | -0.024 | (0.035) |
| Area other crops | 0.035 | (0.102) | -0.011 | (0.097) |
| Time parcel capital | 0.001 | (0.003) | 0.001 | (0.002) |
| Value agricultural assets until 1999 | 0.000 | (0.000) | 0.000 | (0.000) |
| Organisations before year 2000 | 0.215 | (0.203) | 0.180 | (0.154) |
| Years that household reside in locality | 0.032** | (0.015) | 0.003 | (0.011) |
| Constant | -0.722 | (1.024) | 0.301 | (0.925) |
| | Number of ob = 102 | | Number of ob = 113 | |
| | LR $chi^2(9) = 10.13$ | | LR $chi^2(9) = 4.11$ | |
| | Prob > $chi^2 = 0.3399$ | | Prob > $chi^2 = 0.9042$ | |
| | Pseudo $R^2 = 0.0845$ | | Pseudo $R^2 = 0.0277$ | |

Note: Standard errors in parentheses; * significant at 10%; ** significant at 5%; *** significant at 1%.

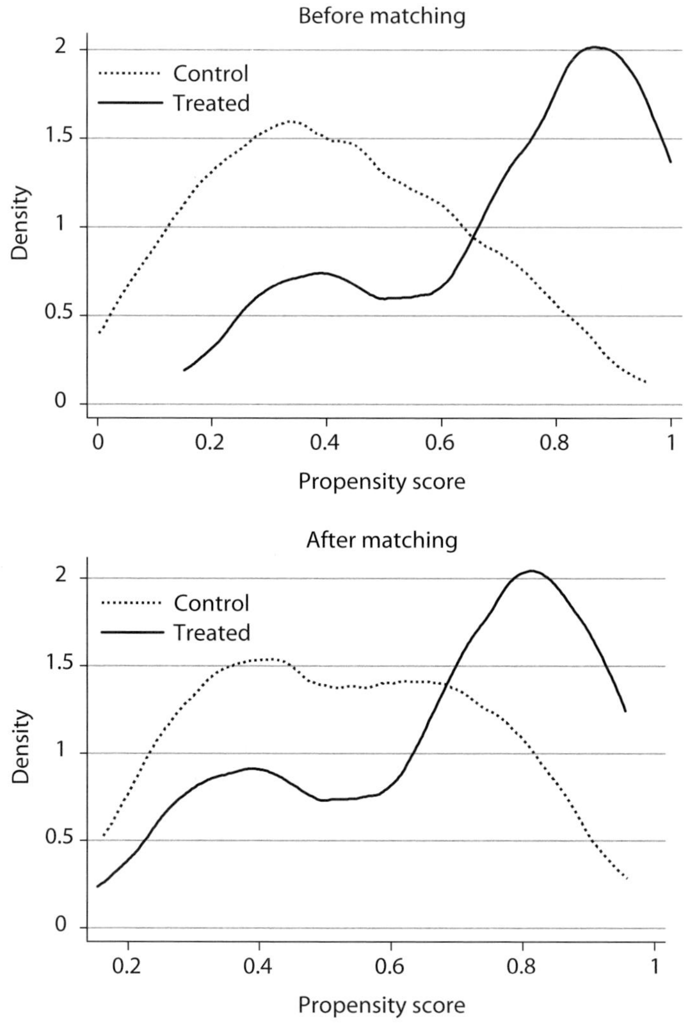


*Figure A1. Organic coffee: distribution of propensity scores.*

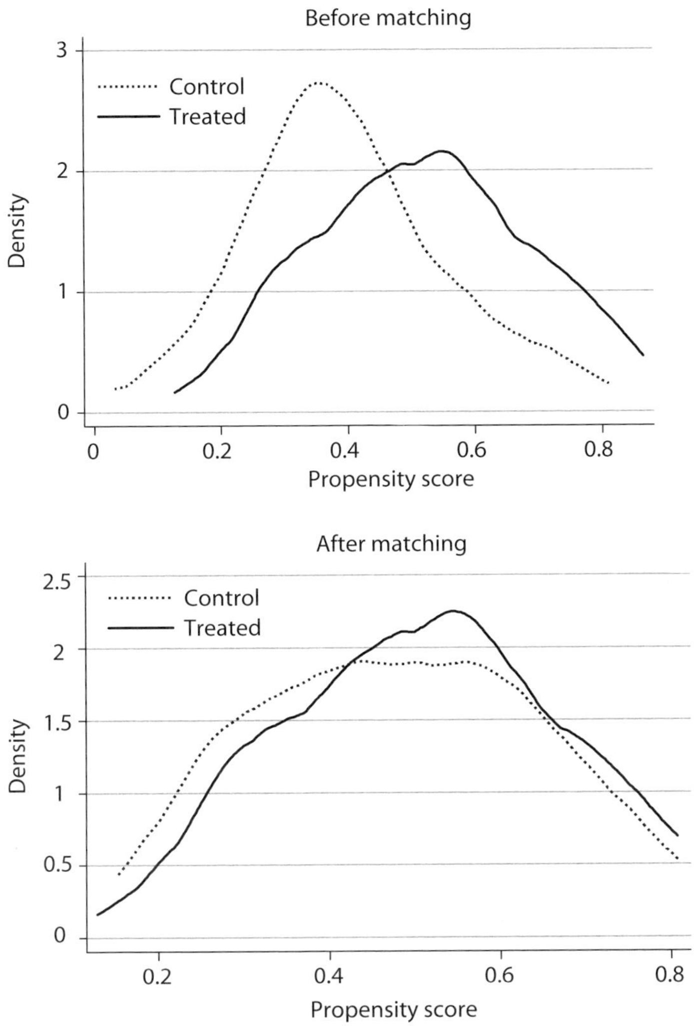


*Figure A2. Conventional coffee: distribution of propensity scores.*

*Table A5. Matching by cooperative (organic production).*

| Variable | La Florida | | | Pangoa | | | Ubiriki | | |
|---|---|---|---|---|---|---|---|---|---|
| | Difference | S.E. | T-stat | Difference | S.E. | T-stat | Difference | S.E. | T-stat |
| Profit coffee production | 521 | 2,986 | 0.17 | 1,288 | 2,160 | 0.60 | 523 | 2,532 | 0.21 |
| Price weighted average | -0.49 | 0.59 | -0.83 | 0.38 | 0.27 | 1.42 | 0.29 | 0.25 | 1.18 |
| Production gross coffee | 590 | 2,773 | 0.21 | -781 | 2,094 | -0.37 | 159 | 2,431 | 0.07 |
| Household expenditures | 428 | 1,678 | 0.25 | -2,514 | 2,364 | -1.06 | -4,175 | 1,899 | -2.20** |
| Credit access | 0.28 | 0.26 | 1.08 | -0.14 | 0.21 | -0.66 | -0.41 | 0.16 | -2.62** |
| Amount of credit | -1,689 | 1,711 | -0.99 | -2,557 | 1,258 | -2.03** | -3411 | 1,438 | -2.37** |
| Value agricultural assets since 2000 | 2,388 | 1,695 | 1.41 | 987 | 693 | 1.42 | 1,241 | 1,542 | 0.80 |
| Economic perception1 | 0.11 | 0.28 | 0.40 | -0.59 | 0.29 | -2.03** | -0.03 | 0.20 | -0.14 |
| Economic perception2 | -0.22 | 0.26 | -0.85 | -0.45 | 0.21 | -2.22** | -0.38 | 0.16 | -2.43** |
| Risk attitude | 0.55 | 0.54 | 1.03 | -0.37 | 0.37 | -0.98 | 0.74 | 0.29 | 2.57** |

Note: * significant at 10%; ** significant at 5%; *** significant at 1%.

Table A6. Matching by cooperative (conventional production).

| Variable | La Florida | | | Pangoa | | | Ubiriki | | |
|---|---|---|---|---|---|---|---|---|---|
| | Difference | S.E. | T-stat | Difference | S.E. | T-stat | Difference | S.E. | T-stat |
| Profit coffee production | -8,011 | 3,261 | -2.46** | 433 | 2,640 | 0.16 | 3,457 | 2,853 | 1.21 |
| Price weighted average | -0.44 | 0.35 | -1.25 | -0.08 | 0.18 | -0.43 | 0.11 | 0.26 | 0.41 |
| Production gross coffee | -5,801 | 2,670 | -2.17** | 1,248 | 1,700 | 0.73 | 1,172 | 2,181 | 0.54 |
| Household expenditures | -1,052 | 2,065 | -0.51 | 317 | 1,376 | 0.23 | 1,786 | 1,912 | 0.93 |
| Credit access | 0.10 | 0.17 | 0.56 | 0.31 | 0.16 | 1.90* | 0.09 | 0.14 | 0.64 |
| Amount of credit | -124 | 3,542 | -0.03 | 503 | 1,477 | 0.34 | 545 | 1,630 | 0.33 |
| Value agricultural assets since 2000 | 3,574 | 2,330 | 1.53 | -315 | 471 | -0.67 | 1,969 | 1,713 | 1.15 |
| Economic perception1 | 0.29 | 0.30 | 0.95 | -0.10 | 0.24 | -0.43 | -0.59 | 0.24 | -2.45** |
| Economic perception2 | 0.33 | 0.28 | 1.20 | 0.10 | 0.20 | 0.52 | -0.18 | 0.19 | -0.96 |
| Risk attitude | 0.71 | 0.46 | 1.54 | -0.24 | 0.37 | -0.67 | 0.53 | 0.38 | 1.39 |

Note:* significant at 10%; ** significant at 5%; *** significant at 1%.

# Chapter 4

## The impact of Fair Trade in banana production of Costa Rica

*Guillermo Zúñiga-Arias and Fernanado Sáenz-Segura*

### 1. Introduction

While Fair Trade has been widely studied for coffee production (Ponte, 2002a,b; Rice, 2001), there are far less field studies available for bananas. This paper attempts to use the knowledge gained of Fair Trade coffee to better understand its potential impact in banana production. A possible explanation of the limited availability of studies on FT bananas might be related to the fact that original Fair Trade requirement were strongly oriented towards smallholder farms and their organisations. Small-scale family farms produce over 70 percent of the world's coffee in a wide array of Latin American, Asian, and African countries (Brown *et al.*, 2001). Many smallholder coffee producers live in highland areas and manage agro-ecosystems located in some of the world's most culturally and biologically diverse regions (Bacon, 2005).

However, in banana production middle-size and larger exploitations are more common features. This implies that either outgrower arrangements or wage labour contracts are applied. Banana production is mostly located in lowland areas close to a harbour, and tends to be far more a monoculture crop with little or no additional diversification activities. Production activities are also rather continuous, while crop maintenance, irrigation and disease control (especially *sigatoka*) require a substantial permanent labour force.

Fair Trade in banana production means that producers obtain a price which covers the cost of production and an additional price premium to be invested in social or environmental activities or for quality improvements. Consumers purchase FT bananas with the assurance that a higher percentage of the retail price goes to the farm families, and that the premium is benefiting social, environmental and other community services, like housing, education and health care.

The Fair Trade standards stipulate that banana importers pay a price that covers the costs of sustainable production and enable better livelihoods, signing delivery contracts that encourage long-term planning and socio-economic stability, particularly through the provision of pre-harvest finance (FLO, 2003). In the case of coffee and cocoa, mainly small-scale producer organisations became eligible for certification. However, for crops like bananas, citrus fruit and tea the certification has been expanded to include large agricultural enterprises that maintain minimum standards regarding labour practices, environmental care and union organisation. Certification standards thus vary between crop type and social organisation (large farm or cooperative), but share common characteristics with respect to perceived social and economic development principles.

Given the vulnerability of banana production and the complex nature of banana trade, some authors are rather critical on its FT perspectives (Getz and Shreck, 2006). FT bananas are increasingly viewed as sustainable alternatives to the conventional food system, with its many negative social and environmental externalities. Operationalising these goals for organic and Fair Trade food via certification can be a complex and difficult process. Specifically, the implementation of certification frequently creates a disconnect between expectations raised by labels and the 'lived experience' of the producers (Rice, 2001; Goodman, 1999). Certification may even exacerbate socio-economic inequality and disrupt local social norms by creating a hyperfocus on surveillance. The certification process priorized the demands of the market to such a degree that farmers remain largely unaware that they are participating in anything 'alternative'. The appeal of certified labels rests most on the integrity of what the label represents to consumers, but a robust analysis of how certification intersects with and affects local spaces, cultures and communities at the point of production is largely absent.

The main issue addressed in this paper is to assess the impact of Fair Trade at the household level. Previous research gave an idea of the main pros and cons that the Fair Trade banana faced when dealing with the spot market. We will try to assess the impact of Fair Trade on the wealth of the household. The socio-economic implications of Fair Trade are not necessarily straightforward. Since the strategy relies on working both 'in' and 'against' the market, FT organisations must constantly seek a balance between opposite demands: (a) the requirements of the global agro-food system which relies on impersonal exchange relations and exploitative practices on the one hand, and (b) the expectations of an alternative model of trade based on social and environmental justice on the other hand. Reconciling both demands asks for a large transparency in trade practices and mutual bargaining on investment and pricing regimes

The remainder of this article is structured as follow: Section 2 provides some general information and presents earlier evidence on impact measurement in FT banana systems. In Section 3, the case studies selected for the FT assessment in Costa Rica are presented. Section 4 outlines the field work materials and method and explains the statistical procedures for matching. Section 5 presents the empirical results, followed by a discussion on the implications for further strengthening FT impact in the Costa Rican banana farms.

## 2. Fair Trade and bananas

Proposed as an alternative system of trade, Fair Trade initiatives seek to create positive social change by altering what happens at each end of the commodity chain while shortening the social distance between producers and consumers. For small-scale banana producers, the Fair Trade market represents a critical export outlet for their product, and perhaps the last hope for their future as independent banana producers (Shreck, 2002). Fair Trade organisations have created a system of certification and labelling that provides consumers with a guarantee that products are grown by disadvantaged producers under healthy social and environmental conditions. In return, consumers are willing to pay a premium for this guarantee with an expectation that it will be returned to producers. Growing interest in alternative trade over the past few years is noted by its success in the market, with global sales estimated at $ 400 million each year (Fair Trade Federation, 2000)

Consistent with its history as a colonial commodity produced for the North by the South, the contemporary export banana industry continues to extract profit for transnational corporations while returning little to the communities producing the fruit (Raynolds and Murray, 1998). The sector epitomises all that is being denounced by oppositional movements as unfair, unsustainable and pursued for the sake of corporate profit at the expense of people and the environment. Moreover, the entire banana industry frequently meets a state of crisis resulting from overproduction (Banana Link, 2000).

As the crisis intensifies, small-scale producers and plantation workers are the most seriously affected. During the mid-1990s, roughly 15,000 small farmers were forced out of the banana sector in the Windward Islands and in the latter half of 2000, approximately 10,000 plantation workers were laid off in Costa Rica alone (Banana Link, 2000; IADB, 2000). While the large-scale plantations, on which bananas destined for export markets are typically grown, have never been ecologically sustainable, agrochemical abuse has intensified, especially in the past fifty years. Intensive production methods and pesticide overuse in the banana industry has proven devastating to both communities and ecosystems (Bourgeois, 1989; Henriques *et al.*, 1997).

The international banana trade is oligopolistic in structure, with two vertically integrated corporations - Dole Food and Chiquita Brands - controlling over 50 percent of the world market (Banana Link, 2001). Production for exports is concentrated in Central and South America and international trade is valued at roughly five billion dollars (FAO, 2000). Between 1988 and 1998, world exports doubled to 12 million tons (Liddell, 2000). Only twelve percent of revenues from this market, however, remain in producing countries and small producers receive a small fraction of the profits (Chambron, 2000).

Alternative production and marketing in the banana sector has taken off dramatically since the mid-1990s, in part as a response to falling profit margins in the conventional trade. More than simple marketing strategies, these initiatives attempt to improve the exploitative conditions of production (FAO, 2000). Currently, there are at least five different certification schemes in operation, each making specific claims about improving the social and/or environmental soundness of banana production. The diversity of these efforts and the participation of industrial giants in these schemes, suggest that we may be witnessing the transformation of the alternative trade market from a niche activity operating at the margins, to a mainstream operation.

The FLO Fair Trade banana initiative is one of the more widely known efforts. Bananas from both independent small-scale producers and plantations can be certified to carry the Fair Trade label, though each group must meet a different set of criteria. The first Fair Trade bananas arrived in the Netherlands from a plantation in Ghana in 1996. They were an instant success, gaining ten percent of the market within a few months of going on sale (Banana Link, 1997). Five years later, Fair Trade bananas from seven registered producer groups were available in eight European countries. By April 2002, FLO reported banana sales from 2001 reaching 29,065 tonnes, signalling the third year in which growth of 25 percent was recorded (FLO, 2002).

Producer associations are central to Fair Trade initiatives and consequently an understanding of the role they play can help determine the implications of and challenges to the initiatives. According to FLO's certification criteria, small-scale producers can participate in Fair Trade through collective organisations (i.e. democratically-controlled cooperatives and/or associations) (FLO, 2000). The close contact between the producers and the company is unusual when compared with the relationship between other exporters and growers in the region, notably because none of the other exporters offer contracts to producers.

Small-scale production of a highly perishable fruit like bananas for a market dominated by a few multinational corporations is challenging, and is one of the reasons Fair Trade is being adopted in this sector. Since it is difficult for small farmers to compete with plantations in the conventional market, the Fair Trade market may represent the only viable option for these growers to continue cultivating bananas. The reasons for this are closely related to difficulties that small farmers face for meeting export market's quality expectations. In general, smaller producers lacking the resources of larger plantations are unable to benefit from expensive technologies, like cable systems for transporting stems or from a permanent and trained labour force to care for the trees prior to harvest. A shortage of capital may also prevent growers from applying the optimal amounts of inputs or irrigating regularly. Each of these factors contributes to a consistent harvest of acceptable quality. This suggests that access to the Fair Trade market may provide many critical advantages for producers that receive their certification.

The analysis of Shreck (2002) suggests that market access provided by Fair Trade certification is a significant and positive benefit to the growers. Even though, when asked about the perceived benefits of Fair Trade, many responded with 'not very large'. In terms of economic support, the increased market security is considered most important, but even when farm gate prices are high, sometimes producers are unable to export and then they must settle again for whatever they can capture at the local market. Yet, this price oftentimes fails to even cover the cost of harvesting, let alone production.

The growers' understanding of the Fair Trade initiative is still fairly limited. Finally receiving direct payments of the social premium was the most significant event and provides the Farmers' Association with visible economic benefits from the Fair Trade market. The promise of a future Fair Trade premium encouraged the group's exporter to pre-finance recovery efforts on the farm after Hurricane George, thereby permitting producers to begin exporting sooner. This use of the premium provided critical support needed by the growers and enabled them to recover from the effects of the hurricane far more easily than other producers in the valley.

Growers in other communities were starting to convert land to other crops, explaining that with bananas, the premium had repaid a large debt and was being earmarked for projects targeting the production process and for strengthening the Association. Again, the size of the Fair Trade social premium is substantial. However, it is intended to be distributed in such a way that its benefits reach the community as a whole. Unless the benefits are better distributed to a broader range of households (a challenge that has thus far been impossible to meet given the demands of the market), Fair Trade has the risk to increase inequalities at local level, a phenomenon not uncommon to other non-traditional export agriculture schemes targeting small-scale producers (Glover and Kusterer, 1990; Conroy *et al.*, 1996). Sufficient autonomy and independence of the local organisation are required to guarantee their abilities for an efficient and equitable distribution of the FT benefits.

Despite growers' increasing level of knowledge about Fair Trade, their sense of entitlement to its benefits remained limited to an expectation that high-quality bananas can provide access to higher-paying export market segments which favour fruit coming from small-scale producers. This limited understanding of the Fair Trade program is not unique to this case (see for instance Renard, 1999; Fisher, 1997), but as elsewhere, it may inhibit the growers' role as real partners in an alternative trade relationship. It also prevents the realisation of the broader potential of Fair Trade participation promised to growers. More attention could therefore be given to educating participants about Fair Trade (for which a range of efforts are currently underway), so that they might eventually fill their role as equal partners, rather than as beneficiaries of an aid package and suppliers of a specialty market. Access to the alternative banana market is one of the most immediate benefits of Fair Trade, but the final effects should be assessed considering wider implications for household and community welfare.

## 3. Case studies

We selected two case studies for the comparison of Fair Trade and non-Fair Trade banana production: (1) *Coopetrabasur* in Southern Costa Rica as a major supplier of bananas to the European Fair Trade market, and (b) San Pablo farm as a representative private banana producer linked to the *Corporación Bananera Nacional* (CORBANA). We focus attention in both cases on the income and welfare position of the labourers and their families.

### *3.1. The case of Coopetrabasur (FT)*

*Coopetrabasur* was founded in 1980 by 70 banana workers after the multinational banana company left the southern part of Costa Rica due to opposition of the labour union. From 1980-1995 they signed a contract with a transnational company for selling the banana at a fixed price. This contact covered production cost and the salary of the families of the associates to the cooperative. In 1996, the transnational company broke the contract and started paying below production cost. *Coopetrabasur* owns 500 ha. in total; half of the area is used for producing banana while the other half produces oil palm that generates substantial profits in the past four years. The bananas survive due to the bonus received on the oil palm that makes the cooperative records to be in blue.

Agrofair comes in 1998, supporting the production and commercialisation of banana. In 2003, the cooperative started certification with EurepGAP and ISO 9001. At the same time they initiated business relationships with COOP, a large supermarket chain from Switzerland. Nowadays, the cooperative meets a stable but still difficult financial situation. They are selling 30 to 40% of the total banana production via Fair Trade at an average price of $ 6.8 per box. The rest of the banana had been sold at conventional price $5.7 per box, while production costs are $6.6 per box. The process of exporting to Europe under the Fair Trade label also implied an increase in costs due to investments in improved labour conditions, packing plant and safety, although there were also introduced changes in the production process for reducing pesticide use (Deugd *et al.*, 2005).

One important characteristic of the *Coopetrabasur* banana production is that it is not in hands of individual producers but under a cooperative structure. The cooperative is the owner of the land, and hence the banana plantation is managed collectively. Therefore, stakeholders do not own land but contribute their labour. In this way, the organisational structure of the multinational firm is maintained but now management is in the hands of the producers. The cooperative has 70 members and around 100 employees. All workers are on payroll and the difference in salaries between a worker and a member is 1,500 colons; more or less 2.8 dollar. The activities performed by the workers are rather varied; workers rotate over the activities depending on the demands of the plantation. Women are likely to be involved at the packing plants. The Fair Trade bonus is received by all workers in the cooperative.

There is an ongoing discussion amongst members to determine if they are going to substitute bananas by oil palm. One of the main arguments of keeping banana is that this crop is labour-intensive and hence associate family members can get a job at the cooperative. In the other hand, oil palm is less labour-intensive but generates higher profitability. But many members still remember the banana company time as the good time for the people in the region.

At the beginning of the relationship with the Fair Trade, *Coopetrabasur* gave the FT premium to the workers in their pay roll cheque. After discussion between the producers and administrative staff of the cooperative it became clear that the role of the premium was not very transparent in this way. Producers and workers mostly considered the premium as a form of salary, and when asked about how they used it nobody could give a precise answer. Basically, they did not differentiate between salary and premium.

The cooperative has changed the way of re-distributing the premium and since 2000 they developed a program which distinguishes between three main areas: social, economic and environmental projects. In recent years, when asking workers and producers about the Fair Trade premium, the majority expresses satisfaction regarding the ways it has been invested, mentioning health care, infrastructure, education, painting of houses, sport facilities for students and children among other benefits. In the last three years, the fair-trade bonus has been kept by the cooperative and used in community projects for sport, health, education and nutrition. In 2008, the Fair Trade program provided 600 school material packages to the children of all stakeholders.

### *3.2. The case of Finca San Pablo (non-FT)*

*Finca San Pablo* was established 40 years ago in 1968 by the former *Asociación Bananera Nacional* (ASBANA), an association funded by a group of Costa Rican banana growers. ASBANA later evolved into the *Corporación Bananera Nacional* (CORBANA), which was created by law in 1971 as a public semi-governmental organisation. CORBANA has been designated as the regulatory body of the Costa Rican banana industry, and its mission is to watch over the development of the banana sector. According to that purpose, CORBANA created – amongst others - two important divisions in research and technical assistance. CORBANA is financed by a fee of US$ 0.05 per exported box of bananas coming from 120 associated plantations. Its share capital is made up, in equal parts, by the central Government, the three state banks and the Costa Rican banana producers. The Board of Directors is formed by one member from the Costa Rican Government, two members from the banks and two members from the associated growers. The workers have two organisations to deal with the managers of *San Pablo*, namely the *Asociación Solidarista* and a syndicated-type workers committee.

*Finca San Pablo* has 300 ha, from which 285 ha are under banana production, 12 ha are under forest reserve and the rest is unused land. The total number of labourers ranges from 200 to 220, most of them specialised in different tasks. The production ranges from 50,000 to 70,000 boxes per month (in 2007). Labour availability has been a critical issue, since the plantation is located in a region where other banana and pineapple plantations compete for labourers. Moreover, in the past *San Pablo* offered less attractive conditions for labourers to settle down and poor operational performance. Because in the production and processing of banana labourers perform specialised tasks, shortages of certain type of workers become critical (i.e. for *paleros*, workers specialised in the construction and maintenance of creeks, or *deshijadores*, workers skilled in the selection of the succeeding offspring for mature banana plants). Hence, the mobility of a worker from one task to another is in many cases constraining, bringing up several operational problems.

In 2006 the managerial board of *San Pablo* prepared an integral reconverting plan for the plantation and presented it to the Board of Directors of CORBANA. The plan has two components, namely an agronomic component aimed to improve the productivity of the plantation, and a social component aimed to make attractive the plantation's facilities to workers, especially to workers with a family. Regarding the former component, the ongoing plan improved the production yields with about 25%, and the latter component implied the following actions: (1) an increase in the base wages per tasks for all workers, (2) a new canteen, (3) a new *comisariato* or mini-supermarket, (4) improvement of the soccer field, (5) refurbished meeting hall and housing facilities, (6) bus service for school and high-school students, and (7) medical services without charge. The plan is co-financed by CORBANA and by the *San Pablo* firm. According to the plantation managers, a quarter of the plan has been performed with promising results.

Certifications have been implemented in *San Pablo* since 1999, mostly due to changes in the international markets. ISO-14001 was the first certification to be achieved, coming through a trade relationship with the transnational Banana Development Corporation (BANDECO) and Del Monte Corp. In the year 2003, EurepGAP was achieved due to a trade relation with Fyffes (a transnational exporting to EU). In this case, having previously achieved ISO-14001 was helpful to adapt the operations in the plantation for gaining the certification. *San Pablo* was the first private banana plantation in the world to gain the EurepGAP. The last gained certification was Rain Forest Alliance, since it was required within a trade relationship with Chiquita. In summary, certifications were used by *San Pablo* to guarantee access to specific banana market segments that would otherwise not be available to them.

All production is sold to one single banana broker, that is selected after gaining a public tender each year. Consequently, given the market dominated by large fruit corporations, the production is never sold independently,. The selling procedures are very structured: the *San Pablo* managers start by preparing a selling plan to be approved by CORBANA. Hereafter, the public tender is designed taking as a reference the minimum selling price fixed by the Costa Rican Government. Once the tender is performed, they negotiated with participants and select the best offer. The *San Pablo* managers regard the activities with promising future. Even while bananas remain a polemic issue in the trade negotiations with the European Union, they did not receive by now any negative signals from the markets or their brokers.

## 4. Materials and methods

To assess the impact of Fair Trade on the banana production we use two organisations one with FT (*Coopetrabasur*) and another without FT (*Finca San Pablo*). We first present some descriptive analysis and then performed a matching analysis to identify the positive or negative impacts of FT for the households and the production system in each organisation. The sample size consists 58 questionnaires for the FT organisation and 55 for the non-FT organisation. We search to control for significant differences in most of the household characteristics to guarantee an un-biased assessment of the FT impact.

Bland and Altman (1994) explain matching as that for every case there is a control who has the same (or closely similar) values of the matching variables. Matching should be based on exogenous characteristics like sex, age, location, ethnic group, etc. We rely on matching to ensure that the controls and the treatment cases are similar in variables which may be related to the variable we are studying but are not of influenced by FT involvement themselves. It should be noted that there are also certain disadvantages to matching, since we can only use cases for whom we have matching controls. The more variables we match, the more difficult it may be to find such controls. Another practical difficulty with matched pairs is that if we want to adjust for other non-matched variables, the analysis requires more complex regression procedures.

Descriptive statistics are performed to check for the main differences between the case studies. The t-test assesses whether the means of two groups are statistically different from each other (Field, 2002). This analysis indicates whether it is appropriate to compare the two groups, and especially to guarantee that the analysis of the post-tests permits the two-group randomised experimental design. Results are presented in Table 1.

The results indicate that the people involved with the Fair Trade have been part of the community for longer periods of time compared to the workers for the non-Fair Trade firm, and hence their sense of belonging and identity identification tends to be higher. It is also clearly confirmed that workers and associates of *Coopetrabasur* feel to be better off than the people working at the non-FT firm, both with respect to current welfare as well as regarding their future welfare expectation.

It is important to notice that people involve in the non-FT segment possess their own production plots and also have other activities besides the agricultural work in banana production. Consequently, they receive slightly higher salaries compared to the people working in the FT farm (although this does not result in significant differences in

*Table 1. Significant differences between Fair Trade and non-Fair Trade farms.*

| | Fair Trade | Non-Fair Trade | Significance [2] |
|---|---|---|---|
| **Household characteristics** | | | |
| Family size | 3.96 | 4.04 | 0.824 |
| Family average age | 26.80 | 24.69 | 0.193 |
| Family head age | 36.88 | 34.47 | 0.847 |
| Family head education | 2.27 | 2.28 | 0.951 |
| Years living at the region | 31.17 | 17.96 | 0.001 *** |
| Years living at the community | 21.68 | 11.74 | 0.001 *** |
| **Income (colons)** | | | |
| Family head contribution | 110,193 | 141,566 | 0.004 *** |
| Family contribution | 186,263 | 195,481 | 0.538 |
| Annual income | 2,318,464 | 2,537,222 | 0.312 |
| Annual expenditures | 2,214,850 | 2,242,514 | 0.853 |
| Profits | 37,528 | 207,441 | 0.425 |
| Male contribution | 146,340 | 169,098 | 0.143 |
| Female contribution | 93,658 | 107,536 | 0.195 |
| **Expenditures (colons)** | | | |
| House maintenance | 1,086,109 | 1,218,353 | 0.095 * |
| Education | 139,547 | 44,742 | 0.001 *** |
| Savings | 42,207 | 58,691 | 0.557 |
| **Risk and organisation perceptions [1]** | | | |
| Organisational perception | 4.67 | 4.53 | 0.160 |
| Risk perception | 3.08 | 3.29 | 0.070 * |
| Satisfaction with Technical Assistance | 8.19 | 7.91 | 0.474 |
| Satisfaction with Trade | 8.91 | 8.71 | 0.114 |
| Actual Economic perception | 1.33 | 1.76 | 0.002 *** |
| Future Economic Perception | 1.34 | 1.62 | 0.036 ** |

[1] Organisational perception (1 = weak, 5 = strong); risk perception (1 = risk acceptance, 7 = risk-averse); satisfaction (1 = little satisfied, 10 = very satisfied); economic perceptions (1 = improved, 3 = deteriorated).

[2] *** significance <0.01; ** significance <0.5; * significance <0.1.

terms of total income or expenditures). Only the family head income contribution to the household is significantly larger for the non-FT segment. This result indicates that FT involvement is not directly resulting in increasing incomes or salaries.

In terms of expenditures, non-FT families tend to invest more in house maintenance, possibly because they have to rent or buy a house in the community, contrary to the FT families where the cooperative provides most of them with houses and covers the maintenance costs. More important, the expenditure analysis reveals that FT workers invest far more in education and training. This is of critical relevance, since investments in educational and social capital are key determinants for breaking vicious circles of exclusion and overcoming poverty traps. This might also explain why FT workers consider themselves better of than five years ago and expects to be better off during the coming five years.

In addition to the socio-economic data, we compared the FT and non-FT workers with respect to several attitudinal variables. We therefore run independent sample t-tests to identify significant differences regarding key variables, like sense of ownership, perceptions regarding the farmers' organisation and individual savings and investment behaviour. As shown in Table 2, workers and associates of *Coopetrabasur* have a substantially stronger sense of belonging and feelings of ownership compared to those in the private non-FT company.

In terms of asset ownership, saving propensity and access to credit, workers in the FT farm have a positive association towards credit access and asset (mainly bicycle) ownership, but in the non-FT company there is a larger positive association towards saving capabilities. As we will explain later, this is largely related to the income composition and the frequency of payments. Access to credit is facilitated by the national banking system as well as through the workers association of the FT Cooperative that gives the guaranty to the credit organisation.

*Table 2. Significant association between Fair Trade and attitudinal attributes.*

| Attribute | Fair Trade | Non-Fair Trade |
|---|---|---|
| Working years | + ** | |
| Working at the cooperative | + *** | |
| Years of living in the region | + ** | |
| Saving capability | | + *** |
| Assets ownership (bikes) | + *** | |
| Access to credit | + *** | |
| Sense of belonging to the organisation | + *** | |
| Workers feels the organisation as theirs | | - * |
| Organisation is efficient | + ** | |
| Actual situation is better than 5 years ago | | - *** |
| Future situation will be better off in 5 years | | - * |

Note: +/- = positive/negative effect of the association;
significance levels: *** sign. <0.01 (1%); ** sign. <0.05 (5%); * sign. <0.1 (10%).

### *4.1. Fair Trade premium in* Coopetrabasur

Members and workers of *Coopetrabasur* generally believe that Fair Trade offers more benefits than conventional production (91% of respondents). Some of the benefits that are most mentioned are: minimum wages (15%), access to social security (9%) and better working conditions (15%). We also asked the associates and workers about the importance of the FT premium for them and 86% of the respondents confirmed that the premium was considered important. However, 71% of the respondents said that they have not been consulted about the use and allocation of the premium money.

When we asked how the premium should be used, respondents forwarded options like improvement of wages (22%), community infrastructure (31%) and better working conditions (12%). In practice, the Fair Trade premium of *Coopetrabasur* has been used in several ways during the last eight years. In the beginning, the Fair Trade premium was given to the members and workers as part of their weekly salary, although in the salary form the amount of premium was separately specified. This procedure reduced the consciousness regarding Fair Trade benefits, and therefore nowadays *Coopetrabasur* developed a program to use the Fair Trade premium within three defined areas of work. addressing economic, social and environmental issues. The premium use is controlled and manages by the cooperative board. Most members are now more aware about the impact of Fair Trade for their community.

In the absence of fully reliable information on the current spending of the FT premium, we presented *Coopetrabasur* members and workers several options for the preferred allocation (see Table 3). Investments in health care, education and infrastructure are generally most appreciated, whereas premium use for credit provision and technical assistance receive considerable lower priority. Most likely, the absence of public programs related to infrastructure, education and health have biased the answers

*Coopetrabasur* has been working in line with these main trend asked by members for FT premium investments. There are several ongoing projects for improving the quality of life of the members and workers within the cooperative (i.e. maintenance

*Table 3. Preferences regarding Fair Trade premium use.*

| Area | Resource allocation (in %) | | Priority ranking (1 = high, 5 = low) | |
|---|---|---|---|---|
| | Average | Standard deviation | Average | Standard deviation |
| Technical assistance | 13 | 7.5 | 3.6 | 1.4 |
| Education | 23 | 13.6 | 2.6 | 1.3 |
| Credit provision | 17 | 9.1 | 4 | 1 |
| Health care | 26 | 15 | 2.2 | 1 |
| Infrastructure | 25 | 17 | 2.6 | 1.4 |

of communal green areas, construction of a saloon for meetings), a health area is constructed and investments in a communal water source managed by the cooperative have been realised. In addition, an ambulance has been bought and a small communal clinic managed by the Health Ministry is realised for better controlling diseases like malaria, cholera, among others. Part of the FT premium has been invested in promoting women entrepreneurial training, school maintenance, school food program for children, educational materials, and general training programs for the whole community. It is important to notice that these communal improvements in quality of life issues have been done after changing the FT retribution system from direct monetary transfers through weekly salary to an establish cooperative program where the premium is concentrated and invested in major socio-economic and environmental activities.

## 5. Impact assessment

The survey is based on a total number of 110 valid observations suitable for analysis. We first run a Probit regression to capture the main exogenous attributes differentiating between Fair Trade and non-Fair Trade producers. The result of the Probit are presented in Table 4.

It is important to notice that a main attribute to define the likelihood for Fair Trade participation of a particular household is related to the number of years living in the community. This variable refers to the identity and the sense of belonging. In addition, to be able to participate in membership of a (cooperative) organisation is required. *Coopetrabasur* membership that can be obtained over time, by invitation or inheritance.

It also seems that smaller as well as older families are more likely to belong to a Fair Trade organisation. Family heads are on average somewhat older when belonging to the

*Table 4. Fair Trade discriminant attributes (Probit regression).*

| Likelihood Fair Trade (1.0) | Coefficient | S.E. | Significance |
|---|---|---|---|
| Years of working at the organisation | 0.6933 | 0.0386 | 0.072 ** |
| Farm household head age | 0.0533 | 0.0202 | 0.008 *** |
| Family size | -0.0411 | 0.1050 | 0.696 |
| Household head contribution | $-8.22*10^{-6}$ | $3.32*10^{-6}$ | 0.013 |
| Years living at region | 0.0575 | 0.0176 | 0.001 *** |
| Years living at community | 0.01952 | 0.016 | 0.223 |
| Constant | 0.9438 | 0.7672 | 0.219 |

Note: * Sign. <0.1; ** Sign <0.05; *** Sign <0.01; Pseudo $R^2$ = 33.03%.

Fair Trade organisation compared to the workers at *Finca San Pablo*. Lack of mobility and more local stability – as reflected by the number of years living in a particular region or community – seem to indicate that FT families are usually well established.

After conducting the Probit regression, we perform the *propensity score matching* procedure to identify the impact of Fair Trade on the selected outcome variables (i.e. total assets, expenditure in education, organisation perception, risk perception, total income, total expenditure, profits, savings and household expenditure).

We only present in Table 5 the most significant outcomes. We find consistent outcomes by running three different matching possibilities (kernel, one-to-one and nearest neighbours). Because of this consistency, we only discuss the latter estimates using the *nearest neighbour* procedure (looking for the cases that are similar or equal to each other).

The most significant outcome is that in the case of banana the impact of Fair Trade is particularly positive when referring to wealth. Differences in tangible and non tangible assets are significant and show a positive impact on household and community welfare. Wealth is constructed as an asset index and Costa Rican banana farmers experience a positive impact of FT on assets. This implies that even while no significant income differences are registered, wealth differences (resulting from other expenditure preferences) are the most notable result.

Another important outcome is that – with similar income levels – FT farmers devote significantly more resources to educational expenditure, illustrating the revealed preference that FT farmers highly value education as a key element to break the poverty trap. This illustrates the importance given to human capital (in addition to social capital) for improving quality of life for the smallholding communities.

At the same time it is important to note that the perception regarding the organisational performance under FT is higher than under non-FT conditions. This indicates that FT farmers appreciate the role of good governance within their organisations as a key attribute for reaching a positive FT impact. The stronger sense of belonging and co-ownership are play a critical role in enabling stakeholder identification with FT.

Finally, the female contribution to the household income is significantly larger for the non-Fair Trade farmers. This may be partly explained by the more decisive recruitment policies applied in *Finca San Pablo*, that tries to maintain and attract families by providing additional opportunities and facilities for women to work, including higher salaries.

In general, Fair Trade members are better off compared to their counterpart in the comparable non-FT enterprise. This is most strongly related to the sense of belonging that they experience, the impact of the cooperative in their day to day life, as well as to the amount of assets acquired by the members and the social programs provided by

*Table 5. Matching analysis of Fair Trade banana in Costa Rica.*

| | Kernel | | | One-to-one | | | Nearest neighbour (3) | | |
|---|---|---|---|---|---|---|---|---|---|
| | Diff. | S.E. | t-stat | Diff. | S.E. | t-stat | Diff. | S.E. | t-stat |
| **Income** | | | | | | | | | |
| Annual income | 240,843 | 365,236 | 0.66 | 255,676 | 414,331 | 0.62 | 265,369 | 372,025 | 0.71 |
| Annual expenditures | 139,880 | 205,882 | 0.68 | 110,585 | 221,349 | 0.50 | 187,352 | 219,816 | 0.85 |
| Profits | 222,942 | 350,101 | 0.64 | 360,859 | 326,637 | 1.10 | 190,444 | 336,883 | 0.57 |
| Total assets | 1,260,671 | 655,206 | 2.27** | 1,835,684 | 692,502 | 2.65** | 1,249,114 | 608,432 | 2.05** |
| Female contribution | -29,264 | 17,133 | -1.71* | -36,615 | 16,185 | -2.26** | -26,744 | 16,419 | -1.63* |
| **Expenditures** | | | | | | | | | |
| House maintenance | -153088 | 113,009 | -1.35 | -257,514 | 118,543 | -2.17** | -140,973 | 108,581 | -1.30 |
| Education | 62370 | 27,856 | 2.24** | 55,632 | 32,932 | 1.69* | 609,47 | 27,710 | 2.20* |
| Savings | 20214 | 40,824 | 0.50 | 678,46 | 42,053 | 0.90 | 12,718 | 425,44 | 0.30 |
| **Risk and organisation perceptions** | | | | | | | | | |
| Organisation perception | 0.17 | 0.15 | 1.16 | 0.10 | 0.19 | 0.52 | 0.11 | 0.15 | 0.75 |
| Risk perception | -0.12 | 0.16 | -0.74 | -0.16 | 0.22 | -0.72 | -0.14 | 0.17 | -0.85 |
| Satisfaction tech. assistance | 0.47 | 0.61 | 0.78 | -0.08 | 0.82 | -0.09 | 0.27 | 0.62 | 0.43 |
| Satisfaction trade | 0.49 | 0.42 | 0.97 | 0.21 | 0.57 | 0.36 | 0.44 | 0.41 | 1.05 |
| Actual economic perception | -0.60 | 0.21 | -2.81** | -0.41 | 0.29 | -1.43 | -0.59 | 0.23 | -2.55** |
| Future economic perception | -0.53 | 0.21 | -2.53** | -0.59 | 0.30 | -1.98* | -0.53 | 0.23 | -2.27** |

Note: significance levels: * Sign. <0.1; ** Sign <0.05; *** Sign <0.01.

the cooperative. In words of one stakeholder '... *while the cooperative stands, we will have work and food for our families...*'.

## 6. Discussion and conclusions

*Coopetrabasur* is in a moment of critical decisions, because many of the members are trying to move to palm oil due to the boom of the bio-fuel, while others are still keeping bananas as their main livelihood strategy. Palm oil production is far less labour-intensive and prices in the market are higher; therefore *Coopetrabasur* profitability increasingly depends on palm oil. Banana production, on the other end, is more labour- intensive and at this moment production is hardly profitable, not even considering the Fair Trade premium. At this moment there are two different options: (1) some members are willing to fully change production to palm oil giving priority to private financial-economic arguments, and (2) other members are willing to maintain some less profitable banana area by increasing the amount of labour per hectare (even beyond the average number per hectare), in an effort for keeping and giving work to many people in the cooperative and community.

Current practice is that the palm oil production provides a subsidy for the banana production. Palm oil has been highly profitable during the last years and its revenues are used to compensate for the losses in bananas. Conventional prices of banana at $5.5 per box and for Fair Trade banana at $6.8 per box hardly compensate the production costs of $6.6 per box at *Coopetrabasur*. Break even performance requires that at least 40% of the bananas most be sold through Fair Trade.

When FT premium payments are given as part of the salary, the impact was not clear in the eyes of the beneficiaries, mainly because the additional income is directly transferred to consumption. The positive impact became greater when the premium became managed by the local organisation and invested in local projects as defined by the board of the cooperative and the assembly. The Fair Trade premium becomes more important to the organisation when international prices of banana are low or when there is a crisis in the sector. With rising global prices, the difference between international conventional price and Fair Trade price is small, and under these circumstances the additional effort for producing Fair Trade banana is not well rewarded in the eyes of the cooperative stakeholders.

One important issue that is worthy to mention again is that in this case study the behavioural preferences towards investment in education seem to be the most fundamental difference between FT and the non-FT farmers. The high importance given to education may, however, in the long run enable their children to become engaged in other, non-agricultural activities. Education might thus contribute in breaking the vicious poverty circle, eventually even escaping from banana production.

The data analysis shows that most banana workers in the Fair Trade farm are still fully working just at the banana plantation, whereas workers from the non-FT company have already more diversified income sources. Since no significant differences in terms of risk attitudes are observed, the engagement in FT may thus serve as an alternative insurance strategy that reduces prospects for household income diversification.

## References


Bacon, C.M. (2005). Confronting the Coffee Crisis: Can Fair Trade, Organic and Speciality Coffees reduce Small-scale Farmer Vulnerability in Northern Nicaragua? *World Development* 33: 497-511.

Banana Link (1997). Fair Trade Breakthrough Rattles Big Boys. *Banana Trade News Bulletin*, p. 1.

Banana Link (2000). ¿2001: Hacia Un Nuevo Siglo Bananero? Availabale at: http://www.bananalink.org.uk/ 2001_doc/2001_doc.htm.

Banana Link (2001). *Best of the Bunch! Fair Trade bananas: From producer to consumer.* Norwich: Banana Link.

Bland, J.M. and D.G. Altman (1994). Statistical Notes: Matching. *British Medical Journal* 309: 1128.

Bourgeois, P. (1989). *Ethnicity at Work: Divided Labor on a Central American Banana Plantation.* Baltimore: Johns Hopkins University Press.

Brown, O., C. Charavat and D. Eagleton (2001). *The Coffee Market: A Background Study.* London: Oxfam.

Chambron, A. (2000). *Straightening the Bent World of Bananas.* Maastricht: EFTA.

Conroy, M., D. Murray and P. Rosset. (1996). *A Cautionary Tale: Failed U.S. Development Policy in Central America.* Boulder: Lynne Rienner Press.

Deugd, M, G. Beluche and I. Villalobos (2005). *Sistema de crédito COOPETRABASUR-AFAD.* Informe Final Centro de Estudios para el Desarrollo Rural, San José.

Fair Trade Federation (2000). Fair Trade Facts. Available at: http://www.fairtradefederation.com.

FAO (2000). *Ad-hoc Expert Meeting on Socially and Environmentally Responsible Banana Production and Trade.* Rome: FAO

Field, A. (2002). *Discovering Statistics. Using SPSS for Windows.* SAGE Publications, London.

Fisher, E. (1997). Beekeepers In the Global 'Fair Trade' Market: A Case From Tabora Region, Tanzania. *International Journal of Sociology of Agriculture and Food* 6: 109-159.

FLO - Fair Trade Labelling Organization (2000). Fairtrade Banana Criteria. Available at: http://www.fairtrade.net/banana.html.

FLO - Fair Trade Labelling Organization (2002). Sales in 2001. *FLO Fairtrade Fruits Newsletter* 1.

FLO - Fair Trade Labelling Organization (2003). Standards in general. Available at: http://www.fairtrade.net/sites/standards/general.htm.

Getz, C and A. Shreck (2006). What Organic and Fair Trade labels do not tell us: towards a place-based understanding of certification. *International Journal of Consumer Studies* 30: 490-501.

Glover, D. and K. Kusterer (1990). *Small Farmers, Big Business: Contract Farming and Rural Development.* New York: St. Martin's Press.

Goodman, D. (1999). Agro-food studies in the Age of Ecology': Nature, corporeality, bio-politics. *Sociologia Ruralis* 39: 17-38.

Henriques, W., R. Jeffers, T. Lacher and R. Kendall (1997). 'Agrochemical Use on Banana Plantations in Latin America: Perspectives on Ecological Risk'. *Environmental Toxicology and Chemistry* 16: 91-99.

IADB - Inter-American Development Bank (2000). *Social Protection for Equity and Growth*. Washington, DC: IADB.

Liddell, I. (2000). *Unpeeling the Banana Trade*. London: Fairtrade Foundation.

Ponte, S. (2002a). The Latte Revolution? Regulation, Markets and Consumption in the Global Coffee Chain. *World Development* 30: 1099-1122.

Ponte, S. (2002b). Brewing a Bitter Cup? Deregulation, Quality and the Re-organization of Coffee Marketing in East Africa. *Journal of Agrarian Change* 2: 248-272.

Raynolds, L. and D. Murray (1998). Yes, We Have No Bananas: Re-Regulating Global and Regional Trade. *International Journal of Sociology of Agriculture and Food* 7: 7-44.

Renard, M. (1999). 'The Interstices of Globalization: The Example of Fair Coffee'. *Sociologia Ruralis* 39: 484-500.

Rice, A. (2001). Noble Goals and Challenging Terrain: Organic and Fair Trade Coffee Movements in the Global Marketplace. *Journal of Agricultural and Environmental Ethics* 14: 39-66.

Shreck, A. (2002) Just Bananas? Fair Trade Banana Production in the Diploma Republic. *International Journal of Sociology of Agriculture and Food* 10: 13-23.

# Chapter 5

## Assessment of the effect of Fair Trade on smallholder producers in Costa Rica: a comparative study in the coffee sector

*Fernando Sáenz-Segura and Guillermo Zúñiga-Arias*

### 1. Introduction

The Fair Trade movement was established in 1992 out of several founding organisations, as a coordinated initiative aimed to contribute to the improvement of quality of life among primary producers in the developing world. It is categorised both as a social movement and market-based model. There is a myriad of international organisations involved in Fair Trade, all of them pursuing broadly similar social development objectives (Ronchi, 2002). These organisations basically administrate the Fair Trade Certification (FTC) by performing two basic activities: (1) supervision of production operations in developing countries, and (2) guaranteeing to consumers in developed countries that the products originated in developing countries fulfil the FT philosophy. Some of these organisations also administrate special Fair Trade stores in the developed world. In 1998, FINE was created as an informal association of four main Fair Trade networks: Fairtrade Labelling Organization International (FLO), International Fair Trade Association, Network of European Worldshops and European Fair Trade Association.

The Fair Trade certification regime operates in a fairly simple manner: primary producers receive a procurement price that is generally higher than the conventional market price (premium price). Consumers in the developed country are willing to pay such a higher price, just because they want to contribute to the welfare of producers in the South and their families. Hence, the philosophy behind FT is more than simple trade and has certain ethical and solidarity dimensions (see also Chapter 11).

On the other hand, producers in developing countries applying for FT must fulfil certain requirements. First, they should be regarded as small growers who depend mainly on family labour for production. Producers should be organised and operating their organisations along democratic lines. The implemented decision-making process should be extended to the destiny of the additional capital resources resulting from participation in the FT movement (Rice, 2001). Moreover, FT is expected to have a positive impact on farmers organisations. Since these organisations directly receive the premium payment, they can operate social-oriented development projects, such as investment in education, infrastructure and credit programs for agricultural and non-agricultural activities. Hence, we can expect a strengthening of farmers' organisations around the administration of this capital, and a positive spill over effect in terms of purchase of inputs and bargaining power capacities.

The FT philosophy essentially differs from the neo-classical point of view. At theoretical level, FT is sometimes considered as a price distortion that affects well-functioning markets, where equilibrium prices are set by supply and demand reaching maximum utility (see disscussion in Chapter 10). At ideological level, it may be regarded as a pathway that condemns farmers to poverty, as FT artificially keeps them into non-profitable activities (Fridell, 2007). These critical views are hardly assessed with empirical field data. Instead, a political economy analysis of FT will argue that markets are already heavily distorted and that FT supply chains try to modify transaction costs and risk distribution amongst farmers, traders, processors and retailers.

On the other hand, some authors criticise the linkages between FT agencies and farmers' organisations and wonder if the premium prices really benefits farmers and their communities. It has been said that the real impact of the Fair Trade on the quality of life of primary producers is mostly due to the organisational development supported by Fair Trade agencies (Ronchi, 2002). However, under certain circumstances this organisational development may fail in the proper administration of the fair price and/or in the provision of supporting services. This situation may hide the potential Fair Trade benefits and could contribute to growing distrust between producers and agencies involved in the Fair Trade. Moreover, financial services and other supporting activities may be absent or scarcely developed at the interface between smallholder farmers, primary peasant organisations and secondary trade agencies, thus contributing to deviations from the original purpose of the Fair Trade movement.

In this paper we present an integrated assessment of the impact of Fair Trade for smallholder coffee producers in Costa Rica. The remainder of the paper is organised as follows: Section two reviews the basic ideas behind the FT and its origins. Section three discusses the experiences of Fair Trade in coffee production and trade. Section four describes the selected case studies. In section five we outline the field work methodology and the matching procedures. Section six presents major outcomes. Finally, in section seven we discuss their implications for policy and development practice.

## 2. Fair Trade as an alternative trade model

The early foundations of Fair Trade (*Comercio Justo*) started in 1946 when Ten Thousand Villages, a North American broker of craftsmanship, started buying embroideries from Puerto Rico, with the idea to generate employment and income among poor people. In 1949 the Sales Exchange Refugee Rehabilitation and Vocation (SERRV), a non-profit organisation, started buying products from countries in South America. By 1958 opens the first Fair Trade Store in United Sates. In the same decade, the movement started in Europe led by Oxfam GB, which bought crafts from Chinese refugees. By 1967 in Europe the first importer that administrated the Fair Trade seal was established. By 1969 the first 'World Shop' - better known as Fair Trade stores - opened their doors, playing an important role in the promotion of the Fair Trade philosophy among consumers in the developed world (IFAT, 2002).

According to Vizcarra (2002), during the 1960's and 1970's Fair Trade evolved into a more coordinated movement between organisations from the North and the South. This coordination basically sought alternative market chains for producers that for some political or economic reasons where excluded from classical spot markets. 'Trade, not Aid' was the slogan at that time, which meant that developing countries needed an alternative way to trade under equal conditions with the developed world. In this sense, it was based on the so-called 'alternative trade' paradigm that sought to fight poverty in the developing world. The Dutch '*Solidaridad*' was the first organisation aiming to certify Fair Trade imports through the *Max Havelaar* seal. In the 1980's the European Fair Trade Association (EFTA) and the International Federation of Alternative Trade (IFAT) were established. Coffee was the initial FT target activity because international prices were severely depressed at that time, leaving the producers with almost no feasible options for profitable trade. In 1997, several agencies conform the Fair Labelling Organization (FLO) in an effort to streamline certification activities

There are several terms and definitions used to characterise Fair Trade. 'Partnership', 'dialogue', 'transparency', 'respect', 'empowerment' and 'fairness' are keywords in most FT definitions. Fair Trade goes beyond the mere exchange of products, since it pursues fairness and changes in the conventional rules that govern in the international commerce. It puts the people above the earnings (IFAT, 2002). The philosophy behind Fair Trade is to increase the welfare of families in the developing world by eliminating unnecessary middlemen along the chain, and creating a kind of social conscience amongst retailers and consumers in the target country. This implies a long term relationship between the trading partners, with certain criteria of ethics and solidarity (Lara-Pineda, 2000). FINE gives the following concise definition of Fair Trade:

> *'Fair Trade is a trading partnership, based on dialogue, transparency and respect, which seeks greater equity in international trade. It contributes to sustainable development by offering better trading conditions to, and securing the rights of, marginalised producers and workers - especially in the*

*South. Fair Trade organisations (backed by consumers) are engaged actively in supporting producers, awareness raising and in campaigning for changes in the rules and practice of conventional international trade'.*

Fair Trade seeks to protect the rights of producers and their families, increasing their welfare and preserving cultural values associated to the production of a certain good. Therefore, the idea is to substitute the aid-based relationship between the developed and developing countries, by another based on cooperation and equity. FT functions by establishing a more direct relationship between a producer and a consumer of a good, which is certified by a Fair Trade organisation. Hence, the producer receives a higher price than in the conventional market price for the product. Consumers are willing to pay a higher price, because they are aware that such higher price contributes to improved producer's welfare.

There are several criteria the producers should satisfy before being able to join Fair Trade (Rice, 2001). For instance, they must to be regarded as small growers who depend mainly on family labour for their production. Producers should also be organised and operating their organisations along democratic lines. The implemented decision-making process should extend to the destiny of additional capital resulting from participation in the FT movement. With the fair price, the organisations can provide services that individual producers cannot afford. Hence, access to inputs and credit is an obvious positive effect derived from social organisation at the producers' level. Community cohesion and coordinated actions aiming to further the social interests of the community are also benefits that often come about as 'side' effects of cooperative strengthening and integration.

## 3. Fair Trade coffee

Most studies on FT coffee focus on the price differences between regular and FT sales. Low coffee prices continue to devastate rural economies and threaten the biodiversity associated with traditional production (CEPAL, 2002; IADB, 2002). Permanent employment in Central America's coffee sector has fallen by more than 50% and seasonal employment by 21% (IADB, 2002). Among the consequences are shifts in power to the roasting and retailing end of the commodity chain and declining prices paid to producers (Talbot, 1997).

Bacon (2005) compared Fair Trade, organic and specialty coffees with respect to their potential to reduce small-scale farmers' vulnerability in Northern Nicaragua. In this region, 61% of the surveyed farmers grow half of more of the food they eat. Many coffee farmers also produce maize, beans, bananas, fruits, chayote and yucca, while purchasing off-farm commodities like salt, sugar, oil and meat. Both men and women allocate 80-90% of their maize and beans to household consumption before selling an eventual surplus. In contrast, farmers sold 80-90% of the coffee harvest, generally keeping only the lowest quality beans for their own consumption. Coffee revenues are used to build houses, send children to school, and provide savings and investments for the future. The study supports the conclusion that access to FT certified coffee markets leads to significantly higher (and more stable) prices paid to the farmers and enables them to improve their livelihoods. Certification has an even greater influence on prices than the altitude (related to quality production).

The evidence from this study suggests that participation in alternative trade networks reduces exposure and vulnerability to low commodity prices. In a similar vein, Raynolds (2002) also points to the price premium as a critical element to offset the many other conditions that affect the quality of life. Farmers linked to coffee cooperatives that sell to alternative markets received higher average prices and also felt more secure in their land tenure. However, even then three quarters of all surveyed farmers reported a decline in their quality of life during the last few years. Their responses to the questions about perceived changes in the quality of life showed no significant difference between farmers participating in conventional and alternative trade networks. This finding and the results of the focus groups suggest that income from coffee sales to alternative markets is not enough to offset the many other conditions (e.g. higher input costs, steadily increasing consumer prices, gasoline and communication costs) that have provoked a perceived decline in the quality of one's life.

Many cooperatives allocate a substantial proportion of the price premium offered by Fair Trade and organic markets to investments in productive infrastructure, payments of debts, provision of credit, technical assistance services, coverage of administrative and certification costs, and to funding of housing and education projects in farmer communities. These practices sometimes result in lower direct production costs or subsidised living costs for the producers involved.

It should be note that most farmers sell their coffee to multiple markets (Brown *et al.*, 2001). FT agencies purchase up to 60% of the coffee, while the remainder is delivered through conventional market outlets. Raynolds (2002) registers that farmers delivering to a cooperative connected only to conventional markets are four times more likely to perceive a risk of losing the title to their land due to low coffee prices compared to members of cooperatives connected to FT coffee markets. Community investments made in local projects for health promotion, environment, education and community development are likely to reinforce these ownership feelings.

Access to FT is conditional on a number of selection criteria. Producer groups must consist of smallholder growers that operate their own farm depending mainly upon family labour to produce their coffee. The group must be organised and operated along democratic lines, and the decision-making process extends to the destiny of additional capital resulting from participation in the FT movement (Rice, 2001). Cooperative efforts in the rural countryside are supposed to provide smallholder producers with a range of benefits to overcome the constraints of operating as atomised actors within their local milieu. Access to inputs and credit is an obvious positive effect derived from social organisation at the production level. Larger cooperatives can reach economies of scale in purchase, thus potentially cutting transaction costs related to the provision of inputs, services and credit.

Community cohesion and coordinated actions aimed to further strengthen the interests of the community are also benefits that often perceived as 'side' effects of the cooperative organisation. Producers often make long-term (forward) contracts prior to harvest time to deliver their coffee to the processor or marketing cooperatives (Rice, 2001). If prices remain stable until harvest, the marketing cooperative should be able to pay all the money due to the grower and may collect a margin for covering operational expenses and financial costs. Of course, if prices decline during the 'waiting period' between signing the contract and the delivery of the harvest, the growers receive their guaranteed floor price and might be willing to wait some time until the marketing cooperative is able to cancel the second part of the payment in due order (*ibid.*).

## 4. Case studies

We selected two coffee processors in the central-western part of Costa Rica for an in-depth impact analysis of FT. We started by making a brief survey of nine cooperatives belonging to the consortium COOCAFE, which unites 3,500 coffee producers under Fair Trade Certification. COOCAFE is one of the first and oldest partners in the FT coffee program (Ronchi, 2002). We selected *Coopemontes de Oro R.L.* as a representative case study, since it shows average performance. It sells the coffee to different importers in the United States, Canada, Germany, France, Switzerland and The Netherlands and reports an average yearly production of 230 tons.

As control case *Café de Altura S.A.* is selected, with quite similar operations to *Coopemontes de Oro R.L.* It is an interesting case study, because this enterprise functions under particular organisational arrangements, whit certain criteria of social solidarity and tight cultural roots in the community. While *Café de Altura* is registered as a private enterprise, they consider themselves as an experimental organisational model between classical entrepreneurship and a cooperative firm. Given their legal status as an enterprise, they can not apply for Fair Trade Certification, but part of the coffee is delivered to Utz Kapeh. Table 1 summarises the main characteristics of both case studies.

### 4.1. *Coopemontes de Oro R.L.* (Fair Trade case)

*Coope Montes de Oro R.L.* was established in 1984 as a traditional coffee cooperative, aiming to process all the coffee production from the highlands of the *Cantón* of *Montes de Oro*, Province of Puntarenas. The main facilities of the cooperative are located in the town of Miramar. In 1988, *Coope Montes de Oro* - together with nine other cooperatives - founded the so-called *Consorcio de Cooperativas de Caficultores de Guanacaste y Montes de Oro R.L* (COOCAFE). At the beginning, the consortium

*Table 1. Comparison of case studies.*

| Characteristics | Coopemontes de Oro R.L. | Café de Altura S.A. |
|---|---|---|
| Type of firm | Treatment | Control |
| Year of foundation | 1984 | 2004 |
| Number of members | 286 | 600 |
| Number of workers | 10 | 20 |
| Main commercial activity | coffee | coffee |
| Land area (ha) | 1581.58 | 3240 |
| Land tenure | land owned by each member | land owned by each member |
| Median of farmer's land (ha) | 5.53 | 5.4 |
| Total production (average/year) | 230 tons | 7740 tons |
| Percentage of sales conventional output | 60-70% | 100% |
| FT premium received (%) | 60% | none |
| Others | two processing facilities | one processing facility |
| Certifications | Fair Trade | Practices<br>Utz Kapeh |
| Year of certifications | 1994 | 2005 |
| Implementation of certifications | via overprice (60% of the overprice goes to producers and 40% goes to the cooperative | via prize. It has been won by the enterprise consecutively over two years (70% goes to producers and 30% to different social investments) |
| Other commercial activities or services | hardware store<br>factory of organic fertiliser<br>cafeteria<br>drying of coffee<br>transport of fruit coffee | none |

aimed to provide administrative and financial assistance to its founding members, but later evolved into a secondary level, service-rendering exporting association. By 1989 COOCAFE began to participate into the Fair Trade of coffee (Ronchi, 2002).

In *Montes de Oro,* the production areas of coffee are located at 17 km from the town of *Miramar*. The zone is poorly accessible by a single dirty road. The cooperative has 286 active members, one (outdated) processing facility in the production zone (currently closed), and another plant in Miramar with better technology and a sun-operated machine where the processed coffee can be dried. As most traditional cooperatives, *Coope Montes de Oro R.L.* owns one of the largest hardware stores in town. They have also developed other services, such a factory of organic fertilisers made with the remains of the coffee fruit, dumped after the process. More recently, a small cafeteria has been successfully installed to enhance local people to taste and drink export quality coffee. The cooperative also enables the associates to exchange fresh fruit coffee by the corresponding amount of processed coffee (for personal use). Besides, it owns 53 ha. of undeveloped land with certain potential for tourist development. By 1994 the cooperative received the Fair Trade certification, and the FT premium is supposedly distributed 60% to producers and 40% to the cooperative.

The cooperative has a certain monopolistic positions since is the only coffee processor in the zone. Coffee growers are scattered along one single road axle that connects several small villages until reaching the town of Cedral (the largest village). The production zone is relatively isolated and includes the high part of the Aranjuez river watershed. Due to the geographic characteristics of the watershed, the entire region has only one entrance and one exit through the road. This highly constrains the access to other parts of the country and the connection with larger urban centres. Moreover, coffee producers have to transport their produce with their own means or by hiring private transportation, whereas the cooperative offers transportation services at a small charge. Certainly, all these facts contribute to enhance the central position of the cooperative in front of the producers.

According to Ronchi (2002), the relevant direct impact of FT administrated through COOCAFE is the distribution of the price premium. Thirty percent of this premium is invested in capitalisation funds, while the remaining 70% is devoted to a producers' fund. The resources from the latter fund are directly distributed to the primary-level cooperatives.[1] Each individual cooperative saves half of the capitalisation fund into a so-called Social Capital Fund. The fund is aiming to finance several projects, such as the production of organic fertiliser or the diversification of production activities, as well as educational programs for members and families.

The socio-cultural level of coffee producers in *Montes de Oro* is relatively low in comparison with other production zones, and most farmers only have primary education. Some of these producers consider certifications like Fair Trade as 'an expensive way to access specialised markets' and expressed reserves whether FT might be beneficial in the long term. Some other cannot afford to introduce changes in the productions system. Most producers consider the Fair Trade premium as a safeguard against international low prices. Actually, it helped a lot to guarantee adequate maintenance of the coffee plots. However, during periods with low prices (like the years 2003 and 2006) the adopted strategy is to reduce maintenance of the coffee plantation, move into other agricultural activities and use part of the premium to maintain household consumption. Table 2 shows the distribution of the FT premium price, during the last harvest-periods.

[1] The distribution varies from cooperative to cooperative. In the case of *Montes de Oro*, the distribution is 60%/40%

*Table 2. Coope Montes de Oro R.L., premium fund distribution (in US$).*

| Harvest-period | Certifications | Technical assistance | Investment in technology | Total |
|---|---|---|---|---|
| 2004-2005 | 3,884.54 | 3,884.54 | 3,884.54 | 11,653.62 |
| 2005-2006 | 4,352.93 | 2,418.30 | 2,901.95 | 9,673.18 |
| 2006-2007 | 4,316.44 | 4,316.44 | 4,316.44 | 12,949.32 |
| Total | 12,553.91 | 10,619.18 | 11,102.93 | 34,276.12 |

Over the last three periods, 37% of the total premium was allocated to pay certifications, while around 30% was allocated to technical assistance and technological upgrading, respectively. From the period 2004-2005 to 2005-2006 the total amount of the premium was reduced in 10%, but it increased again with 40% by the period 2006-2007. It is interesting to note again that around a third part of the total premium is used to pay back the certification itself. For a small and constrained cooperative like *Coope Montes de Oro*, this share may be too costly. Moreover, the remaining 64% is supposedly devoted to technical assistance and technology investments. However, in both cases the total amount of money is lower than the yearly income of a local agricultural technician.

There are no major differences in quality between the coffee from Miramar and the coffees of the Central Valley (Hard Bean and Strictly Hard Bean). According to Ing. Alex Díaz, of the agency of Minister of Agriculture and Livestock (MAG) in Cedral (with 25 years of working experience in the zone) the coffee of Miramar is wrongly classified as Pacific, while the quality of the cup is similar to the coffee cup of the western part of the Central Valley. This is because most of the coffee lies around 1,000 m. above sea level and there are no strong differences in terms of soil quality and climate compared to the western part of the Central Valley (San Ramón). Unsuccessfully, the MAG has been attempting to change the qualification of the coffee of Miramar from Pacific to Central Valley. Moreover, *Coope Montes de Oro* has done little effort on this.[2]

The relationship between the cooperative and its associates is somewhat difficult. Inadequate past decisions and deficient management in general led the cooperative through several crises in the past, arriving even at the edge of bankruptcy. This has increased the level of distrust amongst the producers, who consider uncertain their future trade relationship with the cooperative. Moreover, the cooperative is challenged to distribute proper information regarding selling prices, payment of premiums, technical assistance, quality and destination of the production. However, since the cooperative is the only buyer in the zone, the producers feel a high dependency and would benefit from alternative options.

[2] Ing. Alex Díaz Porras, personal communication, 2007

### *4.2. Café de Altura de San Ramón Especial S.A. (non-Fair Trade case)*

*Café de Altura S.A.* was created as a private enterprise in the year 2004 when *Coopecafira R.L.* - the traditional coffee cooperative in San Ramón - went into bankruptcy. The Cantón of San Ramón is located in the Western Central valley of Costa Rica and is one of the most important regions of coffee production of the country. *Coopecafira R.L.* was until 2004 the most important coffee processor in San Ramón, whit nearly 1,700 associated smallholder coffee producers. It functioned as a normal coffee plant, using traditional processing techniques. However, the cooperative never implemented a clear strategy to sell its coffee to specialised markets, but continued to rely on traditional market chains. Moreover, wrong managerial decisions led the cooperative into a spiral of indebtedness, from which it never recovered.

In subsequent years, the enterprise started moving into environmental certifications. Therefore, it became part of the SUSCOF consortium (together with six other cooperatives), and joined projects led by *Fundecooperación para el Desarrollo Sostenible* and CGESTI (an NGOs that promotes sustainable development). These projects provided training to staff of the cooperative, with the objective of making changes in the production process and gain the ECO OK, ISO 14000 and Utz Kapeh certifications. These certifications allowed a substantial reduction of production costs. However, several factors pushed the cooperative into a financial crisis: (1) the price crisis in international spot markets, (2) obtaining the ISO 14000 certification implied an investment of one million dollars in a residual-water treatment plant, (3) poor performance in international sales and (4) other unplanned investments in expensive equipment. All these factors together led the cooperative to interrupt its financial obligations with the banks. By June 2004, the cooperative was declared bankrupt with a global remaining debt of five million dollars.

A few months before *Coopecafira R.L.* disappeared, a large group of associates joined forces to look for a solution. Coffee is considered a highly esteemed cultural value in San Ramón, thus the people of the community refused the idea to loose their local coffee processor and deliver coffee to outsiders. A committee led by the current manager of the present *Café de Altura S.A.* prepared a recovery plan of two phases and presented it to the Assembly of Associates. The first part of the plan was to convince the Banco Nacional de Costa Rica (major mortgagee) to get into a deal by promising the payment of US$ 30.000 in pending interests. Such debt was paid with the harvest 2004-2005, after most of the former members of *Coopecafira R.L.* agreed to deliver coffee without any payment in advance. The second phase was to define a new institutional model for the organisation that was approved by the assembly of associates. By June 2004 *Café de Altura S.A.* was formally established assuming all the assets and debts of the former cooperative. The new company exhibits the following characteristics and rules:

- Associating to the enterprise requires to have a coffee farm in the Cantón of San Ramón.

- The enterprise only accepts coffee grown above 1,000 meters above sea level and under natural shadow.
- The number of actions of each associated is determined by their production.
- There is not a general management. Everything is decided in the Committee Board, which is appointed by the General Assembly.
- Any associated can have no more than 1.7% of the total pool of actions. This prevents the concentration of power inside the enterprise or the purchase of actions by a larger company.
- US$ 10 per delivered fanega is deduced to each coffee producer. This charge is intended to credit the general indebtedness with the Banco Nacional. No utilities are distributed amongst members until the debt is properly honoured.
- 50% of the price defined each year for the payment in advance is retained by the enterprise. This capital is used to buy coffee in areas outside San Ramón as strategy to compete with larger enterprises.
- Coffee is the only activity of the enterprise. There are no interests in other activities. The former hardware store of *Coopecafira R.L.* was turned into an independent company, with capital from the same associates.

The enterprise started with 60,000 actions and by selling most of the coffee to Starbuck's, under the certification 'Practices'. Actually, the enterprise has won twice the prize for quality granted by Starbuck's every year (2005 and 2006). This prize has been distributed for 70% to the producers and 30% is used for different communal projects (health and education), administrated by the company. Because the company cannot be granted a third time by the Starbuck's prize, they plan to continue with the communal projects by deducing a small fee from the associates' earnings. However, not all the processed coffee is sold under the certificates 'Practices' or 'Utz Kapeh'. Instead, the strategy points to diversify sales to different buyers with different quality requirements.

The company is formed by 600 associates, from which only 200 grows coffee under any certification. Additionally, they have around 1000 non-members (e.g. not certified producers) that regularly deliver coffee to the enterprise. The average productivity is 50 fanegas per ha and the average farm size is 3 ha. Even while there is a highly disperse population, there are no large differences in socio-economic characteristics amongst the producers in the region.

## 5. Sampling and matching

Data was collected in October-November 2007 through a field survey applied to selected primary producers and in-depth interviews with local processors. Because the identity and number of the producers were unknown at the beginning of this research, we implemented a non-random sampling method, known as the 'snowball' method (Babbie, 1992). In total, we interviewed 103 coffee producers of Miramar (FT zone) and San Ramón (non-FT zone). Both study areas are traditional coffee production zones with long tradition in producers' organisations. We applied several statistic techniques, including a detailed matching technique, to assess the differences between both populations and identify the effect of FT on coffee producers.

The characteristics of farm households are different in the Fair Trade (FT) and non-Fair Trade (non-FT) zones in several aspects (see table 3). In general, household are younger in the FT zone compared to the non-FT zone. Families in the FT zone are somewhat less educated, and are more recently settled in the FT zone compared to the non-FT zone. This is in line with the history of colonisation of the highlands of Miramar, where coffee production started later. This zone was colonised by settlers coming precisely from the non-FT zone, during the middle of the 20$^{th}$ Century. These settlers brought the coffee with them and are culturally closer to the Central Valley culture and different of the people living in the lowlands of Miramar. No significant differences are observed in farm size, family size and coffee production areas.

Total income and the income derived from coffee are higher in the non-FT zone compared to the FT zone. In a similar vein, food expenditure are also higher in the non-FT zone. The expenditure for self consumption is significantly higher in the FT zone, which may indicate certain level of poverty. Annual profit - defined as the difference between total income (from all sources of income, including income from coffee) and total expenditures of the household – is generally higher in the non-FT zoned.

The performance of the farmers' organisations seems to be better in the non-FT zone. In general, the organisational strength and coherence is regarded better by its members in the non-FT zone, in terms of performance, force and identification. On the other hand, the participation of women in coffee activities seems to be higher in the FT zone, which may indicate that the households use more family labour in coffee production compared to farmers in non-FT zone.

In conclusion, households in the FT zone seem to be younger, less educated, more specialised in coffee and poorer than households in the non-FT zone. This implies that we need to apply stringent matching principles to identify the real impact of FT, correction for the selection bias in the sample.

We used a matching procedure to assess the influence of several exogenous variables on the likelihood of engagement in Fair Trade. Results are shown in table 4. The analysis allows us to identify major differences between FT and non-FT producers. The matching test (Table 4) show significant differences between both samples in terms of actual coffee area, age and education, and period of residence in the region. Most outcomes confirm the tendencies shown in the previous single t-test analysis.

In general, FT producers are of more recent settlement and have larger coffee areas (but similar farm size) with plots suffering some slight soil erosion. The initial Probit regression confirm that FT producers are more likely to be younger with less educated

*Table 3. Farm household characteristics according to market segmentation.*

| | Fair Trade | Non-Fair Trade | t-stat. | Sign. |
|---|---|---|---|---|
| **Household characteristics** | | | | |
| Family size | 4.10 | 3.84 | 0.423 | |
| Family age average | 35.80 | 44.04 | 0.006 | *** |
| Family education >15 years | 6.44 | 7.77 | 0.026 | ** |
| Farm household head age | 49.67 | 59.04 | 0.001 | *** |
| Farm household head Education | 3.94 | 4.11 | 0.587 | |
| Years living at the region | 36.52 | 47.15 | 0.006 | *** |
| Initial area | 4.04 | 5.04 | 0.470 | |
| Actual area | 5.53 | 5.40 | 0.945 | |
| **Income (colons)** | | | | |
| Coffee income | 2,011,833 | 3,179,127 | 0.105 | * |
| Other agricultural income | 474,975 | 693,968 | 0.536 | |
| Non-agricultural income | 242,531 | 485,451 | 0.229 | |
| Total income | 2,729,338 | 4,358,546 | 0.065 | * |
| Self consumption expenditure | 6,542 | 3,333 | 0.078 | * |
| Food expenditure | 78,846 | 99,300 | 0.057 | * |
| Other expenditures | 24,342 | 47,276 | 0.001 | *** |
| Annual expenditures | 1,592,310 | 2,486,756 | 0.002 | *** |
| Profits | 1,366,631 | 2,581,481 | 0.079 | * |
| Coffee dependency | 75.90 | 79.24 | 0.561 | |
| **Savings and credit (colons)** | | | | |
| Credit | 257,312 | 1,080,727 | 0.235 | |
| Savings | 164,133 | 444,068 | 0.140 | |
| **Risk and organisation perceptions** | | | | |
| Identification with organisation | 3.48 | 4.12 | 0.004 | *** |
| Functioning of the organisation | 3.92 | 4.15 | 0.024 | ** |
| Organisational force | 3.40 | 4.17 | 0.001 | *** |
| Organisational perception | 3.60 | 4.14 | 0.001 | *** |
| Risk perception | 2.01 | 2.13 | 0.335 | |
| Actual economic perception | 1.62 | 1.58 | 0.797 | |
| Future economic perception | 1.60 | 1.78 | 0.266 | |
| **Gender and environment** | | | | |
| Agricultural production decisions | 1.44 | 1.38 | 0.713 | |
| Food consumption decisions | 2.22 | 2.36 | 0.372 | |
| Home maintenance decisions | 2.22 | 2.43 | 0.265 | |
| Children education decisions | 2.41 | 2.56 | 0.412 | |
| Credit decisions | 1.98 | 2.00 | 0.493 | |
| Woman participation in certified seed use | 1.98 | 2.00 | 0.295 | |
| Woman participation in fertilising | 1.94 | 2.00 | 0.065 | * |
| Woman participation in association of products | 1.94 | 1.98 | 0.265 | |
| Woman participation in plot cleaning | 1.87 | 1.98 | 0.036 | ** |
| Woman participation in harvesting | 1.67 | 1.98 | 0.001 | *** |

Note: *** significant at 1%; ** significant at 5%; * significant at 10%.

*Table 4. Factors influencing FT engagement (Probit regression).*

| Variable | Coef. | Std. Error | t-stat. | Sign. |
|---|---|---|---|---|
| Constant | 3.58 | 1.08 | 0.001 | *** |
| Living in community (years) | -0.015 | 0.009 | 0.09 | * |
| Average family education | -0.276 | 0.084 | 0.001 | *** |
| Number of household members | 0.145 | 0.092 | 0.116 | |
| Age of household head | -0.037 | 0.042 | 0.009 | *** |
| Educational level of household head | 0.092 | 0.163 | 0.572 | |
| Initial access to land (ha) | -0.010 | 0.023 | 0.644 | |
| Actual coffee area (ha) | 0.082 | 0.044 | 0.065 | * |
| Time from plot to town (minutes) | -0.008 | 0.005 | 0.130 | |

Note: *** = sign. at 0.01; ** = sign. at 0.05; * = sign. at 0.1.

families compared to non-FT producers (see also Table 3). This means that FT may be targeted to farmers that are open to learn alternative strategies for production and trade. Stated otherwise, in the FT segment prevail younger producers that are more flexible to understand the implications of having coffee production under a FT certification, and that require substantial training to compensate for their limited educational background.

## 6. Results

The matching tests (Table 5) show significant differences between both samples in terms of land area, total and non-agricultural income, food and self consumption, expenditures, perceptions on the farmers' organisation, household decisions, and participation of women in coffee activities.

In general, non-FT coffee producers reach higher income – both from coffee and from other activities - and realise higher expenditures levels, controlling for differences in exogenous characteristics. Moreover, they have a better perception on their organisation, a higher female participation in on-farm activities and more shared decision-making within the household. Conversely, the FT farmers exhibit lower overall expenditures (even with larger coffee production areas) and a higher degree of food self-consumption. Interestingly, however, even with these lower expenditures FT farmers spend considerable more on education. This may be regarded as a type of investments that could enable their children in the future to diversify into Non-farm activities.

FT producers have slightly larger actual coffee area but their plots suffer from some slight soil erosion. Dependency on coffee is considerably higher amongst FT

*Table 5. Differences between FT and non-FT production zones (matching analysis).*

| | Kernel | | | One-to-one | | | Neighbour (3) | | |
|---|---|---|---|---|---|---|---|---|---|
| | Diff. | S.E. | t-stat | Diff. | S.E. | t-stat | Diff. | S.E. | t-stat |
| **Farm characteristics** | | | | | | | | | |
| Actual area | 1.57 | 1.56 | 1.01 | 3.40 | 1.31 | 2.60** | 2.01 | 1.83 | 1.10 |
| Expenditures in inputs | 25,073 | 25,158 | 1.00 | 25,489 | 18,722 | 1.36 | 22,881 | 19,310 | 1.18 |
| Risk of flooding | -0.13 | 0.10 | -1.38 | -0.2 | 0.10 | -2.06** | -0.16 | 0.09 | -1.80* |
| Drainage conditions (1=slight) | -0.002 | 0.16 | -0.01 | 0.11 | 0.18 | 0.61 | 0.01 | 0.14 | 0.10 |
| Soil erosion (1= slight) | 0.46 | 0.19 | 2.39** | 0.51 | 0.21 | 2.47** | 0.37 | 0.18 | 2.00** |
| Mountainous land (2= slight) | 0.24 | 0.18 | 1.39 | 0.02 | 0.21 | 0.11 | 0.26 | 0.18 | 1.42 |
| **Household characteristics** | | | | | | | | | |
| **Income and expenditures** | | | | | | | | | |
| Coffee income | -308,510 | 734,016 | -0.42 | 166,246 | 573,138 | 0.29 | -177,921 | 798,924 | -0.22 |
| Other agricultural income | -141,796 | 589,724 | -0.24 | 313,614 | 383,847 | 0.84 | 49,902 | 422,216 | 0.12 |
| Non-agricultural income | -397,685 | 202,924 | -1.96* | -282,205 | 354,477 | -0.80 | -254,223 | 251,365 | -1.01 |
| Total income | -847,990 | 1,129,003 | -0.75 | 197,655 | 661,477 | 0.30 | -382,242 | 1,043,908 | -0.37 |
| Self consumption expenditure | 2,663 | 2,446 | 1.09 | 3,304 | 2,422 | 1.36 | 2,184 | 2,462 | 0.89 |
| Food expenditure | -28,038 | 13,295 | -2.11** | -13,615 | 14,750 | -0.92 | -19,596 | 15,298 | -1.28 |
| Education expenditures | 40,314 | 28,145 | 1.43 | 47,346 | 24,683 | 1.92* | 38,244 | 21,926 | 1.74* |
| Other expenditures | -28,856 | 8,913 | -3.24*** | -10,627 | 12,822 | -0.83 | -27,214 | 9,633 | -2.83** |
| Annual expenditures | -814,404 | 379,484 | -2.15** | -296,186 | 365,718 | -0.81 | -718,566 | 427,656 | -1.68* |
| Profits | -559,702 | 1,042,543 | -0.54 | 366,327 | 524,915 | 0.70 | -245,822 | 1,074,550 | -0.23 |
| Coffee dependency | 0.25 | 0.06 | 3.86*** | 0.16 | 0.08 | 2.06** | 0.23 | 0.062 | 3.75*** |
| **Savings and credit** | | | | | | | | | |
| Credit | 0.25 | 0.12 | 2.02** | 0.22 | 0.17 | 1.31 | 0.28 | 0.13 | 2.12** |
| Savings | 0.27 | 0.13 | 2.07** | 0.16 | 0.17 | 0.89 | 0.27 | 0.14 | 1.97* |

Note: t-test = 1.67 or higher up to 2 is significant at 10%; t-test = 2 or higher up to 2.66 is significant at 5%; t-test = 2.66 or higher is significant at 1%.

*Table 5. Continued.*

| | Kernel | | | One-to-one | | | Neighbour (3) | | |
|---|---|---|---|---|---|---|---|---|---|
| | Diff. | S.E. | t-stat | Diff. | S.E. | t-stat | Diff. | S.E. | t-stat |
| **Risk and organisation perceptions** | | | | | | | | | |
| Identification with organisation | -0.56 | 0.24 | -2.08** | -0.64 | 0.31 | -2.06** | -0.68 | 0.27 | -2.55** |
| Function of the organisation | -0.28 | 0.14 | -1.99* | -0.10 | 0.19 | -0.52 | -0.23 | 0.15 | -1.52 |
| Organisational force | -0.68 | 0.16 | -4.18*** | -0.60 | 0.20 | -3.04*** | -0.73 | 0.16 | -4.52*** |
| Organisation perception | -0.51 | 0.15 | -3.47*** | -0.44 | 0.17 | -2.55** | -0.55 | 0.15 | -3.75*** |
| Risk perception | -0.10 | 0.19 | -0.50 | -0.15 | 0.15 | -0.96 | -0.19 | 0.20 | -0.97 |
| Actual economic perception | 0.22 | 0.22 | 1.00 | 0.11 | 0.27 | 0.41 | 0.12 | 0.22 | 0.55 |
| Future economic perception | -0.07 | 0.23 | -0.32 | -0.11 | 0.29 | -0.38 | -0.04 | 0.24 | -0.16 |
| **Gender and environment** | | | | | | | | | |
| Agricultural decisions production | -0.07 | 0.28 | -0.25 | -0.07 | 0.39 | -0.17 | -0.11 | 0.30 | -0.37 |
| Food consumption decisions | -0.42 | 0.23 | -1.82* | -0.57 | 0.21 | -2.66** | -0.46 | 0.24 | -1.92* |
| Home maintenance | -0.61 | 0.27 | -2.23** | -0.60 | 0.28 | -2.16** | -0.56 | 0.27 | -2.04** |
| Children education decisions | -0.37 | 0.24 | -1.57 | -0.30 | 0.22 | -1.37 | -0.24 | 0.22 | -1.12 |
| Credit decisions | -0.49 | 0.28 | -1.75* | -0.57 | 0.35 | -1.60 | -0.37 | 0.28 | -1.29 |
| Woman participation in fertilising | -0.04 | 0.04 | -1.00 | -0.03 | 0.03 | -1.00 | -0.03 | 0.03 | -1.00 |
| Woman participation in plot cleaning | -0.07 | 0.08 | -0.92 | -0.10 | 0.11 | -0.87 | -0.07 | 0.09 | -0.77 |
| Woman participation in balanced feeding | -0.03 | 0.07 | -0.44 | 0.00 | 0.11 | 0 | -0.02 | 0.08 | -0.30 |
| Woman participation in harvesting | -0.26 | 0.11 | -2.44** | -0.30 | 0.13 | -2.29** | -0.23 | 0.11 | -2.18** |

Note: t-test = 1.67 or higher up to 2 is significant at 10%; t-test = 2 or higher up to 2.66 is significant at 5%; t-test = 2.66 or higher is significant at 1%.

producers, and they have significantly better access to credit and save more money than producers in the control zone. In short, FT seems to enhance in the short run certain specialisation in coffee, partly because other income-earning options are scarce. In addition, it seems that the certification has a positive effect on both credit use and savings amongst the FT producers which may further reinforce this specialisation process. On the other hand, investments made in education may indicate that their long-turn options are inclined to include other non-agricultural activities.

The non-FT production zone (Cantón de San Ramón) is a wealthier area in comparison with the FT production zone (Miramar). Therefore, we expect to find farmers with commercial activities other than coffee. Besides, in the non-FT zone at least three competing buying firms (*Café de Altura S.A.*, *Palmichal S.A.* and *Orlich S.A.*) are operating, while in Miramar only one single cooperative is active. The competitive nature of the processing firms in the non-FT zone and the higher perception of farmers' organisations may indicate a better bargaining power distribution between processing firms and producers. Conversely, the FT farmers are poorer and more dependant of a single monopsonistic buyer,[3] and therefore exhibit less positive perception about the functioning of their organisation.

Finally, women appear to participate more in key households decisions in the non-FT households. Good infrastructure and well developed townships, as well as a better access to different commercial options and educational opportunities, enhance women's position within and options outside the households.

## 7. Discussion and conclusions

The main conclusion we can draw from this analysis is rather straightforward: the expected positive effect of the Fair Trade participation are at first sight rather disappointing and not directly observable. About half of the coffee producers in the FT region do not perceive any benefit from the certification, while a third part does not know about the premium. If we accept that the cooperative pays the premium price with the yearly harvest, we can conclude that the FT benefits are somewhat hidden. Stated otherwise, the FT producers do not really perceive the positive effects of their FT engagement, since they cannot observe differences in their annual income. This is mainly an institutional problem: even while the cooperative fulfils with the distribution of the premium payments, the farmers cannot attribute this to FT.

Households in the FT zone are younger, less-educated and usually poorer than households in the non-FT zone. The fact that women in the non-FT zone devote less time to coffee production may indicate that they can be engaged in other activities, and that their labour force is not required to maintain the coffee harvest. This also implies that non-FT farmers have more options for income diversification.

[3] Monopsonistic means that in the market only one or a few single buyers are active.

Farmers located in the FT zone also face more disadvantages compared to farmers in the non-FT production zone. They are poorer and more dependant on one single crop and one single buyer. The FT certification thus provides assistance to farmers living in less-developed areas, with few alternative livelihood options (like those in Miramar), but also may lock-in these farmers into a monopsonistic situation with limited bargaining power.

These findings point to the necessity of further discussions on the expected role and performance of FT cooperatives in monopsonistic settings. The FT organisations may initially enable the step towards successful market integration, but can end up in a perverse monopsony market situation, which limits further development options for stepping out of poverty. New options for alternative FT schemes could certainly be helpful to enlarge the bargaining position of the members *vis-à-vis* their cooperative association, and to strengthen the market position of the cooperative itself. This strategy should address critical issues like access to information, marketing and upgrading options, and strategies for balancing individual and collectively-based decision-making regimes.

## References


Babbie, E. (1992). *The Practice of Social Research.* Wadsworth: Belmont, CA.

Bacon, C. (2005). Confronting the Coffee Crisis: Can Fair Trade, Organic, and Specialty Coffees Reduce Small-Scale Farmers Vulnerability in Northern Nicaragua? *World Development* 33: 497-511.

Brown, O., C. Charavat and D. Eagleton (2001). *The Coffee Market: A Background Study*. London: Oxfam.

CEPAL (Comisión Económica para América Latina y el Caribe) (2002). *Centroamerıca: El Impacto de la Caıda de los Precios del Café (LC/MEX/L.517).* Mexico: CEPAL.

Fridell, G. (2007). *Fair Trade Coffee: the Prospects and Pitfalls of Market-driven Social Justice.* Toronto: University of Toronto Press.

IADB - Inter-American Development Bank (2000). *Social Protection for Equity and Growth.* Washington, DC: IADB.

IFAT (2002). Estándares para las Organizaciones de Comercio Justo. Available at: http://fongdcam.org/uploads/docsInteres/comercio_justo/articulos.

Lara-Pineda, O. (2002). El Comercio Justo en Europa: Evolución, Funcionamiento, Estructura Institucional y Tendencias. Available at: http://www.ciat.cgiar.org/agroempresas/pdf/comercio_justo_europa.pdf.

Raynolds, L. (2002). Consumer/Producer Links in Fair Trade Coffee Networks. *Sociologia Ruralis* 42: 404-424.

Rice, A. (2001). Noble Goals and Challenging Terrain: Organic and Fair Trade Coffee Movements in the Global Marketplace. *Journal of Agricultural and Environmental Ethics* 14: 39-66.

Ronchi, L. (2002). *The Impact of Fair Trade on Producers and their Organizations: a Case Study with COOCAFE in Costa Rica.* Poverty Research Unit Working paper No 11. Brighton: University of Sussex.

Talbot, J. (1997). Where does your Coffee Dollar go? The Division of Income and Surplus along the Coffee Commodity Chain. *Studies in Comparative International Development* 32: 56-91.

Vizcarra, G. (2002). El Comercio Justo: una Alternativa para para la Agroindustria Rural de América Latina. Available at: http://www.ciat.cgiar.org/agroempresas/pdf/comerjus.pdf.

# Chapter 6

## The impact of Fair Trade in banana plantations in Ghana: income, ownership and livelihoods of banana workers

*Ruerd Ruben and Lucie van Schendel*

### 1. Introduction

Fair Trade was initially mainly associated with small-scale production and cooperative organisation. When the portfolio of Fair Trade products was expanded from typically smallholder crops like coffee and cocoa to include other crops like bananas, mangoes and tea where medium- and large-scale production systems prevail, the position of plantations poses new challenges to the Fair Trade movement (Murray and Raynolds, 2007: 10). The perishability of bananas makes the storage, shipping and handling much more demanding compared to other Fair Trade commodities, since technical and capital requirements account for substantial economies of scale. In addition, Fair Trade deliveries to mass outlets and supermarket increasingly demand reliable year-round supply of large volumes of high quality that are difficult to guarantee through a network of smallholder producers.

The expansion of Fair Trade banana sourcing from fruit plantations and the subsequent FLO certification framework for hired labour in plantation crops asks for new methods and procedures for defining Fair Trade impact. Tropical fruits (bananas, citrus, mango and pineapple) are nowadays the major Fair Trade product represent more than 60% of total certified volume and roughly a quarter of total Fair Trade value (Raynolds and Long, 2007: 26). International trade in bananas has traditionally been controlled by multinational companies, with Chiquita, Dole and Del Monte dominating production, cooled transport, ripening and distribution. Their historical record in terms of labour rights violations, repression of labour unions, chemical poisoning, water contamination and political manipulation in the so-called 'banana republics' is well-documented (Ellis, 1983; Striffler and Moberg, 2003; Human Rights Watch, 2002).

In subsequent periods, the transnational companies partly withdrew from primary production, while maintaining control over shipping operations. Banana outgrower schemes and cooperative associations were able to conquer space. Increasing stress from *black sigatoka* infestations also motivated relocation into new production areas. In addition, EU import licensing policies provided advantages for establishing production in Caribbean and African countries. After the breakdown of the Wall, the expectation of further growth of the world market set the stage for a new scramble for banana plantations. While this proved to be rather disappointing, prices at the international banana market became highly volatile, regularly suffering from overproduction but periodically also facing shortages (when production areas are hit by hurricanes or other natural disasters).

Fair Trade sales of bananas for the European market started in 1996 with the establishment of Agrofair, a mixed ownership company with half of its shares owned by producers in developing countries and the other half of the capital provided by northern NGOs and ethical investors. To guarantee deliveries, Agrofair (through Solidaridad) invested in the recovery of the VREL banana plantation as a subsidiary firm in Ghana. In a similar vein, banana sales from the Latin American plantations in the United States started in 2004 through Wild Oats stores in an agreement with Transfair USA. In both markets, discussions on 'upscaling' and 'mainstreaming' Fair Trade banana deliveries actually lead to heated discussions on options for cooperation with the multinational companies (Lamb, 2008; Raynolds, 2007). In this context, it is of key importance to better understand the real differences in welfare, attitudes and working conditions in order to be able to acknowledge the Fair Trade impact.

This study provides a comparison of Fair Trade and private company banana production, focussing on the socio-economic income and welfare effects for workers and their families. We conducted field surveys amongst 50 workers of each type of enterprise, controlling for differences in family size, own land area and assets. This balanced sample of observations can subsequently be used to compare differences in income level and composition, and to assess workers' opinions on job satisfaction and corporate identification.

The remainder of this chapter is structured as follows. Section 2 provides a short characterisation of two banana plantations in Eastern Ghana, located at the border of Volta River: the Fair Trade plantation Volta River Estates Ltd. (VREL) and the privately owned company Golden Exotics Ltd. (GEL). Section 3 outlines the analytical framework for comparing both plantation, focussing on aspects like salaries and working conditions, household income, risk attitudes, job satisfaction and ownership feelings. Results from the field work are presented in Section 4. Finally, Section 5 provides a discussion on the major differences between Fair Trade and conventional banana production and outlines some prospects for further reinforcing and deepening Fair Trade within a plantation context.

## 2. Setting

The field study is based on the comparison between the Fair Trade plantation Volta River Estates Ltd. (VREL) and the privately owned company Golden Exotics Ltd. (GEL).

### *2.1. Volta River Estates Ltd (VREL)*

The Ghanaian banana company Volta River Estates Ltd (VREL) was established in 1988 as a Ghanaian/Dutch joint venture with assistance by the Dutch Finance Corporation for Developing Countries (FMO). VREL became the first Fair Trade company for production of bananas for the European market under the Oké label since 1996. VREL is one of the leading agricultural companies in Ghana, and an important employer in the Eastern Province. VREL plantation consists of 180 hectares of cultivated banana area divided over five different sites. Production includes conventional and ecological bananas (former VREL organic), and has recently been expanded with pineapples (in a separate Bio Fair Fruit company). Investments are mainly raised from subordinated loans provided by main current private and corporate shareholders, and through Fair Trade bank loans. New expansion and upgrading projects are funded through the Dutch PSOM program.

The competitive position of VREL strongly depends on continuous production, stable quality and company reputation. All three aspects require permanent attention. Plans for further expanding the banana area are made to enhance economies of scale. Quality management is critical for maintaining market shares and premium payments. Reputation will become more relevant when more stringent FLO standards are applied for plantations and co-ownership might become a key feature for Fair Trade certification. Since 1996, a quarter of the shares of VREL are legally owned by the Dutch NGO Solidaridad (and administered through Agrofair) and were recently handled over as a trust to the local Fair Trade Premium Committee (FTPC), with the intention to transfer this ownership ultimately to the company workers. Given the fragile financial performance and the critical balance sheet composition of VREL, further deepening of the ownership structure needs to be addressed during coming years.

The current workforce of VREL includes 560 employees, with 93% field workers (including 70 people for securities), 3% workshop staff and 4% office staff. Labour productivity is relatively low, with about 2 workers/ha and 500 boxes/worker at a yearly base.[1] Female employees represent 12% of the workforce. Employment conditions are relatively favourable compared to other farms in the region. Workers receive a stable salary which is ten percent higher than the national minimum wage, and additional provisions include social security, health insurance (only for workers), maternity leave,

[1] Labour productivity is fairly below standards of Latin American plantations (1-1.2 workers/ha), partly due to the organic character of part of production, but also because no clear productivity standards are defined.

pension fund, education subsidy and allowances for funerals.[2] Moreover, through the Fair Trade premium workers received a bicycle, Christmas allowance and they can benefit from a low-interest loan facility.

### 2.2. Golden Exotics Ltd. (GEL)

Golden Exotics Ltd. was created in 2003 as a sub-division of the French *Compagnie Frutieres*, originally for the production and export of pineapples. The company took over already existing operations from Paradise Farm, and is now co-owned by Dole with 40% of the shares. Propagating material came from their plantation in Ivory Coast. In the first year, GEL exported 33 tons, growing in 2005 to 2,880 tons and in 2006 to 8,440 tons. Export projections are to raise volumes to over 16,000 tons of pineapples (Danielou and Ravry, 2005).

In 2005, GEL started a new farm for the production of bananas, using tissue culture coming from a laboratory in Ivory Coast. The plantation has a size of 813 hectare and provides employment to 1,300 employees. Current yields are 60-70 tons/ha. The farm is located in the Volta delta at 70 km from Tema harbour. Soils have a fertile clay content and year round supply of water is guaranteed through five dams along one of the tributaries of Volta river. The original irrigation system was development by the Government in the early nineties to promote the production of rice and sugar cane. This was, however, not very successful and many small farmers were unable to make a living, thus leaving the land idle. GEL has been able to use the available infrastructure and through modern pumps and ingenious drip irrigation systems the banana plants are supplied with water and nutrients.

The GEL plantation counts with mechanised internal transport lines that bring the bananas to five packing stations where selection, grading, cleaning and packing takes place. The better quality bananas are exported. Plans for expanding the company size exist, but depend on better transport, stocking, warehousing and harbour facilities in Tema.[3] GEL employees have full-time employment and are subject to tight labour organisation. Nominal wages are slightly higher, but fringe benefits are lower compared to VREL.

## 3. Approach

We conducted a field study with a random sample of 50 VREL and GEL employees during the 2007 agricultural cycle. The survey builds on earlier research (March-May 2007) amongst the VREL workforce that covered a total of 266 VREL workers,

[2] In earlier years, the salary bonus used to be larger, but due to inflation and exchange rates the difference with other employers is now smaller.

[3] With support of the World Bank, plans are made to built a fruit terminal in Tema harbour for improving storage facilities under adequate temperature and humidity conditions.

representing 47.5 percent of the total workforce. Stratified random sampling was used to select participants from each of the five production sites. In most cases, workers were visited at their house, but sometimes the interviewer met the workers at their working location, such as the banana plant or the office. Participation was anonymous and voluntary. The interviews were conducted with the help of local interpreters that received an intensive training. Additional interviews with GEL employees were held in October-November 2007, focussing on a more detailed insight in their income and employment conditions.

A standardised field questionnaire was used to collect both general information on the VREL and GEL workers and their living conditions, and information on their attitude towards the company. The following type of data was collected:

- *Individual characteristics*: gender, age, household size, dependency rate and level of education.
- *Household characteristics*: assets per capita, outstanding loans, accumulated savings, total family income, income sources, proportion VREL/GEL salary to total income.
- *Workforce variables*: tenure (years of work at the company), salary, fringe benefits, engagement in other off/non-farm activities.
- *Benefits*: salary payments and fringe benefits (additional rewards, like pensions, insurance, loans, school fee contribution, bicycles), benefits derived from the Fair Trade premium, working conditions (working hours, sanctions)
- *Attitudes* regarding risk and time preference, job satisfaction, sense of ownership and Fair Trade awareness/importance (only for VREL workers).

This set of variables can provide insights in the welfare position and livelihood strategies of the employees in both firms and could also enhance understanding on less tangible behavioural and attitudinal aspects of the employment relationship.

Most analyses regarding the impact of Fair Trade focus attention on directly observable phenomena like wages, working conditions and premium allocation. For an adequate understanding the Fair Trade implications in a plantation context, this is considered insufficient. With international companies penetrating the Fair Trade market, asking occasionally for the certification of their plantations by independent agencies, the traditional supply base of deliveries by a limited group of certified producers is considerably broadened and the critical stance towards multinational companies may be gradually eroded. When differences in production and trade conditions become less tangible, the new frontier of Fair Trade identity shifts towards ownership and governance issues. Worker's job satisfaction and feelings of distributive justice, alongside corporate identification and co-ownership prospects tend to become key markers for Fair Trade (Fransen and Ruben, 2007). These aspects therefore received most attention in our participatory impact assessment of the attitudinal implications of Fair Trade involvement.

To assess worker's attitude towards their company, the survey contained a series of questions on time preference of the participants, their sense of ownership, ownership beliefs, job satisfaction and job security, and (for VREL workers) the attitudes toward Fair Trade. These variables have been operationalised as follows (see Annex for details).

### *3.1. Sense of ownership*

The analysis of sense of ownership is based on studies by Van Dyne and Pierce (2004) and Pierce *et al.* (1991), that include statements like: 'I sense that this is my company', and 'I sense that this is our company'. In total, four statements were used to measure sense of ownership, and responses were recorded on a scale ranging from 1 (totally disagree) to 5 (totally agree).[4]

### *3.2. Corporate identification*

The degree of workers' identification with company goals is constructed on the basis of the methodology developed by Wagner *et al.* (2003). We used statements like: 'If I work hard, the company makes more profit', 'If the company has a problem, I should contribute to the solution', and 'When the company has a financial problem I should share in the consequences'. For measurement, four statements were used, recording responses on a Likert scale ranging from 1 (totally disagree) to 5 (totally agree).

### *3.3. Job satisfaction*

Different statements were used to measure job attitudes, sing a Likert scale with five categories (1 = totally disagree, 5 = totally agree). The statements focused on job security and job satisfaction with different components of the work. The statements are derived from social exchange theory (Mulinge and Mueller, 1998; Lovett *et al.*, 2004) that considers work satisfaction as a balance between inputs (effort, skills, experience) and outputs (salary, intrinsic and extrinsic rewards). Job security is thereby perceived as an important extrinsic reward (Taber and Alliger, 1995; Locke 1995), whereas distributive justice refers to feelings of 'fairness' regarding the received rewards and/or the sanctions applied in case of misconduct.

### *3.4. Attitudes toward Fair Trade*

Attitudes toward Fair Trade can be split into two subscales, one measuring Fair Trade awareness, and one measuring Fair Trade importance. These attitudes were measured both on Likert scales and with yes/no questions. For example: 'Do you know VREL is a Fair Trade farm?', and 'How important is it to you that VREL is a Fair Trade farm?'

[4] We did not address the potential *implications* of sense of ownership for workers' salaries or labour productivity (see: Pierce and Rodgers, 2004 for a further analysis). Given the explorative nature of this study and the preliminary stage of transition towards workers co-ownership, these outcomes are not yet tangible.

The Fair Trade premium was included in the statements as well. For example: 'Are you familiar with the Fair Trade premium?', and 'Is the Fair Trade premium important to you?' Finally, some open ended questions were added to investigate what meaning the VREL workers add to the concept of Fair Trade.

### *3.5. Time preference*

Time preferences are measured by means of a simple game. Participants were given the choice between either receiving an amount of money instantly, or waiting one year and receiving a larger amount of money. The amounts were adjusted to the local monetary unit (Cedis) and represented more or less a monthly salary for the participants. The amount of money they could get after waiting increased with fifty percent for every trial. Higher preference for instant amounts is considered to be related to household poverty.

Statistical t-tests, factor and regression analysis techniques are used to identify the variables that proved to be different between both type of companies. The two sub-samples have been controlled for differences in family size, own land area and assets in order to prevent selection bias. In the subsequent analysis, we discuss the underlying determinants of these behavioural differences and provide an outlook of the future potential of collective action within the context of Fair Trade banana plantations.

## 4. Results

The data analysis has been conducted in four stages. First, a balanced sample of VREL and GEL employees was selected, controlling for equal composition in terms of selected exogenous characteristics (e.g. household size, value of assets, and own land area). Second, differences in income levels and income composition between VREL and GEL employees are analysed. Third, a comparison is made of behavioural and attitudinal perceptions amongst VREL and GEL workers, Fourth and finally, a detailed analysis is presented of the importance and awareness of Fair Trade amongst the VREL workforce.

### *4.1. Matching*

In order to guarantee that the sample composition is sufficiently balanced in terms of fixed household characteristics, we selected 50 cases from the larger VREL survey that exhibit similar wealth characteristics (see Table 1). Household size, own land area and assets are slightly higher for VREL employees, but the value distribution in both groups guarantees that these differences are not significant. Other characteristics, like age, education and gender are broadly similar amongst VREL and GEL workers Average age is around 36 years, 80% are males (females mainly work in the packing station) and about half of the workers received education up to junior secondary

*Table 1. Matching VREL and GEL employees (mean and standard deviation).*

| | VREL | GEL | Sign. |
|---|---|---|---|
| Household size (persons) | 5.76 (2.66) | 4.88 (2.68) | ns |
| Average age (years | 22.9 (0.03) | 24.3 (0.03) | ns |
| Highest education level (scale 0-4) | 1.94 (0.38) | 2.12 (0.38) | ns |
| Own land acre (acres) | 1.88 (1.59) | 1.36 (1.69) | ns |
| Asset value (thousands of cedis) | 194,421 (80,074) | 155,507 (496,798) | ns |

Note: ns = no significant difference

or middle school level (but a quarter has no education at all and females received substantially less education).

### 4.2. Income and welfare

Income levels and sources of income differ substantially between VREL and GEL workers. While the former maintain a daily work schedule till noon, the GEL workers are expected to work a the farm till 4 p.m. Moreover, VREL workers deliver their services during 20-21 days a months but get paid for 27 days; at GEL the normal obligation is to work and get paid during 27 days a month. Consequently, working conditions at VREL are relatively lean (shorter working days; more off-days).

About half of the workforce employed by GEL and VREL receive monthly salaries equivalent to 32-40 Euros. Headmen, workshop staff and security officials receive somewhat higher salaries, and a quarter of the GEL employees earn monthly salaries in the range between 48-64 Euros (for VREL, most employees are in lower scales).

In addition to the salary, the collective labour arrangement with the General Agricultural Workers Union (GAWU) of the Trade Union Congress of Ghana also includes a whole range of fringe benefits. These include sick leave payments, maternity leave, free medical care, school fees and study allowances for children and funeral grants. The gross value of these allowances may be equal tot around 20 percent of the salary. VREL employees receive on average four different fringe benefits against 2.5 for GEL employees. Most workers primarily consider wages, giving far less consideration to fringe benefits and other bonus arrangements.

Table 2 provides an overview of monthly family income from different sources. While GEL employees receive on average a third more salary, VREL employees raise more additional income through the sales of products. Even while family income of GEL employees is considerably higher, family expenditures between both groups are not significantly different. This is likely to be explained by the higher non-monetary revenues that VREL workers earn through food production on their subsistence home

*Table 2. Income composition of VREL and GEL employees (in thousands of cedis).*

| | VREL | GEL |
|---|---|---|
| Salary VREL/GEL | 7,215 (2,336)* | 9,828 (3,954)* |
| Other wage income | 694 (2,387) | 649 (2,343) |
| Casual work | 56 (346)* | 635 (2,216)* |
| Sales of products (own plot) | 3,323 (6,084)** | 1,013 (2,917)** |
| Business income | 757 (2,476)** | 2,033 (5,528)** |
| Income transfers | 29 (141) | 334 (1,764) |
| Pensions | 0 (0)** | 240 (1,188)** |
| Other income | 257 (1,715) | 108 (764) |
| Total family income | 15,026 (8,126)* | 19,544 (11,863)* |
| Family expenditures | 26,441 (14,561) | 27,701 (21,929) |

Note: means and standard deviation between brackets; ** = sign. at 0.05; * = sign at 0.5.

plots. They have more off-time available for home activities and leisure due to the shorter work schedule. Dividing salaries by effective working hours, VREL workers are clearly better off.

Income diversification is notably high amongst both categories of workers, where the banana salary covers around 50 percent of household income and a third to a quarter of all household expenditures. This may be an indication that many workers are strongly risk-averse and consider the salary income from the banana plantation mainly as a sound basis for undertaking other non/off-farm activities, particularly by the female family members. This implies that the stable and guaranteed income from banana production is a vital component for stabilising their livelihoods that permits subsequent engagement in (more rewarding) other trade and small-scale business activities.

### *4.3. Attitudes*

In addition to the monetary assessment of the fair impact on household income, considerable attention has been devoted to understand differences in attitudes and behavioural motivation between VREL and GEL employees. Annex gives an overview of the statements that were used for measuring job attitudes, corporate identification and sense of ownership. Table 3 provides the summary results.

The time preference game yields information on whether or not the participants had a turning point on which they were willing to wait for a larger amount of money instead of receiving a lower amount instantaneously. The higher the score, the less risk-averse people are. The mean score on this variable for VREL workers proved to be significantly higher than for GEL workers, indicating that they have better capacities

*Table 3. Attitudinal comparison VREL and GEL employees.*

| | VREL | GEL |
|---|---|---|
| Risk attitude/time preference | 5.92 (3.74) ** | 4.86 (2.84)** |
| Job security | 4.76 (0.63) | 4.52 (01.13) |
| Job satisfaction | 4.45 (1.10) ** | 4.78 (0.82) ** |
| Distributive justice | 4.0 (0.8) | 3.9 (1.3) |
| Corporate identification | 4.47 (1.02) * | 3.46 (1.82) * |
| Sense of ownership | 4.41 (1.12) * | 3.48 (1.83) * |
| Fringe benefits (amount) | 3.9 (1.0)* | 2.6 (1.1)* |
| Salary payments ($10^3$ cedis) | 7,215 (2,336)* | 9,828 (3,954)* |

note: means and standard deviation (between brackets).
** = sign at 0.05; * = sign at 0.10

for engaging in risky activities. Amongst the VREL participants, a third rejected all offers, while the others reached the turning point at a 150-200 percent of returns to investment. Differences in time preference (or, alternatively, relative risk aversion) are likely to be related to household income and family composition (e.g. families with more dependent family members can take less risk). In this particular case, however, the lower VREL salary does lead to less risk aversion amongst VREL workers, thus indicating that their employment with the company provides a suitable floor income for guaranteeing household livelihoods.[5]

### 4.4. Job security and job satisfaction

Attitudes towards job security and distributive justice (fairness) are generally higher for VREL workers, even while no significant differences are found (see Figure 1). Job satisfaction is slightly higher amongst GEL workers. Job security and job satisfaction are positively related to each other in both firms. Furthermore, job satisfaction is strongly influenced by the salary payments (mainly at GEL), but is hardly favoured by access to fringe benefits (Van Schendel, 2007). Within VREL, workers with a lower time preference are more satisfied with their job. Most importantly, a positive and significant relationship has been observed between job satisfaction/security and sense of ownership (Fransen and Ruben, 2007). This implies that further steps towards co-ownership could substantially contribute to reinforcing job satisfaction.

[5] Fransen and Ruben (2007) find that risk attitudes by VREL workers are negatively related to the factors 'corporate identification' and 'job satisfaction'. This implies that workers that are less identified with the company and less satisfied with their current work are inclined to take more risk (i.e. searching a job outside VREL).

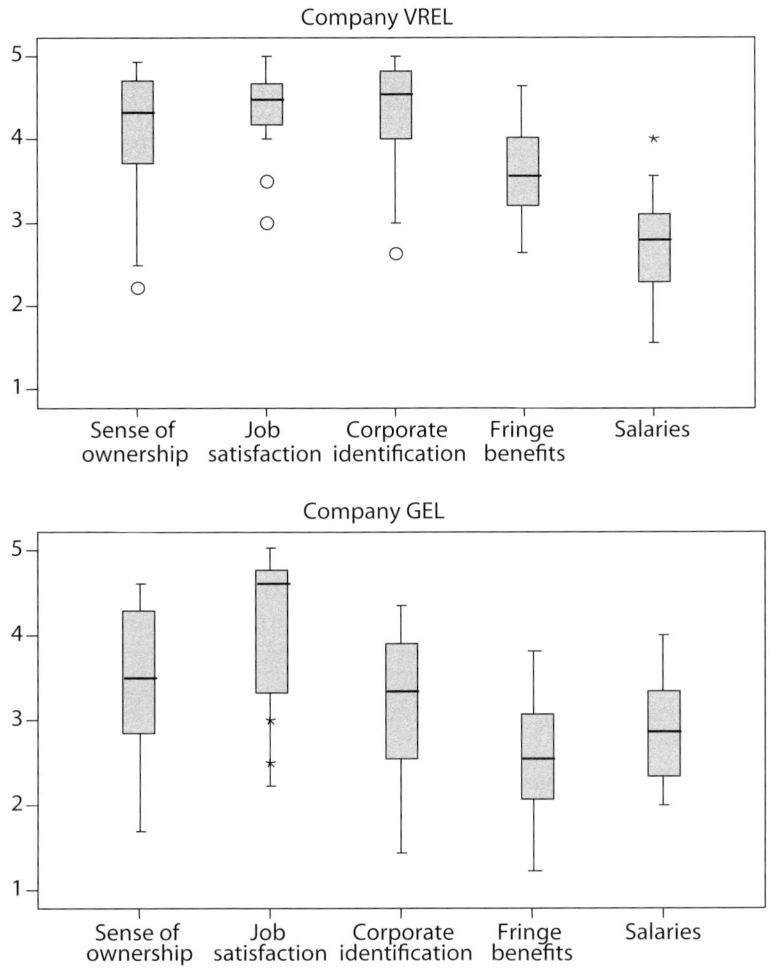


*Figure 1. Comparison VREL and GEL worker satisfaction.*

### *4.5. Corporate identification*

The degree of workers' identification with the company is substantially higher at the VREL plantation. VREL workers experience a higher sense of co-responsibility with the corporate goals and ambitions, probably because the management better informs the workers in the current state of affairs. In a similar vein, VREL workers express more responsibility for the corporate success, which in their view is mostly related to quality performance and banana yields.

#### 4.6. Sense of ownership

The sense of (co-)ownership is significantly higher amongst the VREL workers, in particular amongst employees that have already a long trajectory of working with the enterprise (on average more than 6 years). Sense of ownership proved to be particularly high with older employees and for large families with a high dependency rate (where the salary represents the major source of income). The sense of ownership is positively influenced by feelings of corporate identification ($r=0.38$, $p<0.01$) and further reinforced by better job security ($r=0.26$, $p<0.01$).

#### 4.7. Fair Trade

Attitudes toward Fair Trade have been measured by a set of questions and statements (see Annex). Factor analysis is used to identify two main dimensions that together explain 51% of the total variance. The two factors can be labelled as 'Fair Trade awareness' ($\alpha = 0.74$) and 'familiarity' with the Fair Trade premium ($\alpha = 0.84$). The importance attached to Fair Trade, as expressed by the VREL workers, was measured on a Likert scale (1 = low, 5 = high). Mean score on this variable was 4.17 (SD = 0.96): 93% declared to be familiar with the concept of Fair Trade. However, on the open questions whether workers know what the function of Fair Trade is, a quarter had no answer and another 16.5 percent gave incorrect answers (e.g. 'Fair Trade is the sticker on the bananas').

The importance attached to Fair Trade by the VREL workforce is stronger amongst male workers with a higher position in the enterprise and owning more assets (see Table 4). Workers that express more identification with corporate goals also give more importance to the Fair Trade affiliation. Job satisfaction appears to be inversely related to Fair Trade importance, indicating that workers that are more satisfied with their current work give less attention to Fair Trade aspects. On the other hand, Fair Trade awareness is positively related to job security, illustrating that workers are quite confident in the long-term potential of the Fair Trade market engagement. Finally, no significant relations were found for any of the variables with familiarity with the Fair Trade premium. Very few workers (22%) attend the meetings about Fair Trade, and 94% of the workers indicated that they wanted to know more about the concept of Fair Trade.

It should be noted that the Fair Trade premium in VREL is mainly used for providing specific items (like the purchase of bicycles, health kits and school subsidies) to the workforce. Given the difficulties of attending a large number of employees living scattered over several rural villages, available resources are not sufficient to permit fixed investments in schools, electrification or roads at all place simultaneously. In practice, a major part of the premium money is maintained on a bank account and used for providing interest-free loans to the workers. Strange enough, this is done without any coordination with other local (in)formal financial institutions, like the savings and credit union and the funeral associations. Consequently, hardly any multiplier effects are generated from the Fair Trade premium fund.

*Table 4. Factors influencing Fair Trade attitudes (OLS regression).*

| Variable | Fair Trade importance | Fair Trade awareness | Premium familiarity |
|---|---|---|---|
| Constant | 1.95 (0.59)*** | 1.41 (2.76) | 1.06 (1.94) |
| **Attitudes** | | | |
| Sense of ownership [1] | -0.52 (0.07) | 0.01 (0.40) | 0.12 (0.24) |
| Corporate identification [1] | 0.36 (0.10)*** | 0.05 (0.48) | 0.37 (0.32) |
| Job satisfaction [1] | -0.92 (0.04)** | -0.14 (0.23) | -0.10 (0.15) |
| Job security [1] | 0.07 (0.06) | 0.74 (0.22)** | -0.24 (0.24) |
| **Individual and household characteristics** | | | |
| Gender [3] | 0.27 (0.14)* | -1.12 (0.89) | -0.23 (0.55) |
| Age | 0.01 (0.01) | -0.04 (0.04) | 0.12 (0.03) |
| Assets per capita | 0.00 (0.00)** | 0.00 (0.00) | 0.00 (0.00) |
| Dependency rate | 0.25 (0.31) | -0.94 (1.82) | 0.20 (1.05) |
| Outstanding loans [2] | 0.13 (0.11) | 0.07 (0.59) | -0.17 (0.40) |
| Savings [2] | 0.14 (0.11) | 0.42 (0.59) | 0.17 (0.40) |
| Proportion VREL income | -0.03 (0.07) | -0.65 (0.62) | -0.07 (0.28) |
| **Workforce characteristics** | | | |
| Tenure (years) | 0.02 (0.01) | 0.13 (0.09) | -0.02 (0.04) |
| Working position [4] | 0.45 (0.16)** | 1.74 (1.17) | -0.49 (0.50) |
| Pseudo $R^2$ | 0.21 | 0.18 | 0.04 |

Note: * $p$ <0.10; ** $p$ <0.05; *** $p$ <0.01.
[1] 1 = low, 5 = high.
[2] 0 = no / 1 = yes.
[3] 0 = female, 1 = male.
[4] 0 = low, 1 = high.

## 5. Discussion and outlook

The comparative analysis of differences in welfare, livelihoods and attitudes between workers in the VREL Fair Trade plantation and the privately-owned Golden Exotics enterprise reveals a number of remarkable results. Since both plantations are located in the same region and draw on a similar pool of labour resources, competition amongst them is based on careful management of employment conditions. In fact, key elements from the VREL collective labour agreements are usually implemented one year later by GEL. The labour union thus guarantees that many of the Fair Trade benefits become available to a wider range of workers. Workers at GEL receive a higher basic salary, but have to work more hours and receive less fringe benefits. Subjective feelings regarding job safety, job satisfaction and fairness are broadly similar amongst the workforce of both plantations. VREL workers are, however, able and willing to take more risk, especially because their livelihoods are based on a more diverse portfolio of activities.

Banana production in Eastern Ghana remains a highly vulnerable activities. Plantations are sometimes heavily affected by storms or suffer from irregular supply of electricity that can interrupt irrigation systems. Moreover, crops are frequently affected by different root and fruit diseases, and therefore quality is highly variable. Finally, insecure reefer lines make the planning of harvesting operations difficult, and long waiting times in case of delays further reduce fruit quality. Efforts to diversify fruit operations (from bananas to pineapple in VREL, and from pineapple to bananas in GEL) have a limited success. Current experiments with outgrower schemes meet strong limitations due to scarce entrepreneurial capacities of local smallholders.

### *5.1. Prospects for co-ownership*

The VREL experience is particularly interesting to review the options for further deepening Fair Trade through direct worker involvement in co-ownership. In the current situation, VREL workers are fairly well identified with their enterprise but little informed about enterprise management and Fair Trade aspects. In the short run, improvement of working conditions and reinforcing workers' corporate identification (e.g. promotion of transparency and identity feelings) can be expected to yield better returns that the formal and premature shift towards co-ownership.

The transition towards employee co-ownership brings in the dilemma between global interconnectedness (through Fair Trade) against local hierarchy (i.e. the strong tradition of vertical management and established positions). Formal changes in the ownership structure can only bring about the expected results when simultaneously efforts are made towards real democratisation of enterprise management. The implementation of a VREL employee co-ownership scheme can be helpful to contribute simultaneously to the following goals: (a) it becomes a recognisable part of the corporate identity and is 'marketed' towards the consumers; (b) it is effectively perceived by the workers of the company as a tangible aspect of their working conditions, thus providing incentives for improving productivity and quality; and (c) it is considered by the company board as an effective strategy towards enhancing workers' involvement and empowerment.

The envisaged VREL employee ownership scheme could be based on the following core components:

a. Instalment of workers co-ownership through the emission of individual (but non-transferable) shares, preferably at the household level,[6]
b. assignment of employee shares based on transparent criteria related to the duration of employment with the company,
c. deposit of the employee shares-certificates (in trust with a regional Credit and Savings cooperative), using these as a collateral for borrowing; where deposited share-certificates give workers the right to draw on loan facilities (initially up to

[6] Transferable to family members and with pay-back rights (e.g. for retiring employees) against company reserve fund.

the intrinsic value of the share, but in subsequent years the multiplication factor can increase to 150 or 200% with proven credibility);

d. deposited shares can also be used as an endowment fund for counterpart funding to local voluntary networks (particularly funeral associations) and for community investments (schools, etc). This will likely trigger the investments made by the Fair Trade premium committee; and
e. yearly dividend distribution in accordance with the distribution of share ownership (with preference for employee shares) and options for share schemes (i.e. additional emissions as bonus) coupled with the productivity performance of the workforce (eventually by block or site) and measured against a site-specific standard base year.[7]

Linking of employee ownership with short-term borrowing options (through local community organisations) and medium-term capital growth schedules is of critical importance for the acceptance and success of Fair Trade co-ownership. These issues deserve careful consideration and should be addressed fully before further steps can be taken towards launching the employee ownership scheme. Moreover, within the (hierarchical) Ghanaian culture, special attention should be given to leadership development and worker training.

## References


Danielou, M and C. Ravry (2005). *The rise of Ghana's pineapple industry, from successful takeoff to sustainable expansion.* Washington D.C.: Worldbank. Available at: http://www.worldbank.org/afr/wps/wp93.pdf.

Ellis, F. (1983). *Las transnacionales del Banano en Centroamerica.* San José: Editorial Universitaria Centroamericana.

Fransen, S. and R. Ruben (2007). *Prospects for Co-ownership in Fair Trade Supply Chains: an Exploratory Analysis for Banana Plantations in Ghana.* Contributed paper XXII Congress of the European Society for Rural Sociology, Wageningen, August 2007.

Human Rights Watch (2002). *Tained Harvest: Child Labor and Obstacles to Organizing on Ecuador's' Plantations.* Washinton/New York: Human Rights Watch.

Lamb, H. (2008). *Fighting the Banana Wars and other Fair Trade battles.* London/Sydney: Rider.

Locke E. A., (1995). The Micro-analyses of Job Satisfaction: Comments on Taber and Alliger. *Journal of Organizational Behaviour* 16: 123-125.

Lovett S., T. Coyle and R. Adams (2004). Job Satisfaction and Technology in Mexico. *Journal of World Business* 39: 217-232.

Mulinge, M. and C.W. Mueller (1998). Employee Job Satisfaction in Developing Countries: The Case of Kenya. *World Development* 26: 2181-2199.


[7] VREL employees need to build up co-ownership by receiving shares as part of their income or as an incentive bonus (related to individual or joint productivity). This can be further complemented by a savings-related share options scheme (called Share-save).that permits employees to gradually increase their co-ownership. See for a complete overview of employee ownership options: National Center for Employee Ownership (NCEO) and IfsProShare.org.

Murray, D.L. and L.T. Raynolds (2007). Globalization and its Antinomies: Negotiating a Fair Trade Movement. In: L.T. Raynolds, D.L. Murray and J. Wilkinson (Eds.) *Fair Trade: The Challenges of Transforming Globalization*. London: Routledge, pp. 1-14.

Pierce, J.L. and L. Rodgers (2004). The Psychology of Ownership and Worker-owner Productivity. *Group Organization Management* 29: 588-613.

Pierce, J.L., S.A. Rubenfeld and S. Morgan (1991). Employee Ownership: a Conceptual Model of Process and Effects. *Academy of Management Review* 16: 121-144.

Raynolds, L.T. (2007). Fair Trade Bananas: Broadening the Movement and Market in the United States. In: L.T. Raynolds, D.L. Murray and J. Wilkinson (Eds.) *Fair Trade: The Challenges of Transforming Globalization*. London: Routledge, pp. 63-82.

Raynolds, L.T. and. M.A. Long (2007) Fair/Alternative Trade: Historical and Empirical Dimensions. In: L.T. Raynolds, D.L. Murray and J. Wilkinson (Eds.) *Fair Trade: The Challenges of Transforming Globalization*. London: Routledge, pp. 15-32.

Striffler, S. and M. Moberg, (Eds.) (2003) *Banana Wars*. Durham: Duke University Press.

Taber T.D. and G.M. Alliger (1995). A Task-level Assessment of Job-satisfaction. *Journal of Organizational Behaviour* 16: 101-121.

Van Dyne, L. and Pierce, J.L. (2004). Psychological Ownership and Feelings of Possession: Three Field Studies Predicting Employee Attitudes and Organizational Citizenship Behaviour. *Journal of Organizational Behaviour* 25: 439-459.

Van Schendel, L. (2007) *Makes Fair Trade a Difference: Comparison of a Fair Trade and a non Fair Trade Plantation in Ghana*. Nijmegen: CIDIN.

Wagner, S.H., Parker, C.P. and Christiansen, N.D. (2003). Employees that think and act like Owners: Effects of Ownership Beliefs and Behaviors on Organizational Effectiveness. *Personnel Psychology* 56: 847-871.

## Annex. Behavioural statements

Job satisfaction
- I really like my job
- I am very satisfied with my job
- My job offers me sufficient opportunities

Job security
- I will be able to keep my job as long as I wish
- I am sure that I receive my salary every month
- My job is not secure
- GEL /VREL is offering me a secure job

Distributive justice
- I receive a fair salary for the work that I do
- I receive a fair salary for the experience that I have
- I receive a fair salary for the amount of hours that I work
- The punishments given for misconduct are fair

Corporate identification
- If I work hard, the company makes more profit
- If the company has a problem, I should contribute to the solution
- I feel responsible for the financial successes of the company
- When the company has financial problem I should share in the consequences

Sense of ownership
- If I talk about VREL/GEL to other people, I talk about THE/MY company
- I sense that this is OUR company
- Most people that work at the company feel as though they own the company
- sense that this is MY company
- It is hard to think of this company as MINE

Fair Trade
- Do you know VREL is a Fair Trade farm?
- How important is it to you that VREL is a Fair Trade farm?
- A Fair Trade farm has benefits above a regular farm
- Are you familiar with the Fair Trade premium?
- Is the Fair Trade premium important to you?

Note: all statements apply Likert 5-points scale (from 1 = totally disagree to 5 = totally agree; some questions use reverse order).

# Chapter 7

## Fair Trade impact of banana production in El Guabo Association, Ecuador: a production function analysis

*Ruerd Ruben, Luud Clercx, Dario Cepeda and Thomas de Hoop*

### 1. Introduction

Banana production in a smallholder setting is usually characterised by a high heterogeneity amongst farmers (in terms of farm size, resources and experience) and consequently large differences in yields and income. This makes impact assessment rather difficult, since socio-economic performance may differ both amongst the Fair Trade farmers and between Fair Trade and non-Fair Trade producers. In a similar vein, differences in location and production systems could be major sources of income variability and the analysis of the Fair Trade impact can thus easily be biased.

The El Guabo Association in Ecuador provides an unique setting for exploring differences between Fair Trade and non-Fair Trade smallholder banana production, since it covers a wide geographical area with affiliated members and their non-member neighbours residing closely together. This implies that – in principle – a straightforward comparison of their production performance can be made. We are mainly interested to analyse differences in land and labour productivity as underlying determinants of the farm-household income dynamics. To guarantee an un-biased assessment, we controlled for other differences in farm-household characteristics (i.e. farm size, assets).

The analysis presented in this chapter focuses on the impact of farmers' engagement in Fair Trade on their production systems and organisation. It is usually supposed that guaranteed Fair Trade market outlets and stable prices provide incentives to producers to realise on-farm investments, intensify input applications and enhance labour use (Ellis, 1993). The presence of delivery contracts with an European import firm (Agrofair) and the possibilities to supply large quantities of bananas at regular intervals makes El Guabo an appropriate partner for trade and co-investment. Further improvement of local production systems requires that smallholders are able to reduce the risks and are capable to mobilise the scarce factor capital (Saenz-Segura and Ruben, 2004; Kuyvenhoven and Ruben, 2002). Possibilities for intensification of production and quality upgrading in smallholder regimes are strongly related to the contractual terms provided in the market (Key and Runsten, 1999; Ruben and Saenz-Segura, 2008). Fair Trade certification may thus have the potential to alter production practices that reinforce smallholder livelihoods.

The remainder of this chapter is structured as follows. First, we provide a short overview of the El Guabo producers' association, its historical roots, internal organisation and current performance. Hereafter, we outline the analytical approach used in this study. Main attention is given to the procedures for estimating separate production functions for Fair Trade and non-Fair Trade producers, and the identification of the underlying determinants of the registered productivity differences. Next, the empirical results from the field survey are presented and implications for further expansion of Fair Trade production are discussed. Finally, we outline possible pathways for reinforcing the impact of Fair Trade in a context of highly diversified agroecological conditions that is typical for many other peasant communities.

## 2. Setting

The *Asociación de Pequeños Productores Bananeros 'El Guabo'* (hereafter: Asoguabo) is located in the province El Oro, in the region that includes the cities of El Guabo, Machala and Arenillas. The association incorporates 15 local groups with a total membership of some 400 producers covering a net banana production area of approximately 2,000 hectares. Asoguabo is the main supplier of bananas to AgroFair. The association was founded by 14 small banana producers of the city El Guabo, who started to export their fair-trade bananas to AgroFair in 1998. In 2006, Asoguabo supplied 31,328 ton of bananas (1,727 million boxes), covering 46% of the total banana sales volume of AgroFair. Farm sizes range from 2 to 20 ha while farming systems vary also strongly, from rainfed agroforestry subsistence systems of banana and cacao in the hills to irrigated banana cultivation in the dry lowlands. About one third of the sales volume of Asoguabo concerns organic certified bananas.

Presently, Asoguabo exports bananas of its members, provides technical assistance in banana cultivation and post-harvesting and administers social and environmental projects implemented with the Fair Trade premium. To be better positioned for meeting the future challenges, Asoguabo is currently undergoing some restructuring. Recently a foundation, called *Fundación Asoguabo*, was registered to administer and manage projects financed by the Fair Trade premium received by Asoguabo. Furthermore, Asoguabo registered a company, named OKEGUABO Ltda, which will initially serve as a joint investment vehicle for Asoguabo and AgroFair to set up a new PSOM project (co-funded by the Dutch government). Asoguabo will continue to exist to look after the interests of its members and represent them as board member of the various related entities.

Ecuador is the main exporter of fresh bananas with a production area of 186,000 ha. The export of bananas from Ecuador has grown steadily, from 214 million boxes (4.23 million tons) in 2001 to 256 million boxes (4.65 million tons) in 2006. With an export volume of 2.2 million boxes (40,000 tons) in 2007, Asoguabo ranks 20$^{th}$ among exporters of Ecuador. World exports of organic bananas account for approximately 1% of total banana trade and 2.5% of the European market. Ecuador is the second largest producer is Ecuador with about 5.4 million boxes of organic bananas exported in 2007. Asoguabo is currently the third largest exporter of organic bananas with 630,000 boxes of organic bananas (see Figure 1).

Banana production is highly variable between seasons and type of producers (Cepeda Bastidas *et al.*, 2008). Additionally, the export markets in Europe and the USA experiment a structural seasonal behaviour. Demand and prices tend to drop between July and November because of the harvest of local fruit like apples, pears and cherries. This also affects the performance of Asoguabo (see Figure 1). The El Guabo region consists of different agro-ecological zones, ranging from (semi-)humid and dry lowlands to more humid upland areas. Average banana yields vary been 20 and 33 boxes per ha per week. Farms with limited technologies produce around 20 boxes/ha, semi-technified farms are at 25 boxes/ha and highly technified production can reach 40-45 boxes/ha. Four production systems have been identified - characterised as conventional banana monoculture, conventional agroforestry, organic monoculture and organic agroforestry – that differ widely in terms of planting density, input applications and banana yields. Banana production is frequently challenged by the

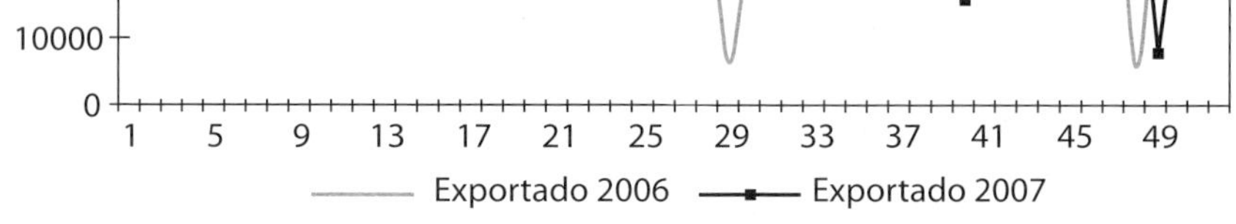


*Figure 1. Weekly banana export volumes (boxes), 2006-2007.*
*Source: www.asoguabo.com.ec.*

Black Sigatoka disease.[1] Other major differences refer to farm size stratification (average farm size of 10.5 ha, with a SD of 14.5 and a quarter of producers owning more than one farm) and organic certification (58% of the farms are devoted to organic production). The average banana area is around 5.5 ha. Most producers have their own packing station at the farm and irrigation systems, but organic agroforestry farmers notably lack access to sufficient water resources and good roads, and have scarce availability of complementary infrastructure (warehouses, toilets and washing places, mandatory for EurepGAP certification).

Given its considerable size and FT-certified banana volumes, El Guabo receives substantial financial benefits from Fair Trade (Salinas and Matamorros, 2007). Conventional banana producers receive US$ 4.50/box (38% more than other smallholder producers) and the price paid to organic producers raises till US$ 6.70/box. In terms of Fair Trade premium, according to the FLO standards, Agrofair pays US$ 1 per box, of which 20% is used for credit provision to enhance further technification and 80% is channelled towards different social and environmental programs (i.e. school fees, childcare, health and social insurance). The latter activities also include workers and other community members. The premium fund received since 2004 represents a total amount of US$ 6,170,169. El Guabo receives technical support from several (non)governmental development organisations (SNV, GTZ, CORPEI, CTM, PSOM and AFAD) to support business development and to guarantee the effective use of the premium funds.

## 3. Approach

For the comparison of differences in yield and labour productivity between FT and non-FT banana farmers, we relied on a so-called production function approach. A production function describes the technical relationship between variable input(s) and an output and estimates the amount of production that is generated with a certain (combination of) inputs.[2] Input are mainly agricultural land, labour, chemical inputs, irrigation, and machinery or equipment, while the output refers to the total amount of banana production per farm per hectare, in terms of exportable banana boxes of 18.14 kg).

[1] Control of Black Sigatoka is very important for the quality of bananas. Black Sigatoka is a fungal disease that causes dark leaf spots that eventually enlarge and coalesce, causing turning yellow and brown of the leaf area resulting in yield losses of more than 50%, premature ripening and serious defects in the exported fruit. The fungus that causes Black Sigatoka is formed under high moisture conditions and is disseminated by wind, rain and irrigation water. The disease is difficult and expensive to control and best results are obtained by frequently applying fungicides mixed with spray oils to leaves by spraying with airplanes or helicopters in combination with cultural practices.

[2] For a basic introduction to the principles of production function analysis in agriculture economics, see Ellis (1993).

The basic underlying idea is that both types of producers face different external marketing options and therefore their internal production organisation is also likely to be different. This is expected to lead to significant higher factor productivity in FT farms, giving the incentives to further improve banana yields through better/more input use or improved labour allocation. We first outline the analytical framework and then provide a technical specification of the estimated model.

### *3.1. Analytical framework*

Differences in production systems between FT and non-FT producers (located in the same region and thus facing similar agroecological conditions) are likely to be determined by access to markets and information. Farmers that meet lower output prices and/or difficulties to obtain better inputs are obliged to rely on production technologies that yield lower returns to land and labour. Otherwise, improving access to input and output markets and providing better technical information about possible production alternatives enables farmers to reach higher returns.

Whereas technical change is usually depicted as a shift along the production function, the transition from non-FT to FT production is better envisaged as a complete change of production systems. Improved access to market outlets and higher and more stable prices could enable producers to realise substantial in-depth investments in their banana farms. Labour productivity can thus improve due to better access to complementary inputs (Ruben *et al.*, 1998, Heerink and Ruben, 1996). The differences between the FT and non-FT production function are illustrated in Figure 2. As can be seen, non-FT production is only attractive for smallholder producers in the segment of relatively low input use and when the input/output price relation (depicted by the straight line $p_1$) is high. Otherwise, when output prices rise compared to input costs (= $p_2$ line) farmers are inclined to shift towards the FT production function that guarantees higher yields and better labour productivity.

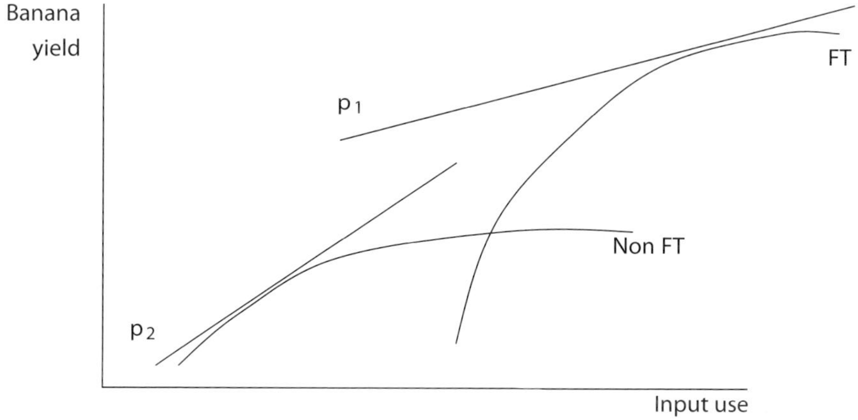


*Figure 2. Fair Trade and non-Fair Trade production functions.*

Empirical studies using separate production function for different categories of farmers usually distinguish between two different strategies (Reardon *et al.*, 1996; Boserup, 1965): (a) labour-led intensification based on intensive use of (family) labour to increase production, and (b) capital-led intensification, where farmers augment their production by combining labour with capital inputs (mainly fertilisers and irrigation). Whereas the former strategy easily leads to over-use of labour ('involution' in the words of Geertz) and declining marginal returns, the latter strategy that guarantees improvements in yields and labour returns as well as more sustainable resource management should be preferred. This implies that higher input use and capital investments that also require more labour use (in harvesting and packing) eventually result in improved labour productivity. Intensification in banana production can thus pay off in terms of simultaneously increasing returns to labour. In practice, however, labour can be scarce, both in the highland areas (due to competition with other crops, like cocoa, and migration tendencies to the lowlands) as well as in the lowland areas (migration tendencies towards urban areas). Consequently, both capital and labour constraints, and lack of good roads (important since harvesting takes place every week), can hinder further intensification in banana production.

### *3.2. Model specification*

The econometric techniques applied for estimating the FT and non-FT production functions rely on Ordinary Least Squares (OLS) regression analysis, using the Chow test and t-tests to verify whether differences between both groups are statistically significant. We use the common Cobb-Douglas specification of the production function that permits direct estimation of factor productivity. The formula for the Cobb-Douglas production function is:

$$Y = a.K^{b}.L^{c} \tag{1}$$

where Y= yield, K = capital inputs, L = labour input, and a, b, and c are coefficients. On both sides of the equation, the ratio variables are transformed into log-variables. Log-linearisation simplifies the function, and facilitates variable interpretation by separating the components. In the Cobb-Douglass production function the elasticity of substitution between capital and labour is assumed to be 1 for all values of capital and labour (Cobb and Douglas, 1928; Douglas, 1976). The elasticity of substitution describes the % change in input substitution given a 1% change in the price of the inputs.

The production function is estimated empirically by means of an Ordinary Least Squares (OLS) regression analysis. The simplest form of a regression model can be written as follows:

$$Y = a + b.K + c.L + ... + e \tag{2}$$

where Y is the dependent variable (productivity), K and L are independent variables (e.g. capital and labour inputs), a is the constant, and e is the error that can not be explained by the regression (i.e. sampling error). The parameters b and c are the regression coefficient. These coefficient can be positive as well as negative, and indicate the effect of the predictor on the dependent variable. For example, when a is 0.5, this means that for every unit of additional capital or input use, yield increases with a factor 0.5. Because outputs and inputs are transformed to logarithms, b and c can be interpreted as elasticities that represent the percentage change in Y as a result of a 1 percent change in K or L.

Since it is very likely that the regression results are not equal for Fair Trade farmers that belong to Asoguabo and other non-Fair Trade producers, we apply the Chow test (Chow, 1960). The Chow test reveals whether or not different groups within the sample - which share certain farm characteristics - have different production functions that should be estimated separately. Consider again the simple regression model (Equation 2). For different (FT and non-FT) sub samples, the regression model can be split into:

$$Y_1 = a_1 + b_1.K_1 + c_1.L_1 + \dots + e_1 \tag{3}$$

and

$$Y_2 = a_2 + b_2.K_2 + c_2.L_2 + \dots + e_2 \tag{4}$$

The hypothesis tested in the Chow test is that the coefficients $a_1$ and $a_2$, $b_1$ and $b_2$, and $c_1$ and $c_2$, (etc.) are equal or different from each other. If the coefficients are indeed different, the production function should be estimated separately for each group. In addition. Independent sample t-test analysis is used to verify if the mean scores of the two different groups on specific continuous variables differ significantly.

## 4. Results

We draw from a wider survey amongst Asoguabo members and neighbouring farms with a representative sub-sample that includes 283 observations (190 Fair Trade and 93 non-Fair Trade farms). Given the heterogeneity in local production conditions, we limited the sample to farmers with banana monoculture that are located in dry lowland areas and have good access conditions (57 Fair Trade and 63 non-Fair Trade farms). Farmers with agroforestry production, located in humid areas and/or in less accessible areas have been excluded from the sample, since they maintain significantly different types of production systems (as confirmed by the Chow test). From each farm, data were collected regarding banana production, input use, production technologies, household income and selected attitudes. We focus in this chapter on major differences in the production variables

Table 1 provides the descriptive statistics for each of the groups. We notice that FT farmers reach a significantly higher average land productivity, whereas only minor differences in average labour use are registered. The substitution of chemical by organic fertilisers and Sigatoka control measures, and the use of improved irrigation systems, important for nutrient take-up, proves to be a major importance for raising land productivity amongst FT farmers. Major investments in cableways and improved packing stations by FT farmers are important to maintain quality and net exportable output.

Further analysis was made of the determinants of the registered differences in land and labour productivity. Table 2 gives the estimates of the parameters of the Cobb-Douglas production function for both FT and non-FT producers. In the overall sample, the dummy for FT involvement is highly significant, indicating that indeed we have to address both types of farmers as different production systems. This is also confirmed by the significant Chow test, that shows that the two categories of farmers operate on different production functions.

Marginal labour productivity is highly positive for FT farmers but significant negative for non-FT producers, indicating that FT farmers reach higher returns on their labour use, while non-FT farmers already apply too much (family) labour given their existing constraints with complementary inputs. FT production located on good soils in flatland areas is positively influenced by drainage, but suffers from negative returns to irrigation. This may be explained by the fact that the supply of water from different natural sources is not fully reliable and thus less effective. Cepeda Bastidas *et al.* (2008) indeed found a strong correlation between labour productivity with the type of irrigation, particularly for sprinkler systems.

*Table 1. Descriptive statistics of Fair Trade vs. non-Fair Trade farmers.*

| | Fair Trade | | Non-Fair Trade | | t-test |
|---|---|---|---|---|---|
| | Mean | SD | Mean | SD | Sign.[2] |
| Altitude (meters above sea level) | 39 | 16 | 36 | 19 | ns |
| Productivity (boxes/ha) | 1,563 | 524 | 1,309 | 499 | *** |
| Labour (days/ha) | 244 | 139 | 236 | 110 | ns |
| - daily labour | 95 | 70 | 93 | 43 | ns |
| - other labour | 149 | 96 | 143 | 80 | ns |
| Assets (value/ha) [1] | 4,830 | 3,219 | 3,259 | 6,830 | * |
| Conventional fertilisers (value/ha) | 616 | 537 | 943 | 1,032 | ** |
| Organic fertilisers (value/ha) | 193 | 396 | 27 | 125 | *** |
| Organic Sigatoka control (value/ha) | 104 | 242 | 15 | 92 | *** |

[1] Includes irrigation system, water pumps, cable systems and packaging facilities.
[2] Significance level: *** = sign at 0.01; ** = sign at 0.05; * = sign at 0.1 level; ns = not significant.

*Table 2. Fair Trade and non-Fair Trade production functions (dep. var: Ln of banana boxes per hectare).*

| Indicator | Fair Trade (N= 57) | | | Non-Fair Trade (N=63) | | |
|---|---|---|---|---|---|---|
| | Coeff. | SE | Sign | Coeff. | S.E. | Sign. |
| Mean age household members | -0.0100 | -2.96 | ** | -0.0030 | -0.67 | |
| **Inputs** | | | | | | |
| Daily labour (days/ha) | 0.2100 | 3.18 | ** | -0.4800 | -2.94 | ** |
| Other labour (days/ha) | -0.0030 | -0.09 | | 0.0600 | 1.53 | |
| Conventional fertilisers | 0.0200 | 1.02 | | 0.0200 | 1.35 | |
| Organic fertilisers | 0.0200 | 0.97 | | 0.1600 | 1.70 | |
| Sigatoka control | -0.1100 | -2.97 | ** | -0.0700 | -0.80 | |
| Herbicides | -0.0400 | -1.18 | | 0.0100 | 0.27 | |
| **Asset (Value * $10^2$)** | | | | | | |
| Packaging facilities | -0.0060 | -1.61 | | 0.0020 | 1.18 | |
| Drainage channels | 0.0900 | 2.86 | ** | 0.0300 | 0.46 | |
| Motor power | 0.0700 | 1.73 | | -0.0030 | -0.17 | |
| Donkey/horse power | 0.7000 | 2.10 | * | - | - | |
| Other assets | -0.0040 | -0.81 | | 0.0110 | 0.97 | |
| **Agroecology** | | | | | | |
| Temperature | 0.2000 | 3.44 | ** | 0.3900 | 1.28 | |
| Altitude | -0.0200 | -3.62 | ** | 0.0070 | 0.89 | |
| Rainfall | -0.0020 | 1.64 | | -0.0005 | -1.04 | |
| Canal irrigation | -0.6400 | -3.23 | ** | 0.3500 | 0.92 | |
| Well irrigation | -0.4600 | -2.48 | * | 0.5600 | 1.35 | |
| River irrigation | -0.5700 | -2.61 | * | 0.4000 | 0.84 | |
| Soil quality | 0.4700 | 3.12 | ** | 0.1200 | 0.74 | |
| *Constant* | 4.0600 | 2.39 | * | -1.9400 | -0.25 | |
| Adjusted $R^2$ | | 0.5654 | | | 0.0869 | |
| AIC | | 37.99 | | | 93.54 | |

Note: *** sign. <0.01; ** sign. <0.5; * sign. <0.1.

Surprisingly, investments in Sigatoka control also have a negative impact on FT production, but causality is likely to be reverse. Farmers start using Sigatoka control after the occurrence problems; it is thus not the Sigatoka control in itself that leads to lower production, but Sigatoka that leads to lower production and obliges to higher investments in Sigatoka control. This implies that farmers with Sigatoka infestation are strictly controlled and may be temporarily suspended by Asoguabo from export deliveries.[3]

[3] Sigatoka-infested bananas tend to mature early and can also affect other bananas in the same container due to ethylene emissions, thus reducing overall quality.

Other major differences between the group of FT farmers that are members of Asoguabo and their non-FT neighbours are found with respect to asset ownership and equipment, credit access and investment behaviour, and changes in production strategies and related livelihoods (see Table 3). FT farmers receive better and more technical assistance and show favourable performance in terms of improvements in yields, production volumes and banana quality. Moreover, they appear to be more inclined to realise investments for improving production and packaging conditions, are also investing in environmental care, as well as in health care and life insurance.

Even while Asoguabo's banana production systems still have wide room for improvement, the incorporation of non-Fair Trade producers into the association already provides a first step towards higher yields and labour productivity (leading to better household incomes). Current plans to introduce a precision agriculture approach that enables producers to optimise cultivation activities and tailor input use to the requirements of the plants, while simultaneously improve harvesting forecasting schedules in line with market demands (Agrofair, 2008), can further shift the Fair Trade production function into an upwards direction.[4] Fair Trade certification and market linkages thus provide the minimum conditions for farmers to engage in

*Table 3. Main differences between FT and non-FT producers.*

| Indicator (in % of producers by group) | FT | Non-FT | Sign. |
|---|---|---|---|
| Access to technical assistance (%) | 95 | 44 | *** |
| Improvement in yields (%) | 42 | 6 | ** |
| Improvements in production (%) | 45 | 10 | ** |
| Improvements in quality performance (%) | 47 | 22 | * |
| Improvement in employment creation (%) | 23 | 4 | ** |
| Intensification of fertiliser use (%) | 49 | 18 | ** |
| Transition to organic farming systems (%) | 28 | 12 | * |
| Implementation EurepGAP standards | 64 | 8 | *** |
| Investments in irrigation | 60 | 18 | *** |
| Investments in packing station (%) | 65 | 32 | ** |
| Environmental protection (%) | 70 | 42 | ** |
| Private health insurance (%) | 68 | 8 | *** |
| Credit access (%) | 75 | 25 | ** |

Note: *** sign. <0.01; ** sign. <0.5; * sign. <0.1.

[4] Asoguabo will make a start with a system of programmed banana harvests on a communal farm. In this system, banana trees will be planted out from a nursery into the field within a time span of 4-5 months and treated as an annual crop. Harvest takes place after 8 months in the high season during 4-5 months, when demand and prices on the export market are high (see Figure 1).

environmentally sustainable production techniques that are otherwise not accessible for individual smallholders (Melo and Wolf, 2007). This potential win-win situation can certainly be attributed to the initial engagement with Fair Trade supply chains that paves the ways for the subsequent upgrading of local production networks. El Guabo has now reached the required economies of scale enabling further investments in precision agriculture – using and integrated management systems for all farms – that permit to optimise banana growth and to timely detect and control possible quality problems.

We finally assessed the differences in time preferences between FT and non-FT farmers in order to assess their willingness to realise in-depth investments. The experimental design is based on a number of alternative offers for receiving a fixed amount today or waiting for a higher amount after one year (see Table 4). Fair Trade farmers exhibit clearly higher willingness to invest when returns raise to amounts more than double the current returns. The registered differences are highly significant between FT and non-FT farmers, indicating that the perceived certainty of having access to FT market outlets has a strong positive effect on farmers' investment attitudes.

*Table 4. Time preferences of FT vs. non-FT producers.*

| Amount today | Amount in 1 year | Fair Trade (% Today) | Non-Fair Trade (% today) | t-value (sign.) |
|---|---|---|---|---|
| USD 1,000.00 | USD 1,250.00 | 0.91 | 0.94 | -0.50 |
| USD 1,000.00 | USD 1,500.00 | 0.87 | 0.94 | -1.18 |
| USD 1,000.00 | USD 1,750.00 | 0.85 | 0.92 | -1.10 |
| USD 1,000.00 | USD 2,000.00 | 0.70 | 0.88 | -2.26 ** |
| USD 1,000.00 | USD 2,250.00 | 0.63 | 0.86 | -2.66 *** |
| USD 1,000.00 | USD 2,500.00 | 0.59 | 0.80 | -2.31 ** |
| USD 1,000.00 | USD 2,750.00 | 0.57 | 0.78 | -2.29 ** |
| USD 1,000.00 | USD 3,000.00 | 0.52 | 0.75 | -2.03 ** |

Note: *** sign. <0.01; ** sign. <0.5; * sign. <0.1.

## 5. Discussion

Certified Fair Trade bananas from Ecuador represent roughly 40% of the European FT market and El Guabo Association is a major partner in this market chain. Given the strong position of local smallholder producer groups and the effective two-tier organisational structure, farmers are able to reap advantages from their engagement in Fair Trade. Positive effects are registered with respect to banana yields and labour productivity that are directly translated into higher household income. Other less tangible benefits are received through the social activities promoted with the Fair Trade premium.

Further development of the Fair Trade concept in the context of El Oro province can be based on two different – albeit complementary – strategies. First, there is still an important potential of conventional smallholder banana producers living in the same area that can become part and parcel of the Fair Trade network. In Ecuador, more than 5 thousand small banana producers (areas up to 30 ha) exist. (Cepeda Bastidas et.al. 2008). More than half of them live in the Asoguabo region. *Widening* Fair Trade through the involvement of more members is therefore still widely possible. This requires, of course, that these producer develop a kind of loyalty towards the association in order to prevent free-riding problems (e.g. side selling to other exporters in case of temporary higher prices, especially on the volatile Ecuadorian spot market). Second, an adequate quality performance and monitoring system for hundreds of farms is crucial, for controlled growth. Organisational reinforcement and leadership training, including a package of support services (credit, technical assistance, Sigatoka control) tend to be key components to guarantee loyal behaviour.

The second pathway for further strengthening El Guabo is based on *deepening* Fair Trade through the upgrading of production systems towards better quality management and improved timing of harvesting operations.[5] This strategy mainly involves current producers that are encouraged to shift towards precision farming in order to further increase both land and labour productivity. Such a transition requires substantial (external) capital investments that can be mobilised due to the commercial guarantees of long-term Fair Trade delivery contracts. Improving smallholder production systems is thus based on supply chain linkages with the European import partner (Agrofair).

Notwithstanding the many day-to-day difficulties that Asoguabo farmers may experience, the association represents not only one of the earliest but also one of the most challenging examples of dynamic Fair Trade development. This is basically due to the ingenious organisational interfaces between vertically-oriented marketing chains and the horizontally-oriented local associations, that both include effective feedback mechanisms (i.e. Asoguabo being a shareholder in the European FT fruit import corporation Agrofair, and local communities linked to El Guabo Association through the Foundation that manages the premium funds). These structures contribute to mutual trust, checks and balances and risk sharing options that could guarantee continuous innovation of Fair Trade practices.

## References

Agrofair (2008). *Introduction of Precision Agriculture among Smallholder Producers of Fair-trade and Organic Bananas.* El Guabo: PSOM Proposal.

Boserup, E. (1965). *The Conditions of Agricultural Growth: the Economics of Agricultural Change under Population Pressure.* Chicage: Aldine.

[5] Within the coming years, Asoguabo will make important investments in this direction within the framework of the PSOM funded project.

Chow, G.C. (1960). Tests of Equality Between Sets of Coefficients in Two Linear Regressions. *Econometrica* 28: 591-605.

Cepeda Bastidas, D., L. Clercx, E. Rodríguez, F. Montenegro, A Ojeda and C. Tamayo (2008). *Informe de Investigacion – Encuesta Condiciones Agro-socioeconomicas de los pequenos productores bananeros de la zona de influencia de la APPBG.* El Guabo: SIPAE & AFAD.

Cobb, C.W. and P.H. Douglas (1928). A Theory of Production. *American Economic Review* 18: 139-165.

Douglas, P.H. (1976). The Cobb-Douglas Production Function Once Again: Its History, Its Testing, and Some New Empirical Values. *The Journal of Political Economy* 84: 903-916.

Ellis, F. (1993). *Peasant Economics: Farm Households and Agrarian Development* (2nd ed.). Cambridge: Cambridge University Press.

Heerink, N.B.M. and R. Ruben (1996). Economic Approaches for the Evaluation of Low External Input Agriculture. *Tijdschrift voor Sociaal-wetenschappelijk Onderzoek in de Landbouw* (TSL) 11: 294-308.

Key, N. and D. Runsten (1999). Contract Farming, Smallholders, and Rural Development in Latin America: The Organization of Agroprocessing Firms and the Scale of Outgrower Production. *World Development* 27: 381-401.

Kuyvenhoven, A. and R. Ruben (2002). Economic Conditions for Sustainable Agricultural Intensification. In: N. Uphoff (Ed.). *Agroecological Innovations: Increasing Food Production with Participatory Development.* London: Earthscan, pp. 58-70.

Melo, C.J. and S.A. Wolf (2007). Eco-certification of Ecuadorian Bananas: Prospects for Progressive North-South linkages. *Studies in Comparative International Development* 42: 256-278.

Reardon, T., V. Kelly, B. Diagana, J. Dione, E. Crawford, K. Savadogo and D. Doughton (1996). Promoting Sustainable Capital-led Intensification in Sahel Agriculture following Macroeconomic Policy Reform. *Food Policy* 22: 317-338.

Ruben, R. and F. Saenz-Segura (2008). Farmers, Markets and Contracts: Chain Integration of smallholder producers in Costa Rica. *European Review of Latin American and Caribbean Studies* (in press).

Ruben, R., N.B.M. Heerink and E. Mol (1998). Economic Evaluation of Low and High External Input Agriculture: a Production Function Analysis for Malang, Indonesia. In: G.A.A. Wossink, G.C. van Kooten and G.H. Peters (Eds.) *Economics of Agro-chemicals: an International Overview of Use Patterns, Technical and Institutional Determinants, Policies and Perspectives.* Aldershot: Dartmouth Publishing Company, pp. 94-106.

Saenz-Segura, F. and R. Ruben (2004). Export Contracts for Non-traditional Products: Chayote from Costa Rica. *Journal on Chain and Network Science* 4: 139-150.

Salinas, M. and A. Matamorros (2007). *La Historia de PROMESA: Una Alternativa Exitosa para la Distribucion de los Beneficios del Premio Comercio Justo.* El Oro, Ecuador: progresonetwork.org.

# Chapter 8

## The effects of Fair Trade on affiliated producers: case studies from Kenya and Peru

*Leonardo Becchetti and Marco Costantino*

> *Fair Trade is an alternative approach to conventional international trade. It is a trading partnership which aims at sustainable development for excluded and disadvantaged producers. It seeks to do this by providing better trading conditions, by awareness raising and by campaigning (FINE).*

### 1. Introduction

Fair Trade is an original bottom-up approach to international trade that aims to alleviate global poverty and promote sustainability. It advocates the payment of a fair price as well as the respect of social and environmental standards in north-south trading relationships in order to encourage the inclusion of poor farmers and artisans in global product markets and help them to move from a position of vulnerability to security and economic self-sufficiency.

Impact analysis is a powerful tool to evaluate the effectiveness of Fair Trade since it directly measures its effects on its direct (producers and their families) and indirect (local communities) beneficiaries in the poor countries. All the stakeholders involved in the Fair Trade movement are concerned and interested about this kind of studies to get important information about their role in the chain and the results coming from their activities:

- *Producers*, poor farmers and artisans in less developed countries are strongly interested in understanding if affiliation to Fair Trade importers is more or less advantageous than selling to the traditional trading chains.
- *Alternative trade organisations* (ATOs) need to show to their consumers and to national and international institutions the results they get through the fair-trading partnerships with local producers.

- Fair Trade *labelling organisations* are interested in receiving information not only about the respect of Fair Trade's criteria, but also about the long run effects of this initiative.
- Fair Trade's *consumers and volunteers* are concerned about the results of their purchasing or volunteering choice. This is because one of the main problems in Fair Trade is informational asymmetry: the socially and environmentally responsible content of Fair Trade is not an 'experience good' since social responsibility 'cannot be tasted'.
- The national and international *institutions*, before deciding to support the movement, want know their impact on producers' and communities' wellbeing.

Even though for all the stakeholders involved it would be essential to evaluate whether the claims of the beneficial effects generated by participation to the FT circuit are well funded, the literature on FT impact analyses is still surprisingly scarce.

Analysis on the existing literature shows that all existing impact analyses are usually based on non-systematic - though qualitatively very rich - evidence collected in case studies (Castro, 2001a,b; Nelson and Galvez, 2000; Oxford Policy Management, 2000; Hopkins, 2000; Ronchi, 2002), with the exception of a few impact studies testing the statistical significance of Fair Trade as the ones performed by Bacon (2005) on a sample of Guatemalan coffee producers and by Pariente (2000) on the Coocafè cooperative in Costa Rica.

When analysing the methodological tools used in these studies, we find the following trends:

- Among all the Fair Trade's criteria, fair price is by far the most studied. Therefore most of the impact studies analyse foodstuffs, whereas studies about craftsmanship are much more rare.
- Latin America is the most studied continent. It is more difficult to find impact studies about Fair Trade projects in Africa and Asia.
- Control groups and random selection are rarely used. Most of the impact studies use non-structured or semi-structured interviews instead of questionnaires.
- Most of the studies analysed study Fair Trade's impact on the producers (direct impact) and their first level organisations (indirect impact) but not on their families and on the local communities.

As regards the main findings of these studies, we can summarise that:

- Fair Trade's relationships are predominantly with first level producer organisations rather than individual producers.
- The Fair Trade premium is managed by the organisation in order to satisfy the individual's welfare needs (in such cases the evaluation of the impact of FT is dependent on the particular merits of the decision to certify a given local producer organisation).
- The main role of Fair Trade is capacity building, an activity which is deemed crucial to support inclusion of local producers in international trade.

Many of these studies acknowledge the importance of a more rigorous impact evaluation. Nelson and Galvez (2000) conclude their work by arguing that '*as with many organisations involved in Fair Trade MCCH has not yet been able to make an assessment themselves of the longer-term impact of its involvement in cocoa marketing for smallholders and their livelihoods. There is a growing recognition amongst organisations involved in Fair Trade that more attention needs to be paid to impact assessment.*' In a similar manner, Oxford Policy Management (2000) agrees that it would be important to compare (levels and changes of) quality of living indicators of farmers affiliated to Fair Trade with farmers from a randomly selected control sample.

Given this state of art in the literature, the goal of our impact study was therefore to apply rigorous statistical and econometrical tools to Fair Trade's impact study, comparing the levels of a number of social and economical indicators of well-being between a target group (set up by Fair Trade's producers) and a control group (set up by farmers with similar characteristics but having no relationships with Fair Trade at all). We believe that the impact of Fair Trade must be assessed not just on the price rule but also on the whole set of criteria with particular attention to those of price stabilisation, anticipated financing and provision of technical assistance.

So far we have applied this methodology to two case-studies in Kenya and Peru, while two more studies are in progress in Chile and the Philippines. In this chapter we briefly present the results of the first two studies. The chapter is divided into four sections (including introduction and conclusions), presenting and commenting on descriptive and econometric findings from the surveys. In the second section we provide a description of the methodology and the main findings of the Kenyan case-study on the Meru Herbs producers' association (food producers). In the third section we present the Peruvian case-studies with Minka and Allpa organisations (artisans). In the last section we try to summarise and compare our main findings, providing some advices for further research and for the implementation of FT criteria.

## 2. Meru Herbs, Kenya[1]

### *2.1. Project's characteristics*

Beyond the myth which consider Fair Trade as a relationship between importers and the individual producer, the success of the FT initiative depends on a virtuous twinning between cooperation in the North and in the South. In order to evaluate the impact of FT project on Meru Herbs affiliates we must therefore study the rise and development of this organisation.

[1] In this section we summarise the findings of Becchetti and Costantino (2008a). For all detailed results we kindly ask to refer to the paper.

Meru Herbs was originally created by the Ng'uuru Gakirwe Water Committee, an association composed of local farmers who started an irrigation project with the aim of bringing water to houses and farms in the area by canalising the Kitheno River. The Committee originates from a group of 430 families that settled down in various plots (between 10 and 40 acres) which were granted by the Kenyan Government in the 1960s. The plots are in the districts of Meru Central and Tharaka, approximately 200 km from Nairobi, on Mount Kenya's eastern slopes.

Meru Herbs was created in 1991 with the goal of generating income to cover the project's costs by commercialising several food products. As in many other similar groups of marginalised producers selling to Fair Trade a main problem is distance from main markets and from the coast which weakens bargaining power with local intermediaries. Regional commercialisation of these products had normally been under the control of Nairobi traders who also exploit their informational advantage with farmers on the dynamic of world commodity prices. In order to reduce their monopsonistic power and create new trade opportunities, Meru Herbs developed a partnership with Altromercato (the leading Italian Fair Trade importer). The partnership therefore began experimentally in 1991 and continued in 1992 with the delivery of a container of roselle or karkadé to diversify the households' production opportunities. In 2000 the organisation received organic certification from the British company Soil Association Certification Ltd. and today it exports a significant part of its production through the Fair Trade channel.

These first historical coordinates help to understand that Fair Trade often plays an antitrust action in markets in which concentration of transport and financial intermediaries is very high. In the contractual agreement between Meru Herbs and affiliated farmers who have organic certification (or who are in the process of obtaining it), the latter agree to sell part of (not all) their production to Meru Herbs. In turn, Meru Herbs commits itself to provide several benefits in terms of services and technical assistance such as (1) provision of complimentary seeds and organic fertilisers to farmers; (2) sale of fruit trees for production at subsidised prices; (3) organisation of complimentary training courses in the implementation of organic farming techniques and (4) offer of services of two of its employees (the Farmer manager and vice-manager) with the specific task of supervising and providing technical assistance to the affiliated farmers. A problem which occurs also in other projects is that the amount of affiliated farmers' production may be not enough to reach necessary economies of scale for product transportation. This is why Meru Herbs also buys (at the Fair Trade prices) fruit for producing jams from non-organic farmers without requiring the above-mentioned contract.

The above mentioned characteristics lead us to divide Meru Herbs producers into three groups: (1) Bio farmers (organic farmers who have signed a contract with Meru Herbs), (2) Conversion farmers (farmers who have recently signed the contract with Meru Herbs and started, but not concluded, a process of conversion to organic production) and (3) Onlyfruit farmers (farmers who sell fruit for jams to Meru Herbs but have not signed any contract with the organisation and who therefore do not enjoy organisation benefits (1) to (4) described above since the latter apply only to full members such as Bio and Conversion farmers).

The fundamental methodological step in impact analyses is the identification of a control group. In this case we looked for farmers with characteristics close to those of affiliated farmers in the same irrigation area who had no relationship with Meru Herbs. The identification of such group selection was made easier by the homogeneity of the population living in the project area. Farmers affiliated to both control and treatment groups benefit from the *Ng'uuru Gakirwe* Water Project and therefore all of them share the same irrigation infrastructure. They differ only in marketing channels (Meru Herbs with or without FT partnership, local middlemen or direct sale in local markets). The advantage of having four groups, who responded to a 100 question questionnaire in personal interviews, is that we can distinguish between long-term and short-term effects of the relationship with Meru Herbs and FT (Bio and Conversion farmers respectively), relationship with Meru Herbs without the full FT relationship (Onlyfruit farmers) and the absence of any relationship with FT (Control farmers).

### *2.2. Descriptive findings*

In the first phase of the analysis, we provide descriptive statistics of data collected with our survey (see Table 1). A first important element is that the three groups selling to Meru Herbs are markedly different in terms of seniority of affiliation. More specifically, Bio farmers declare a much longer commercial relationship with the organisation (more than 13 years on average), while Conversion and Onlyfruit farmers have initiated such relationship more recently (one and three years on average respectively). This implies that the already mentioned non-full membership of Onlyfruit farmers is therefore also associated with a much more recent commercial relationship with Meru Herbs for Bio farmers, but not for Conversion farmers.

We continue our descriptive analysis by focusing on crop variety, sales conditions and quality of life. In the survey we have information on production, distribution channels (Meru Herbs, traditional intermediaries, directly to customers), sale conditions and price satisfaction concerning the 18 products which represent the whole range of crops produced in the area (see Tables 1 and 2). Evidence on distribution channels confirms that the often heard critique of complete dependence of affiliated farmers from Fair Trade is unfounded. As in many other projects Fair Trade is an important diversification opportunity which does not prevent sales in more traditional channels (direct sales in local markets, sales to local intermediaries). As a matter of fact, Bio, Conversion and Onlyfruit farmers also sell between 17 and 28 percent of their products directly to customers, and between 7 and 12 percent to local intermediaries (see Table 1). However, seniority of affiliation has effects on the relative importance of different trading channels since non-organic farmers not signing a contract with Meru Herbs (Onlyfruit farmers) have a far lower share of products sold to FT importers.

*Table 1. Summary characteristics of the four farmer groups (Meru Herbs, Kenya).*

| | Bio | Conversion | Onlyfruit | Control |
|---|---|---|---|---|
| Age | 48 | 43 | 48 | 38 |
| Average years of commercial relationship with the Meru organisation | 13.3 | 1.1 | 2.8 | 0 |
| Schooling (years) | 6.3 | 9.17 | 7.53 | 8.97 |
| Share of products directly sold to customers (percent) | 17 | 18 | 28 | 38 |
| Share of products sold to intermediaries (percent) | 9 | 7 | 12 | 20 |
| Share of products sold to Meru Herbs (percent) | 60 | 55 | 38 | 0 |
| Avg. varieties of products sold | 8.8 | 7.7 | 6.6 | 4 |
| [95 percent confidence intervals] | [8.00-9.66] | [6.40-9.10] | [5.74-7.85] | [3.05-4.94] |
| Papaw[1] | 5 (20) | 5 (18) | 5 (19) | 5 (1) |
| Mango[1] | 7 (20) | 7 (15) | 7 (25) | - |
| Okra[1] | 26 (6) | 32 (9) | 30 (10) | 31 (11) |
| Karkade[1] | 7 (30) | 7 (1) | 7 (28) | - |
| Sorghum[1] | 12.2 (17) | 11.7 (16) | 12.4 (13) | 10.2 (18) |
| Maize[1] | 12.4 (15) | 12.8 (15) | 13 (21) | 11.7 (18) |
| Millet[1] | 15 (16) | 12 (15) | 16.7 (14) | 13.5 (20) |
| Pilipili[1] | 40 (13) | 30.5 (19) | 30.7 (13) | 14 (4) |
| [95 percent confidence intervals] | [40-40] | [28.54-32.50] | [23.77-37.76] | [7.42-22.02] |
| Guava[1] | 7 (18) | 7 (7) | 7 (8) | - |
| Lemon[1] | 5 (19) | 5 (10) | 5 (14) | - |
| Number of respondents | 30 | 30 | 30 | 30 |

Notes: Group legend: Bio: certified organic farmers with long-term affiliation to Meru Herbs and access to FT export channels. Conversion: Meru Herbs members of recent affiliation undergoing conversion towards organic certification. Onlyfruit: non-affiliated farmers selling fruit to Meru Herbs. Control: farmers with no commercial relationship with Meru or FT who share the same productive environment and advantages of the local irrigation infrastructure with affiliated farmers. The survey was undertaken in January 2005.

[1] Price in Kenyan shillings, with the number of group farmers selling the product on the market in parenthesis (Becchetti and Costantino, 2008a).

The difference between Control farmers and the other three groups is evident already from descriptive statistics when we look at average sale prices and crop variety. Affiliated farmers have a far richer product portfolio (from six to nine products) against an average of four for Control farmers. Here again, affiliation seniority has positive effects on such difference since Bio farmers have the largest number of products sold.

*Table 2. Price and income satisfaction and socio-economic indicators (Meru Herbs, Kenya).*

| | Bio | Conversion | Onlyfruit | Control |
|---|---|---|---|---|
| Weekly household consumption expenditure[1] | 425 | 510 | 429 | 357 |
| Satisfaction of living conditions (percent) | 75.23 | 28.14 | 45.64 | 22.16 |
| Household monthly earnings[1] | 4,972 | 5,257 | 4,394 | 3,195 |
| Equivalised monthly earnings[1] | 974 | 1,168 | 784 | 819 |
| Desired monthly earnings[1] | 26,333 | 28,750 | 31,436 | 28,000 |
| Technical assistance from buyers (percent) | 100 | 100 | 30.00 | 33.33 |
| [95 percent confidence intervals] | | | [12.59-47.40] | [15.42-51.23] |
| Infant mortality (percent) | 14.20 | 17.32 | 7.33 | 29.75 |
| Last child born in hospital (percent) | 93.33 | 83.33 | 60.00 | 60.00 |
| [95 percent confidence intervals] | [83.85-102.80] | [69.17-97.48] | [41.39-78.60] | [41.39-78.60] |
| Child labour | 0.87 | 0.55 | 0.92 | 0.77 |
| [95 percent confidence intervals] | [0.79-0.95] | [0.40-0.70] | [0.75-1.09] | [0.60-0.94] |
| Human capital investment | 0.09 | 0.25 | 0.04 | 0.19 |
| Number of respondents | 30 | 30 | 30 | 30 |

Note: Variable legend. *Equivalised monthly earnings*: household monthly earnings scaled by the number of family members. *Infant mortality*: share of group respondents with a child between 0 and 5 years old who died in the last three years; *child labour*: children between 6 and 15 not attending school expressed in relation to the total number of household children in that age cohort; *human capital investment*: teenagers between 15 and 18 going to school expressed in relation to the total number of household members in that age cohort.

[1] In Kenyan Shillings (Becchetti and Costantino, 2008a). Confidence intervals in square brackets are added when difference among groups are significant at 95 percent.

These results support the hypothesis that diversification benefits crucially depend on Fair Trade and Meru Herbs in-kind benefits which give affiliated farmers trade opportunities and skills, respectively, enabling them to cultivate with success the new products. One of these benefits is technical assistance which is available to all affiliated farmers against only around 30 percent of non members.

The more we get into details of affiliation effects, the more we find evidence that the Fair Trade benefits cannot be just identified with the price premium since the risk diversification benefit is equally, if not more important. To sum up our descriptive evidence on product prices we observe that: (1) FT, in cooperation with Meru Herbs, introduces four new products (mango, karkade, guava and lemon) for affiliated farmers (it is therefore impossible to make a price comparison with the Control group on these products); (2) another subset of local products (sorghum, maize, millet and okra) are produced by all interviewed farmers but sold only on the local market. In this case we find no evidence that FT affiliation increases bargaining power also on local sales since there is no significant difference between treatment and control group; (3) the only product which is both sold to FT by affiliated farmers and produced (and sold through traditional trade channels) by Control group farmers is pilipili (red pepper in Swahili). In this case we find evidence of a significant price premium.

The inspection of socioeconomic indicators highlights some relevant differences among the four groups. Control farmers are older and less educated than the other three groups and exhibit lower weekly household consumption expenditure and lower monthly earnings (Table 2). The first two characteristics signal that it is essential in econometric estimates to control for selection bias effects. The limit of available observations prevents us from using approaches (such as the propensity score matching; see Chapter 2-5 in this volume) which minimise such differences before estimating our model. The only available option is to control ex post for these distortions.

Another relevant difference between treatment and control farmers is that the former declare lower desired monthly earnings and higher level of declared satisfaction about living conditions. We are led to conclude that this finding is consistent with the previously mentioned 'hidden' (not explicitly included in FT criteria) benefits of FT affiliation: greater product diversification and in-kind benefits received by Meru Herbs' farmers.

Fair Trade seems also to have positive effects on health indicators. First, affiliation years are significantly and negatively correlated with days lost for illness at work (the result being particularly relevant since long term affiliated are generally older and less educated). This is an important indicator which links health and productivity and directly measures benefits which the former may determine on local development. Second, the share of Control group farmers declaring episodes of infant mortality during the last three years is markedly higher (around 30 percent) than in the other three groups (between 17 and seven percent). This evidence seems to be related to the fact that 93 percent of Bio farmers had their youngest child born in hospital compared with 83 percent of Conversion, 78 percent of Control and 60 percent of Onlyfruit farmers.

A somewhat surprising result is that there is no difference in child schooling between Control and affiliated farmers. Conversion households have the best figures (0.55 percent for the child labour rate and 0.25 for the human capital investment rate), but Bio and Onlyfruit performance appears to be worse than Control group households (though this difference is not statistically significant). To understand whether affiliation has positive effects on child schooling we need, however, more detailed econometric analysis. More specifically, we need to reconstruct child schooling decisions before and after the affiliation date. The first best would be to repeat our survey at a given distance in time. This is however very costly and severe attrition bias (individuals responding to the first but not to the second survey) may significantly reduce the size our already small sample. A reasonable second best approach is that of creating backast panel data in which we reconstruct time series asking farmers about their children's age, schooling years, first year of attendance and school exit of re-entries. With this information we are able to create a panel with a restricted number of time varying factors (schooling decisions, farmers' age, affiliation years). The main limit of our approach is that the income dynamics is unobservable. An important variable affecting schooling decision is therefore missing.

### *2.3. Econometric findings*

From the previous section we learned that affiliated farmers have more diversified crops, higher food consumption, fewer working days lost for illness, fewer episodes of child mortality and superior income satisfaction. Descriptive evidence does not allow us to conclude that participation *per se* in the FT channel ensured significant effects on these indicators for at least two reasons. First, composition effects and heterogeneous characteristics of the four groups may influence some of our findings and significant differences in age and education in treatment and control farmers may explain part of our results. Second, we must verify whether endogeneity and selection bias in the affiliation to Meru Herbs may alternatively explain what we observe. As it is well known the selection bias may be implicit (more productive farmers may be more likely to affiliate) or explicit (affiliation standards may prevent lower quality farmers from becoming members of the cooperative). The question is therefore whether our findings reflect benefits obtained thanks to the affiliation with Meru Herbs and the FT project, or, alternatively, they measure characteristics which were already present (and, presumably, contributed to the affiliation) at the moment in which farmers became affiliated to Meru Herbs.

In an initial econometric exercise we evaluate whether findings on: (1) price satisfaction; (2) weekly household consumption expenditure; (3) dietary quality; (4) satisfaction about living conditions; (5) infant mortality and (6) child labour are robust to the inclusion of proper control factors. The synthesis results of the effect of Fair Trade affiliation are provided in Table 3. In order to evaluate affiliation effects on prices we look at self declared price satisfaction instead of a simpler index of price conditions. The rationale is that such index may more conveniently include price conditions which can not be captured by a standardised price index.

We regress the index on monthly income and several additional demographic controls to evaluate whether differences among groups in terms of price satisfaction are spuriously driven by other economic, sociologic and demographic factors. Our findings highlight a hierarchy of effects documenting that only full membership provides all those benefits (stabilisation of prices and of trade channels, anticipated financing, price premia on a wide range of products) which contribute to price satisfaction. Onlyfruit farmers are on a lower step, but still better than Control group farmers who are fully excluded from these benefits.

*Table 3. The impact of Meru Herbs and Fair Trade affiliation on selected development indicators.*

| Dependent variable (+ estimation approach) | |
|---|---|
| | **Price satisfaction** (OLS) |
| Bio | 0.171*[0.058] |
| Conversion | 0.174*[0.069] |
| Control | -0.132*[0.059] |
| | **Food consumption** (OLS/treatment regression model) |
| Control | -125.024**[62.365] |
| | **Dietary quality** (OLS/treatment regression model) |
| Control | -0.362* [0.202] |
| | **Life satisfaction** (ordered logit) |
| Bio | 1.052** [0.463] |
| | **Infant mortality** (logit) |
| Bio | -1.942* [1.090] |
| Control | 1.532** [0.632] |
| | **Child labour** (Tobit) |
| Conversion | -1.012* [0.432] |
| Bio | 0.019 [0.536] |
| | **Human capital** (Tobit) |
| Conversion | .901* [0.441] |
| Bio | -0.164 [0.215] |

*Dependent variable legend*: *Index of price satisfaction*: where *muchperc* is the share of products sold for which the farmer declares highest price satisfaction, *enoughperc* (*afewperc*) the share of products sold for which the farmer declares next to highest (next to lowest) price satisfaction. The index is the dependent variables in a Tobit specification since it has upper and lower bounds.
Food consumption *(Foodcons)* is monthly household food expenditure. Dietary quality (*Qualcons)* is an index of nutritional quality built as an unweighted average of frequencies of consumption (more than once a day, once a day, once every three days, once a week, rarely, never) of selected food items (ugali, chapati, rice, maize, beans, eggs, milk, chicken, other meat, fish, tubers (potatoes), greens, fresh fruit). On this basis we build an index of dietary quality giving descending values from a maximum of five to a minimum of one to the above mentioned frequency modalities and, finally, we calculate our synthetic index as an average of the values for each food item. The regression is estimated with a Tobit model since the dependent variable has upper and lower bounds.
Infant mortality *(Infmor)* is a dummy taking the value of one if the respondent had episodes of infant mortality in the last three years and zero otherwise. Life satisfaction *(Livsat)* is based on answers to the following question: Are you satisfied with your household's living conditions? We give the following score to qualitative answers: a lot=3; enough=2 a little=1 not at all=0. The specification is estimated with an ordered logit approach. Ch*ild labour (Childlab)*: children between 6 and 15 not attending school expressed in relation to the total number of household children in that age cohort; Human capital (*Humcap)*: teenagers between 15 and 18 attending school expressed in relation to the total number of household members in that age cohort.
*Significance*: * 90% significance, ** 95% significance. Robust standard errors in square brackets.
*List of controls*: age, gender, education, self consumption, self production, geographical area, marital status, number of people living at home, cattle ownership, ethnic group. (see: Becchetti and Costantino, 2008a).

To evaluate the effects of affiliation on food consumption and dietary quality we use as a benchmark a modified permanent income hypothesis which takes into account peculiarities of our sample (the number of individuals living in the household does not coincide with family members, self consumption and self production have an important role on available resources). We therefore take into account that weekly household food consumption expenditure is a function of the unobserved, permanent, disposable flow of monetary and non-monetary resources (PFMNR) and of the number of family members (given that food consumption cannot be suppressed beyond certain levels, larger families should exhibit higher food consumption expenditure for a given level of household monetary income).

To proxy these variables we refer to an extended set of regressors which includes household monthly income as well as measures of self-consumption and self-production (which should reduce consumption expenditure for a given level of monetary income) and effective number of individuals living in a given household. We further include some demographic variables which may proxy for future changes in productivity affecting permanent income beyond what is captured by current monthly income (age, education, gender) and the dummy for participation in the Control group which measures the effects of not having any kind of economic transaction with Meru Herbs.

Regression findings illustrate that participation to the control group generates a significant and negative effect on weekly household food expenditure, net of the variables controlling for demographic factors and various controls affecting permanent household flow of monetary and non-monetary resources. For individuals close to the poverty line an important indicator of household wellbeing is the dietary quality of their food consumption. With detailed information on the frequency of consumption of a number of local food items we are able to build an index of dietary quality giving descending values (from a maximum of five to a minimum of one) to the frequency modalities. Finally, we define our synthetic index as an average of the values given to each food item.

The dietary quality synthetic index is regressed on the usual set of controls and on measures of affiliation to the project or participation in the control sample. Our main finding here is that participation in the control sample is related to a significantly lower value of the dependent variable. In a second estimate we find a significant and positive link between the dependent variable and the number of affiliation years. The rationale of these findings is that affiliation has increased food consumption effects and entails product diversification which may become *per se* a source of nutritional improvement if part of that production is self-consumed.

If advantages of full affiliation (such as product diversification, price stabilisation and in-kind services) affect quality and quantity of food consumption via an increase of the 'permanent household flow of disposable monetary and non-monetary resources', we are inclined to believe that a significant effect of affiliation on satisfaction concerning living conditions should be found. Our hypothesis is supported by results of the relevant econometric estimate in which the level of satisfaction with living conditions is regressed on several control including affiliation in the Bio project or, alternatively, affiliation years.

The overall picture of the effects of FT on farmers' wellbeing helps to understand why affiliated producers have a relatively lower desired wage. Our intuition is that lower desired wage may be related to a superior provision of public or private goods and services which cannot be measured by the information on perceived income. In our case higher quality of monetary and non-monetary goods and services, in-kind benefits and product diversification are likely to increase satisfaction with living conditions for a given level of monthly income.

A further goal of our econometric analysis is to check whether descriptive evidence showing a nexus between affiliation and health indicators (i.e. reduced child mortality, fewer working days lost for illness) is confirmed after econometric testing. What we observe is that affiliation years are significant after controlling for all other relevant and observable regressors. The interpretation of the finding on child mortality is that both higher disposable income and/or the culture promoted by the Meru Herbs association contribute to a wider use of health services (i.e hospital births) reducing child mortality. Furthermore, the result on working days lost for illness is also consistent with an explicit Fair Trade criteria (creating healthy working conditions).

The only performance indicator which does not seem positively affected by FT affiliation is child schooling. Backpast panel data estimates in which we reconstruct twenty years of schooling decisions of interviewed farmers confirm this conclusion. As it is well known we do not find an explicit ban on child labour products in FT criteria. The pragmatic approach of Fair Trade argues that a ban without the creation of alternative could worsen more than improve child conditions. Fair Trade should contribute to reduce child labour indirectly by increasing household income, consistently with the well known *luxury axiom* (Basu, 1999; Basu and Van, 1998) which establishes that parents decide to send children to school when income overcomes a certain poverty threshold. Consider however that Meru Herbs decided, after the year of our survey, to create a system of scholarship for affiliated farmers. We believe that this is one of the most important results of our, and in general of all, impact studies. Evaluating critically positive as well as negative or not significant effects of a project and, in this second case, leading local organisations to rethink and reformulate the approach for an improvement of its results on the wellbeing of beneficiaries.

### *2.4. The selection bias problem*

A standard approach in the literature used for taking into account the selection bias problem is that of estimating a treatment regression model in which a given standard performance equation is re-estimated together with a selection equation in which affiliation/no affiliation to FT is regressed on a set of individual characteristics. The two-equation system helps to disentangle the impact generated by the project (FT makes affiliated farmers better off in terms of a given indicator) from the selection effect (the superior outcome of affiliated farmers depends on the correlation between affiliation to FT and farmers' high outcome or to characteristics correlated to high outcome). To make it simpler, if Meru Herbs explicitly or implicitly selects higher quality farmers, the difference we observe is in the selection process more than in the effects of affiliation.

Our findings show that two performance variables (nutritional quality and satisfaction in living conditions) are particularly robust with persistent effects of years of FT affiliation, even after controlling for both FT and Meru Herbs selection biases.

## 3. Minka and Allpa, Peru[2]

The study on Kenyan farmers left several questions unsolved. A first one is related to the spillovers and externalities produced by FT affiliation on the local environment. More specifically, we are interested to know whether the local antitrust action of FT is effective in increasing the bargaining power of Meru Herbs farmers also with local intermediaries. In addition to it, we wonder about the impact of FT on non affiliated producers given that, in general equilibrium terms, the entry of a new importer must have effects on local demand and supply of labour and agricultural products (see also Chapter 10). Finally, we are interested in a comparison of Fair Trade prices not just with prices of sales to traditional local intermediaries but also of those to socially responsible travellers. With the impact study on the role of FT in two projects in Peru we tried to collect evidence on these points.

### *3.1. Projects' characteristics*

The first project analysed regards a group of farmers in the district of Juliaca belonging to the national organisation named Minka. The goal of Minka is that of 'promoting the development of producers' organisations by respecting their cultural traditions and the local environment together with the full satisfaction of consumers'. To achieve this goal Minka operates with Fair Trade organisations.

Minka buys products from 61 (first level) groups of producers from different areas of the country (Piura, Callao, Lima, Ayacucho, Puno, etc.). The second largest group (after that working in Lima) operates in the District of Juliaca (Department of Puno) located around the Titicaca lake. Living conditions of producers in the district of Juliaca are close or even below the formal subsistence level (one dollar per day in PPP). The traditional activity in the area is agriculture but its extremely low returns and high risk, due to the local atmospheric conditions (drought in summer and frost

[2] In this section we summarise the findings of Becchetti and Costantino (2008b). For the detailed results we kindly ask to refer to the paper.

in winter), led producers to add craftsmanship to their original activity. For Minka and Fair Trade affiliates craftsmanship has gradually become the main activity.

Minka adopts the following key operating principles which replicate the most important Fair Trade criteria: (1) payment of a price mark-up to local producers with respect to what occurs in transactions with traditional local intermediaries who generally exploit informational asymmetries on market prices, demand conditions and final consumer tastes; (2) commitment to purchase the highest quality wool for producers; (3) provision of anticipated financing up to 50 percent of the production of first level groups with which it concludes contracts; (4) use of part of its revenues to finance training courses and other local public goods (restoration of local council buildings, construction of small scale local facilities, etc.) according to the needs manifested by producers' groups. Last but not least, Minka has recently promoted a circuit of 'socially responsible tourism' which helps local producers to obtain prices still higher than those paid by FT intermediaries and to reinforce their self esteem thanks to a tangible and direct demonstration of the final consumers appreciation for their culture and products.

The second project under observation concerns producers located in a village called Chulucanas (Department of Piura), and affiliated to a trading company called ALLPA. The ALLPA Trading Project was initiated by the Peruvian Institute of Research and Development (IPID) in 1981. In 1986 ALLPA became a private company owned by IPID with other individual partners. Its goal is that of promoting market access of low-income handicraft producers giving them the opportunity to improve their standards of living through the pursuance of a quality and customer oriented vision. As it occurs for most organisations operating in the Fair Trade channel, ALLPA works with Fair Trade organisations but also with other private companies, market importers, department stores and distributors in Europe, North America, Mexico and Australia. On the overall, the Fair Trade share in export is 60-70 percent and the main market is Europe (60% of the total export).

ALLPA has a non negligible market share of the total handicraft export in Peru (2 percent in 2006). Affiliated craftsmen are spread throughout 20 communities and 100 handicraft workshops in different areas of Peru (Lima, Cusco, Huancavelica, Chulucanas, Junìn, Pucallpa, Puno, Ayacucho) and work as subcontractors of the organisation. The four main production lines are pottery (Chulucanas), jewellery, knits and wooden furniture and painted glass. ALLPA aims to behave responsibly toward its main stakeholders (employees, the artisans who work in the handicraft workshops and their customers). The organisation takes care of verifying that all workshops are able to produce high-quality handicrafts maintaining social benefit (health, labour hygiene and security) and fulfilling the Peru's labour legislation. The goal of promoting workers wellbeing is realised by creating a system of social benefits for employees and artisans which include legal assistance, health insurance and paid leave. In order to be efficient and competitive, ALLPA delivers effort to enhance orders and to support technologic innovation and investment for all the workshops to increase productivity, to improve quality and therefore easing artisans' access to the market. ALLPA usually provides anticipated financing for up to 50 percent of the production of workshops, it organises training courses for artisans and employees, it provides loans and offers technical support and supervision.

The place in which we realised our survey (Chulucanas) is a small village whose economy is based mainly on highly organised pottery production. Artisans are organised in small-medium sized workshops with an average of 15 employees within a high management layout and a very well developed production system. The comparative advantage of the area hinges on the development of a type of ceramic pottery based on ancient techniques of 'negative painting'. This places Chulucanas at the top of fine ceramic production in northern Peru.

### *3.2. Descriptive findings*

The rationale for the joint analysis of the two projects lies in the fact that they both concern marginalised producers living in the same country with three qualifying differences: (1) products are different (pottery in Chulucanas and apparel in Juliaca); (2) Chulucanas producers have a more recent affiliation; (3) there is a significant difference in standard of living since Chulucanas producers are far better off than Juliaca ones (which are around the subsistence level). Given the above mentioned features our study may be particularly useful in studying how FT impact changes at different affiliation years and living standards.

Our research is based on direct interviews done on randomly selected control and treatment samples in the two projects. A limit of this approach is that we do not control ex ante in the survey design for heterogeneity between the two groups. We obviously do it *ex post* by introducing controls in our estimates and by controlling for selection bias. However, an alternative is that of reducing heterogeneity *ex ante* with a propensity score matching technique. As it is well know in the propensity sore matching approach any individual of the treatment group is associated with an individual in the control group which is closest in terms of a given set of characteristics to the first individual. The validity of this methodology depends on the possibility of drawing from large sets of potential participants to the two groups. This is not always the case in the kind of impact studies described here.

On the whole we interviewed 240 producers and divided them into three groups: (1) 80 producers from Juliaca, affiliated to Minka (FT organisation); (2) 80 producers from Chulucanas, affiliated to Allpa (FT organisation); (3) 80 producers from Juliaca and Chulucanas (40 from each project), not affiliated to the two Fair Trade organisations (control sample). Given the strong difference in living conditions in the two areas average values must be considered as a mean between low living standards of Juliaca and higher living standards of Chulucanas producers (Table 4). On average producers (including those belonging to treatment and control samples from both projects) earn 396.7 soles per month from their main productive activity and their weekly food

*Table 4. Economic and socio-demographic characteristics (Minka and Allpa, Peru).*

| Dep. Var. | Obs. | Mean | Std. Dev. | Min | Max |
|---|---|---|---|---|---|
| Affiliation years | 240 | 5.92 | 8.94 | 0 | 40 |
| Weekly food consumption | 240 | 81.92 | 43.22 | 10 | 300 |
| Monthly earning from the first activity | 241 | 396.69 | 481.79 | 40 | 1,400 |
| Total income | 240 | 436.88 | 499.59 | 53 | 2,000 |
| Share of producers who have a property house | 241 | 0.64 | 0.48 | 0 | 1 |
| Share of producers who have saved money in the last 3 years | 241 | 0.54 | 0.68 | 0 | 3 |
| Share of producers who have vaccinated the last son born | 187 | 0.95 | 0.21 | 0 | 1 |

Source: Becchetti and Costantino, 2008b).

consumption is 81.9 soles. Earnings from all activities are slightly higher and amount on average to 436.9 soles. Only half of the sample declares to have saved money in the last three years. 64 percent of producers have a property house and the last son born has been vaccinated in the 95 percent of cases.

The first difference between the two projects is in terms of affiliation years (around 15 for Juliaca against 3 for Chulucanas producers). This difference gives us the opportunity of comparing the impact of FT on producers welfare at two markedly different phases of FT affiliation. The living standard divide is remarkable since income from the main activity is 199 against 50 soles in the Juliaca, against 663.7 and 599.5 soles in the Chulucanas case for treatment and control sample respectively (see Table 5). If we consider that the exchange rate with the dollar at the time of the survey was 3.18 soles per one dollar, we may calculate that the control group of Juliaca producers living on the Titicaca lake area is well below the poverty line of one dollar per day, while FT affiliates in the same area are slightly above two dollars per day. Economic conditions in the Chulucanas area are much better since the control group earns slightly less than seven and the treatment group above eight dollars per day. The earning gap is reflected in an analogous one in terms of consumption expenditure (53 against 15.9 soles in the Juliaca and 91.4 against 95.6 in the Chulucanas case for the treatment and control sample, respectively). As expected, the food consumption share on total earnings (an indicator of poverty often more reliable than that based on straightforward income measures) is much lower in the Chulucanas case (50 percent against 61 percent in treatment and control sample) than in the Juliaca one (96 against 99 percent).

It is much more difficult to verify the existence of a price premium consistent with FT criteria in handicraft than in food production, since in the former products are highly differentiated. In the Juliaca project we could identify a standard model of wool gloves sold by both FT and local intermediaries. The price premium on this product is consistent since FT importers pay it four times more than local intermediaries.

*Table 5. Summary characteristics of the four farmer groups (Minka and Allpa, Peru).*

| | Juliaca treatment | Juliaca control | Chulucanas treatment | Chulucanas control |
|---|---|---|---|---|
| Standard product's price | 3.11 | 2.07 | 2.83 | 5.71 |
| Standard product's price from tourists | 17.56 | 6.00 | 10.5 | 12.89 |
| Affiliation years | 14.94 | 0.00 | 3.01 | 0.00 |
| Monthly earning from the first activity | 199.00[b] | 50.00[b] | 663.78[a] | 599.51[a] |
| Total income | 219.91[b] | 64.26[b] | 745.63[a] | 622.21[a] |
| Weekly food consumption | 53.03[b] | 15.90[b] | 91.42[a] | 95.62[a] |
| Share of producers who have a property house | 0.74 | 0.50 | 0.54 | 0.78 |
| Food consumption share on total earnings | 96.12[a] | 99.45[a] | 49.63[b] | 61.36[b] |
| Share of producers who have saved money in the last 3 years | 45.21[a] | 30.15[a] | 78.75[b] | 46.34[b] |
| Share of producers who have vaccinated the last son born | 1.00[a] | 0.83[a] | 0.95 | 1 |
| Perceived relative standard of living | 2.19[b] | 0.75[b] | 2.09[a] | 1.83[a] |

a The difference in means between the control and the sample group within the same project is significant at 90 percent. b The difference in means between the control and the sample group within the same project is significant at 99 percent.
Source: Becchetti and Costantino, 2008b.

Unfortunately we could not collect systematic information on other standardised comparable products and could not identify price premia for Chulucanas producers.

With regard to price comparisons an original finding of this survey is the comparison between the price paid by (socially responsible) tourists and FT importers to Juliaca (Chulucanas) producers. Such price is around 51 (29) percent higher than that paid by FT importers. Hence, socially responsible tourism transfers even more value to local producers than Fair Trade does. This indicates that the strategy of the alliance between Fair Trade and socially responsible tourism (Fair Trade, together with local organisations, promotes 'responsible travelling' in the area) has relevant effects on producers wellbeing.

A final interesting finding is related to the perceived relative standard of living with respect to the average standard of the area. Results on this point show that Juliaca producers judge their standard slightly above average, while the control sample more than slightly below average. The distance is narrower in the Chulucanas case. These results are particularly relevant since the observed difference in the perceived relative standard of living does not depend just on the declaration of FT affiliates, but also on that of control sample producers who acknowledge that their standard of living is below the average (to which FT affiliates significantly contribute since they approximately represent one fourth of producers in both areas).

### *3.3. Econometric findings*

As in the Kenyan study also in the Peruvian case descriptive evidence does not provide fully clear cut results since most of the observed findings may be affected by composition effects. The only way to disentangle the effect of the variable of our interest (affiliation years) from other concurring factors is that of econometric analysis. In our standard specification we take care of including as regressors all the measurable variables which may affect our performance indicators such as standard demographic dummies (i.e. age, gender, education measured in terms of schooling years of the respondent, family status and number of children). These last two types of variables are important to know the number of household members. Finally, we use land size as a proxy of wealth, we consider whether the individual has more than one productive activity and we control for self production and self consumption effects. A main difference we introduce in this study is a specific variable measuring the effect of the number of trading channels as a measure of trade diversification. Since creation of additional trading channels in the area is mainly, if not exclusively, due to the introduction of Fair Trade this variable is an additional measure of the potential benefits of this initiative.

Our findings show at first that FT affiliation years have a positive and significant nonlinear (concave) effect on the yield of the main producer activity in the overall sample estimate (Table 6).[3] The result is confirmed in separate estimates of the two different projects. The nonlinearity of the effect of FT affiliation years was unexpected. We interpret it in two ways. First, capacity building effects of FT may have decreasing marginal returns (strong impact at the beginning which gradually declines over time). Second, the positive spillover of the higher bargaining power with local intermediaries induced by Fair Trade affiliation is typically concave (and mainly determined by a strong initial effect).

The wage equations we used seems to make sense given the significance of age and education years in the (positive) expected direction. Returns to education result to be larger for producers with the relatively higher standard of living (Chulucanas) than for the poorer ones in Juliaca. Two additional significant regressors in the wage estimate, which are typical of this context, are the negative impact of self production (a substitute for market wage) and the positive effect of the number of trading channels. More specifically, when we evaluate the magnitude of the effect we find that an additional

[3] We measure decreasing effects of Fair Trade by introducing a nonlinear specification for the effect of affiliation years, that is, by adding a variable measuring the level of affiliation years and a second one measuring their squared values. If the level is positive and significant and the square value variable is negative and significant we have evidence of a nonlinear concave effect. As it is possible to see in Table 6 this is the case for the effect of affiliation years on income from the first activity, professional self esteem, self declared happiness and perceived relative standard of living for the Juliaca project.

*Table 6. The impact of FT affiliation years and number of trade channels on selected development indicators (Minka and Allpa, Peru).*

| | Juliaca | Chulucanas |
|---|---|---|
| **Income from first activity** | | |
| FT age | 12.85** (4.11) | 95.50** (3.21) |
| FT age (squared) | -0.35** (-3.4) | -4.88** (-2.1) |
| Number trade channels | 27.84* (1.69) | 228.25** (3.81) |
| **Food Consumption** | | |
| FT age | 2.68* (1.88) | 0.81 (0.31) |
| FT age (squared) | -0.07 (-1.53) | 0.10 (0.48) |
| Number trade channels | 11.55 (1.54) | 9.52* (1.84) |
| **Professional Self-esteem** | | |
| FT age | 0.25** (3.54) | 0.27* (2.32) |
| FT age (squared) | -0.01** (-2.58) | -0.02* (-2.06) |
| Number trade channels | 0.85* (2.36) | -0.08 (-0.35) |
| **Perceived relative standard of living** | | |
| FT age | 0.27** (3.32) | 0.50** (3.07) |
| FT age (squared) | -0.01* (-2.2) | -0.03** (-2.41) |
| Number trade channels | 0.63 (1.51) | 1.18** (3.7) |
| **Happiness** | | |
| FF age | 0.044414* (2.01) | -0.112138 (-1.22) |
| FF age (squared) | -0.0014636* (-2.05) | 0.0082036 (1.11) |
| Number trade channels | 0.2561534* (2.24) | 0.2351429** (2.70) |

*Dependent variables*: *Food consumption:* is monthly household food expenditure; *Self-esteem*: self evaluation of the respondents on a 0-10 scale; *Happiness*: self evaluation of the respondents on a 0-10 scale; *Perceived relative standard of living*: perceived relative standard of living with respect to the average standard of living in the area on a 0-4 scale;
*List of controls*: age, gender, education, self consumption, self production, geographical area, marital status, number of people living at home, cattle ownership, number of trade channels. T-stats are in round brackets (Becchetti and Costantino, 2008b).
*Significance*: * 90% significance, ** 99% significance. Robust standard errors in square brackets.

trading channel adds extra 116 soles on the total sample, which become 28 and 228 in the Juliaca and Chulucanas case respectively. Given that, as mentioned above, large part of this effect is due to FT affiliation, this implies that the total FT effect should be close to the sum of the FT affiliation and the number of trading channels effects.

In our consumption estimate we wonder whether the positive impact of FT affiliation on the remuneration of the first activity generates a higher weekly food expenditure. Our hypothesis is confirmed in the overall sample and in the Juliaca, but not in the Chulucanas case. Furthermore, to check if results from quantitative variables are confirmed by qualitative ones we measure the impact of FT affiliation on professional self esteem and self declared 'relative' standard of living compared to the average one in the area.

The decision to take into consideration qualitative indicators stems from the fact that large part of the literature is always more showing that observed quantitative indicators (such as productivity) crucially depend on hidden qualitative factors (self esteem, dignity, social capital) which are increasingly objects of empirical research as hidden sources of wellbeing and economic prosperity. Furthermore, we argue that impact analyses should be always more inspired by a 'triple bottom up' approach looking simultaneously at economic, social and environmental performance. In this perspective, qualitative indicators are an important part when measuring social sustainability of Fair Trade.

In the two estimates on professional self esteem and self declared 'relative' standard of living (compared to the average in the area) we find a significant and positive effect of FT affiliation both in the overall sample and in the project-specific estimates. The magnitude of our coefficients implies that five years of affiliation produce a positive change in the perceived relative standard of living which corresponds to one cross sectional standard deviation of the same variable. Here again, in the case of self esteem, we find a significant and concave effect of FT affiliation, exactly as that on income from the first activity and weekly consumption expenditure.

Finally, we aim to evaluate the general effect of FT affiliation on the most comprehensive qualitative indicator (self declared life satisfaction). According to the recent empirical literature, robust evidence has been found, among others, on the significant effects of income on life satisfaction. More specifically, this variable has positive effects in absolute terms especially when it allows to exit from poverty and, in relative terms (relative income), when it is higher than the average income of peers (Frey and Stutzer, 2002a,b; Clark *et al.*, 2006). Based on this evidence we argue that FT affiliation (beyond a possible direct effect) should affect indirectly life satisfaction via its impact on the food consumption share (a proxy of poverty) and the perceived relative standard of living.

The approach we follow here is the estimation of a three equation system in which the main equation has self declared happiness as dependent variable and the standard controls as regressors. In the two additional equations consumption share (proxy of poverty and/or absolute income) and perceived relative standard of living (proxy of relative income) are introduced as dependent variables. Our findings demonstrate that the overall effect is much more significant for the poorer affiliated farmers of Juliaca than for those of Chulucanas. The estimate of the system also shows that FT has direct positive effects on happiness beyond the two indirect ones with both affiliation year and the number of trading channel variables. Chulucanas results differ in two respects: the direct impact of affiliation years is not significant and the indirect effects as well. The only significant result is the direct effect of the additional trading channel. Overall, this implies that the impact on happiness is much more negligible in this area and around one fourth of that of Juliaca.

### *3.4. The selection bias problem*

In our study on the impact of FT on Peruvian producers we introduced in the survey additional questions in order to implement our strategy against the selection bias. In the Kenyan case we did not have any information on potential discriminatory factors which ruled affiliation to the local organisation working with Fair Trade. What we try to do here is to collect specific information on this point. To this purpose we follow a three step approach. First, we introduce in our survey a question on whether affiliated producers found it difficult to associate. This questions allows to identify potential discriminatory factors directly from producers answers. Consider that, as it needs to be in all surveys, respondents have no idea of how we use this information. This is because we do not ask directly what factors made association difficult, but we retrieve such factors in a second step in which we estimate a logit equation where the dependent variable takes value of one if the response is yes and regress it on a set of controls. Third, we use significant controls as regressors in the selection equation in a treatment regression model in which affiliation to the association working with FT is controlled for.

Results from the second step disclose that the number of children and the presence of an additional source of income affect positively the probability of affiliation, while age (and marriage) are (weakly) negatively. The estimate is obviously run only on the respondents belonging to the two treatment groups. Separate estimates for the two groups confirm these findings. We therefore introduce these four variables in the selection equation. The treatment regression model is therefore estimated on the overall sample by considering this additional information we have and therefore by introducing slope dummies for affiliation years, education and age. However, we find that only the intercept is significant in the treatment equation. This implies that factors affecting selection exist but are unknown and captured by the constant terms. Our estimates also confirm the significant nonlinear effect of FT affiliation on income from the first activity and weekly consumption expenditure (for Juliaca producers only), as well as the linear one on professional self esteem.

### *3.5. The effect on schooling decisions*

The approach followed to test whether affiliation to Fair Trade affected producers' schooling decisions is close to that followed in the Kenyan study. We create backcast panel data by asking to each respondent the number of his/her offspring, the age and the number of schooling years for each of them, the age at which each child entered the school and whether there were cases of exits and re-entries. This information allows us to reconstruct year by year (from 1987 to 2007) schooling decisions of the households and regress them on a set of controls which are time invariant during the panel period (gender, father and mother schooling years, participation to the treatment or to the control sample in one of the two projects) or whose variation can be reconstructed without problems (age, FT affiliation years). More specifically, we build an index of Household Human Capital Investment rate (HHCI) given by the following expression:

$$HHCl_{it} = \sum_{j=1}^{n_i} \frac{TOTSCH_{ijt} \mid Entryage_{ijt} \leq Age_{ijt} \leq Endage_{ijt}}{TOTPOTH_{ijt} \mid Entryage_{ijt} \leq Age_{ijt} \leq Endage_{ijt}}$$

where the $HHCI_{it}$ index is the sum of the children of the i-th farmer in the school age cohort in a given period t who actually go to school ($TOTSCH_{ijt}$), divided by the number of children of the i-th farmer being in the school age cohort in the same period ($TOTPOTH_{ijt}$). The school age cohort has a lower bound in Entryage (5 or 6 year according to the questionnaire declaration). The upper bound (*Endage*) varies according to our investigation goals (we move it from 10 to 18 years according to different estimates).

Our results highlight that, in the Chulucanas case, FT affiliation significantly contributes to the schooling decision from 18 to 14 years. This positive effect declines as far as we lower the upper bound, but it remains significant up to the 14 year threshold. In the Juliaca case the effect vanishes below the 16 threshold and its magnitude is smaller. How to interpret the differences between the two projects? By considering the standard of living gap between the two groups the puzzle can be interpreted in the light of the well known luxury axiom hypothesis establishing that parents start sending children to school when they overcome a given threshold of household income.[4] This interpretation is also consistent with the stronger effect of FT affiliation on food consumption expenditure in the Juliaca project: while farmers close to the subsistence level use large part of the premium to increase food expenditure, better-off farmers can afford to choose other destinations including human capital investment. Another interesting correspondence is with the different effect of human capital investment in the two projects. The impact of FT affiliation on schooling decisions is lower where returns to education are lower.

## 4. Conclusions

Fair Trade supply chains include over 4,000 small-scale producer groups in more than 50 developing countries (FTAO, 2005). Our experience from a few impact studies documents that any projects has its peculiarities and that it is difficult to draw general conclusions from analyses carried out on just a few of them. Even though they cannot offer - when taken individually - the final word on Fair Trade, impact studies are nonetheless very important because they may stimulate the debate on FT criteria and on the improvement of FT practices. To make just an example, results in Kenya

[4] Poverty traps and threshold effects are a well known topic in the development economics literature. For a reference see Carter and Barrett (2006) and Travis and Barettt (2007).

and in Peru show that activity diversification and risk reduction benefits are essential for affiliated producers, even though they are not explicitly mentioned in the official criteria. They also show that Fair Trade is neither an exclusive trading channel, nor it is always the one which provides the best price. They document that the most important effect is that of ensuring stable and long term commitment for an important part of production, thereby reducing producers 'transaction costs of sale' which are incurred when looking for customers. Given that the search of markets entails relevant opportunity costs, the Fair Trade alternative ensures a stable and transaction cost free source of income for producers. In this respect, the price premium adjusted for opportunity costs of producer search of customers, is always positive.

Specific findings illustrated in this chapter show that several other effects add up to the above mentioned one. In the case of the observed Kenyan farmers, our main conclusions are that Fair Trade affiliates develop superior capabilities and enjoy superior economic and social wellbeing with respect to control farmers. We can definitely conclude that Fair Trade creates an additional trading channel, promotes crop diversification and provides in-kind services including technical assistance. As a result, Fair Trade and Meru Herbs members exhibit higher price satisfaction, food consumption expenditure and dietary quality. Given all these findings we interpret the remarkable difference between Fair Trade affiliated and control farmers in terms of income satisfaction as not only due to the higher earned income, but also to a relatively lower desired income which is likely to be determined by a higher supply of complimentary (or cheaper) goods, services and technical assistance. An additional factor determining this result is the risk diversification and risk reduction effect of FT affiliation. Price stability and 'insurance' from price fall below a minimum threshold, combined with the stability of orders which reduce producers 'search costs' of sale channels, should also contribute to reduce the need of precautionary savings and therefore increase the share of income available for consumption and satisfaction of family needs. The less positive side of the analysis is the absence of a positive impact on schooling decisions. The fact that after our research Meru Herbs created a system of scholarships for farmers' children is a good step to improve performance also in this important direction.

Results from the two Peruvian studies are very rich and diversified. We detect a clear positive but nonlinear pattern in the impact of FT affiliation years on producers' income and food expenditure. Such nonlinearity is interpreted in terms of decreasing marginal returns of capacity building and positive FT spillovers in the area. In addition to this first direct nonlinear effect, we also observe a linear one determined by trade channel diversification which must be mainly attributed to Fair Trade.

In addition to it, we identify a spillover effect and an externality. First, we observe that FT has positive and significant effects on affiliated farmers' bargaining power with local intermediaries. Second, we find mixed evidence on the impact of FT introduction on non affiliated producers with a positive effect in one but not in the other project. Finally, we document the effects of the alliance of FT with responsible tourism (whose presence is promoted by FT and whose role is complementary to that of FT) showing that responsible travellers pay even more than FT producers.

Finally, with our backast panel data approach we find that affiliation years significantly and positively affect schooling decisions with one important qualification: consistently with the luxury axiom (parents send children to school only when household income is above a given threshold) better off producers are more effective in translating the price premium into a higher schooling investment for their children.

## References

Bacon, C. (2005). Confronting the Coffee Crisis: Can Fair Trade, Organic, and Specialty Coffees Reduce Small-Scale Farmer Vulnerability in Northern Nicaragua? *World Development* 33: 497-511.

Basu K., (1999). Child Labor, Cause, Consequence and Cure, with Remarks on International Labor Standards. *Journal of Economic Literature* 37: 1083-1119.

Basu K. and P.H. Van (1998). The Economics of Child Labor. *American Economic Review* 88: 412-427.

Becchetti, L. and M. Costantino (2008a). The Effects of Fair Trade on Affiliated Producers: an Impact Analysis on Kenyan Farmers. *World Development* 36: 823-842.

Becchetti, L. and M. Costantino (2008b). Human Capital, Externalities and Tourism: Three Unexplored Sides of the Impact of FT Affiliation. Rome: Universty Tor Vergata (Working Paper).

Carter, M.R. and C.B. Barrett (2006). The Economics of Poverty Traps and Persistent Poverty: An Asset Based Approach. *Journal of Development Studies* 42: 178-199.

Castro, J.E. (2001a). *Impact assessment of Oxfam's Fair Trade activities. The case of Productores de miel Flor de Campanilla.* Oxford: Oxfam.

Castro, J.E. (2001b). *Impact Assessment of Oxfam's Fair Trade Activities. The Case of COPAVIC.* Oxford: Oxfam.

Clark, A.E., P. Frijters and M.A. Shields (2006). *Income and Happiness: Evidence, Explanations and Economic Implications.* Paris Jourdan Sciences Economiques, working paper 2006-24.

Fair Trade Advocacy Office (2005). Fair Trade in Europe 2005. Brussels. Available at: http://www.fairtrade.net/uploads/media/FairTradeinEurope2005.pdf.

Frey, B.S. and A. Stutzer (2002a). *Happiness and Economics. How the Economy and Institutions Affect Well-being.* Princeton: Princeton University Press, New Jersey.

Frey, B.S. and A. Stutzer (2002b). What Can Economists Learn from Happiness Research? *Journal of Economic Literature* 40: 402-435.

Hopkins, R. (2000). *Impact Assessment Study of Oxfam Fair Trade.* Oxford: Oxfam.

Nelson, V. and M. Galvez, (2000). *Social Impact of Ethical and Conventional Cocoa Trading on Forest-Dependent People in Ecuador.* Greenwich: University of Greenwich.

Oxford Policy Management (2000). *Fair Trade: Overview, Impact, Challenges.* Available at: www.opml.co.uk/docs/ACF3C8C.pdf.

Pariente, W. (2000). *The impact of Fair Trade on a Coffee Cooperative in Costa Rica. A producers Behaviour Approach.* Paris: Université Paris I Panthéon Sorbonne.

Ronchi, L. (2002). *The impact of Fair Trade on Producers and their Organizations: a Case Study with Coocafé in Costa Rica*. Brighton: University of Sussex.

Travis, J.L. and C.B. Barrett (2007). Risk Responses to Dynamic Asset Thresholds. *Review of Agricultural Economics* 29: 412-418.

# Chapter 9

## 'Better, but not great': the social and environmental benefits and limitations of Fair Trade for indigenous coffee producers in Oaxaca, Mexico

*Daniel Jaffee*

### 1. Introduction and context

This study, based on extensive ethnographic and survey research in Zapotec indigenous communities in the southern Mexican state of Oaxaca between 2001 and 2005, offers one of the first in-depth investigations of the social, economic, and environmental benefits of Fair Trade. It examines the specific ways that Fair Trade has affected small producers in two coffee-dependent villages during the midst of the recent severe global coffee price crisis. The study compares members of the Michiza producer cooperative in the *Rincón de Ixtlán* region, whose certified organic coffee is sold on the international Fair Trade market, with unorganised conventional farming families in the same region who sell their harvests through local intermediaries. This chapter centers on the results of an in-depth household survey that compares economic, social and environmental conditions for 51 coffee farming families - half of them benefiting from the extra income and the advance credit generated by Fair Trade, and the other half selling their harvests onto the conventional world market in the midst of the worst coffee price crisis in history. It also explores the contradictions that can arise in rural communities where only some households participate in alternative markets offering more favourable terms of trade, and identifies some of the limitations to Fair Trade's social impact at the local level.

#### *1.1. Background*

In Mexico, small farmers dominate coffee production. While there are large mechanised estates, 64 percent of the nation's coffee land is held by peasants who grow less than five hectares (12.3 acres). These very small farms comprise 92 percent of all Mexican coffee farms, the highest proportion of any Latin American nation. Especially notable is the indigenous character of these farmers: about two-thirds of the producers who farm less than two hectares (4.9 acres) of coffee - virtually half of all Mexican coffee farmers - are indigenous people (Porter, 2000).

From 1952 until the 1989 collapse of the International Coffee Agreement, the Mexican Coffee Institute (Inmecafe), a government agency, regulated coffee marketing and production, provided low-cost inputs, and organised small producers across the nation into a type of village-level cooperatives known as UEPCs. The reign of Inmecafe caused a dramatic expansion in coffee acreage in Mexico; between 1969 and 1989, the number of coffee producers in Mexico rose by 289 percent, and the area planted in coffee increased by 220 percent. When the Salinas de Gortari government abolished the agency virtually overnight in late 1989, it suddenly exposed an entire sector of peasant producers to the harsh mercy of an unregulated market. The twin blows of the agency's disappearance and plummeting world prices for the 1989-90 harvest wreaked social and economic havoc on wide swaths of the Mexican countryside. As part of a broader peasant movement in Mexico during the 1980's in which rural communities 'appropriated the productive process', seizing control and marketing of their resources from state institutions and corporate concessions, an independent coffee producer movement had begun to emerge well before Inmecafe vaporised in 1989.

As a result of these dynamics, most Mexican coffee farmers now belong to a producer organisation of some kind. In the late 1990s, CNOC - the national federation uniting all of the independent producer organisations - represented 71,126 farmers, or 25 percent of the national total. Another 31 percent of all coffee farmers belong to the formerly Inmecafe-affiliated organisations, the descendents of the UEPCs. This leaves 44 percent of Mexican producers unaffiliated with any organisation (Porter, 2000). With few exceptions, only the independent CNOC organisations have experienced any success in gaining access to value-added markets for their coffee - such as certified organic and Fair Trade - that can provide some protection from low world prices. The Michiza cooperative, founded in 1986, is one of the pioneering independent producer organisations.

From 1997 to 2004, the protracted global coffee price crisis has exposed these Mexican rural and indigenous communities to the harsh forces of the world market, causing severe economic hardship and threatening the cultural and ecological integrity of this highly biodiverse region. Although coffee prices have risen modestly since 2005, the social and environmental legacy of the recent crisis continues to plague coffee-producing regions worldwide. A pound of coffee is still worth less than half what it was in 1989, in real terms. History shows that price volatility and recurring crises are structural features of the international trade in commodities.[1] When coffee prices drop once more, most of the world's 20 to 25 million coffee growing families will again be fully exposed to the harsh forces of the unregulated global market.

[1] The only exceptions are those in which firm controls are imposed on supply, such as the International Coffee Agreement.

### *1.2. Key questions*

Supporters of Fair Trade assert that Fair Trade not only results in more just prices or living 'wages', ends rural poverty, fosters sustainable farming, empowers poor people and women, and enhances food security, but that it also creates a fundamentally more equitable international marketplace (e.g. Transfair USA, 2006; Oxfam America and Transfair USA, 2004; FLO, 2004; Equal Exchange, 2002; Global Exchange, 2002; Ransom, 2001; Raynolds, 2000). I set out to examine these claims, and to find out how peasant coffee producers are actually experiencing Fair Trade. I was interested in the kinds of tangible benefits that Fair Trade generates, especially when it comes to households' economic well-being and food security, their access to education, the need to emigrate to supplement their income, and the environmental impact of their agricultural practices. Importantly, I wanted to know how families who are reaping the economic advantages of Fair Trade markets fare in direct comparison to similar families in the same communities who sell their harvests on the conventional market through local intermediaries, particularly in the midst of a severe price crisis. While there is a good deal of anecdotal information available regarding the benefits of Fair Trade, this research compares systematically - in quantitative as well as qualitative terms - the differences between small farmer households who participate in Fair Trade markets and those who do not.

## 2. Description of study sites and organisations

This section describes the *Rincón de Ixtlán* and the villages of Teotlasco and Yagavila, which are the setting for this case study of Fair Trade's impact on small indigenous peasant farmers, and profiles Michiza, an indigenous coffee producer organisation participating in the European and U.S. Fair Trade markets. The parallel coffee markets that operate in these isolated communities are a microcosm of the contrasts between the conventional world coffee market and the Fair Trade alternative. I then turn to examine the results from the survey that I conducted with members of Michiza and their conventional coffee producer neighbours, looking at the benefits as well as the complexities that participation in Fair Trade brings for these families and communities.

### *2.1. Study sites*

Oaxaca is the most indigenous state in Mexico. Its sixteen ethnic groups comprise between 50 and 60 percent of the population of 3.4 million. Coffee is grown in 124 *municipios* in Oaxaca, an area that contains 771 indigenous communities. The Mexican government classifies 96 percent of this region as having a high or very high degree of poverty (Bolaños Méndez and De los Santos, 2003). The map of coffee-growing zones in Oaxaca coincides almost exactly with a map of the poorest regions of the state, which in turn are the most indigenous. The *Rincón de Ixtlán* is the epitome of this profile. It is located in the steep *Sierra Juárez* mountain range (part of the Sierra

Madre Oriental) to the north of the capital city. This culturally homogeneous region comprises nine indigenous communities that share a common language (Zapoteco del Rincón or Nextizo). The Rincón is home to approximately 5,200 people, 98 percent of whom are indigenous (INEGI, 2000).

Yagavila and Teotlasco are two of nine indigenous communities in the Rincón, located adjacent to each other on a steep mountainside overlooking the Rio Cajonos. Yagavila has a population of 636 people on a land area of 1,479 hectares, and Teotlasco has 553 residents on its 1,587 hectares. Most of these settlements were in existence at least several hundred years before the Spanish conquest. Because of the Rincón's topography, the traditional and current land base of most of the communities runs in a long, narrow swath from 3,000 meters in elevation down to 500 meters or lower, while virtually all of the inhabited villages are situated in a narrow band between 1,100 and 1,600 meters. This location has allowed the Rincón communities to take advantage of a dramatic 'ecological gradient' ranging from tropical forest to cloud and temperate pine forests, a setting that yields pineapples and mangoes as well as blackberries and potatoes (Tyrtania, 1983). Virtually all of the families in Yagavila and Teotlasco farm milpa, coffee and sometimes other crops on these scattered parcels, and subsistence agriculture still plays a central role in the family economy. The relative abundance of land and the wide variety of microclimates and ecosystems have allowed these communities to survive over more than a millennium. These factors may also play a role in helping the region manage the effects of the recurring coffee crises.

Here in the Rincón, the agricultural system is dominated by coffee and maize. Within the community of Yagavila, according to Oaxacan anthropologist Emma Beltrán, these two crops each occupy exactly 47 percent of the agricultural land, with sugar cane on 4 percent and other crops occupying 2 percent (Beltran, 2000). The average family in the Rincón has 3 parcels of coffee, with most of the parcels either very small (0.25 hectare) or small (1 hectare), and few plots larger than that. In the 2003 survey of 51 families in both Yagavila and Teotlasco, the average family had just over three coffee plots totalling just under 2.5 hectares, and three plots of food crops - maize and beans (milpa) plus sugar cane - totalling 1.9 hectares.

The organisational picture for coffee farmers in the Rincón is a complex one. About 70 percent of the families in Teotlasco and 40 percent in Yagavila are *productores libres* - unorganised or 'free' producers who sell their coffee to one of several local intermediaries, or *coyotes*. Slightly less than half of the families in Yagavila belong to the *Union Fraternal*, a remnant of the producer associations formerly linked to Inmecafe and still affiliated with the national peasant union CNC, which pays prices very similar to those of the *coyotes*. The CEPCO union - which sells some coffee on Fair Trade and organic markets—represents another 19 producers in Teotlasco. Finally, the Michiza cooperative has 20 member families in Yagavila and 24 in Teotlasco; virtually all of their coffee is certified organic, and most is sold at Fair Trade terms.

### 2.2. Michiza Cooperative

Michiza (which is also known by its legally registered title, Yeni Naván) emerged out of the work of liberation theology-oriented Catholic priests and laypeople in the mid-1980s, along with other pioneering Mexican producer unions such as UCIRI, ISMAM and UCI-100. Since its founding in 1986, Michiza has grown to a total of approximately 1,100 member families located in 47 communities dispersed across the state, representing six indigenous ethnic groups: Mixtecos, Chinantecos, Zapotecos, Chatinos, Cuicatecos and Mixes. In most of these communities, as in Yagavila and Teotlasco, only a small portion of the producer families belongs to Michiza. In recent coffee harvests, the organisation has collected between 400 and 500 metric tons (400,000-500,000 kilos) of parchment coffee from its members. Over 80 percent of this total is of export quality - all of which Michiza sells at Fair Trade prices to buyers in Germany, Austria, and now the U.S. - while the remainder fetches lower prices on the Mexican domestic market.

The majority of Mexican producer organisations on the Fair Trade register cannot sell all of their export-grade coffee at Fair Trade prices on the international market. Observers estimate that worldwide, only 20 to 25 percent of coffee produced by cooperatives in the Fair Trade system can be sold on Fair Trade terms; the available supply far outstrips consumer demand (Rice and McLean, 1999). Many producer groups in Mexico and elsewhere must sell the majority of their harvest either at the low world market price or at a smaller premium on the international or domestic markets. Michiza, in contrast, sells 100 percent of its export-grade coffee to European and U.S. buyers at Fair Trade terms. The Fair Trade price premium is the most significant element in the higher prices that Michiza's members receive for their coffee, allowing for greater confidence that the economic differences between the Fair Trade households (Michiza members) and conventional households (non-members) can be attributed to the additional capital from Fair Trade. Michiza's 22-year history as an organisation, and its 16 years of exporting Fair Trade organic coffee, also provide the time-depth necessary for such a study. Michiza has been present in Yagavila and Teotlasco since 1990; some current members have been active since the beginning, and the average length of membership of the respondents is 6.8 years. Thus, these households have had adequate time to show the cumulative social and economic effects that are generated by participation in Fair Trade.

## 3. Research methods and sampling

### 3.1. Study timeline, conceptualisation and design

The field research for this study took place between October 2001 and February 2004, coinciding with the nadir of the recent worldwide crisis in coffee prices. This project was designed as a comparative case study, combining both ethnographic and survey research methods. The comparison in this study - between producers participating in the Fair Trade system through the Michiza cooperative on the one hand, and their neighbours in the same villages who sell their coffee on the conventional market (through local intermediaries or *coyotes*) on the other - is key to establishing the extent of the social, economic and environmental benefits that are associated with participation in Fair Trade.

### 3.2. Research methods

Our study is based on a combination of several research methods:

1. *Semi-Structured Interviews*. The study began with a series of semi-structured, in-depth interviews with a number of key participants, including members of non-governmental organisations (NGOs) in Mexico City and Oaxaca City involved in Fair Trade, rural development, organic coffee production and indigenous community governance; a Catholic priest and advisor to Michiza; researchers from the public university and from research centres in Oaxaca; and members of the Michiza *directiva*. I conducted 15 interviews in Yagavila and Teotlasco, and another 19 interviews in Oaxaca City, Mexico City, Cancún, and in the US, for a total of 34 interviews with 33 individuals (one was interviewed twice).
2. *Participant Observation*. I engaged in participant observation in a wide variety of settings, including attending cooperative meetings at the village, regional and statewide levels, and a wide range of productive activities within the home, on families' *milpas* (subsistence agriculture plots), and in tasks of coffee plot maintenance, harvesting, processing and quality selection. I also conducted a series of 'plot walks' with individual producers in their coffee parcels and *milpas*, asking questions about agronomic practices and features.
3. *Household Survey*. The centrepiece of the study was a household survey, conducted in July and August 2003 with 51 families; 25 were unorganised conventional producers ('*productores libres*') and 26 were Fair Trade producers, (all members of the Michiza cooperative, except for two affiliated with the CEPCO cooperative). Table 1 shows the numbers of survey respondents, broken down by their organisational affiliation and village.

In this hybrid survey instrument, the majority of questions solicited discrete-choice answers and numerical data, but also included many open-ended questions. The survey was 15 pages in length and contained 120 items, many of which included multiple sub-questions. All the surveys were conducted in Spanish, either by myself or a research assistant, and each took between 90 minutes and three hours to complete.

### 3.3. Sampling

The sample of coffee producer households for the survey was drawn from two different methods. In the case of the members of the Michiza cooperative, I utilised the organisation's lists of current members as a sampling frame. I was able to conduct surveys with 100 percent of the Michiza members in both Yagavila and Teotlasco, with the exception of a few members who were out of the village for an extended period.

*Table 1. Number of survey respondents by organisational category and village.*

| Organisation | Yagavila | Teotlasco | Total |
|---|---|---|---|
| Michiza | 14 | 10 | 24 |
| CEPCO[a] | - | 2 | 2 |
| **Subtotal - Fair Trade** | 14 | 12 | 26 |
| Unorganised (libre) | 8 | 6 | 14 |
| New Michiza (nuevo ingreso) | 4 | 1 | 5 |
| Fraternal[b] | 6 | - | 6 |
| **Subtotal - conventional** | 18 | 7 | 25 |
| Total | 32 | 19 | 51 |

[a] *Coordinadora Estatal de Productores de Café de Oaxaca* (State Coordinating Body for Oaxacan Coffee Producers), a large statewide producer union on the Fair Trade register. CEPCO is active in Teotlasco and one other community in the region, and had 19 members in Teotlasco as of July 2003.
[b] The *Asociación Fraternal Yagavila* (Yagavila Fraternal Association) was formerly part of the CNC, Mexico's national peasant confederation, long linked to the PRI party. The Fraternal officially had 78 members in Yagavila as of July 2003. It functions primarily as a coffee marketing body (at prices very close to those paid by the *coyotes*), and also channels funds from government support programs to its members.

However, in each of these two villages, Michiza members represent only between 12 and 28 percent of all households. In the case of the *productores libres*, who constitute the bulk of both villages, sampling was more challenging due to the lack of a viable sampling frame. We opted for a modified snowball method, in which we solicited the names of conventional producers from a variety of sources, and selected households to create a sample that approximated the variability within the community as a whole, on a range of socioeconomic and demographic variables. Our sample of 25 conventional producer households was thus to an extent stratified, but not random; it reasonably approximates the variability within the two villages on a number of key measures.

### *3.4. Analysis of data*

*Survey data.* The quantitative data (categorical and scale variables) from all of the survey questions were analysed with the SPSS statistical analysis package, which I utilised to perform a series of statistical tests - principally t-tests, one-way ANOVA, and Chi-squared. The main interest was to determine the relationship between the independent variable of participation (or non-participation) in Fair Trade, and a series of dependent variables - household income and debt, labour costs, educational levels, food security, migration rates, environmental practices and other issues - as well as the statistical significance of these relationships.

*Interviews and qualitative data.* I utilised both the transcribed interviews and the qualitative component of the survey data (people's verbal responses to the open-ended questions in the survey) to elucidate the complex details of people's lived experience and both to contextualise and triangulate the survey data. The qualitative portion of the survey responses contained the verbatim comments from 89 people (the total number of producers, spouses and adult children who took part in all 51 interviews).[2]

## 4. Findings: the benefits and limitations of Fair Trade

According to Mexican sociologist Josefina Aranda, 'there is a need for sounder empirical evidence on the impact of Fair Trade on the environment and on the labour conditions and well-being of farmers and workers' (Aranda Bezaury, 2000). In an effort to address that paucity of data, this research examines the specific ways Fair Trade has affected small producer households in two coffee-dependent Oaxacan villages - socially, economically, and environmentally - during the midst of the worst price crisis in history. A brief discussion of the major findings of the study follows.

### 4.1. Coffee prices

The most visible benefit of belonging to Michiza is the higher prices that producers receive for their coffee - a difference that is most dramatic during times of crisis. For the large majority of producers in these villages who do not belong to an organisation, several local intermediaries, or *coyotes*, are their only link to the world coffee market. With the *coyotes* paying approximately five pesos per kilogram at the end of the 2002-03 harvest, the Michiza members in transition to organic received twice that much by selling to the organisation, and the families who had achieved organic certification were paid three times more, as Annex Table A1 illustrates. The distinct differences between these two markets persisted until the world 'C' price of coffee began to rise with the 2004-05 harvest, when they began to narrow substantially.

### 4.2. Household profiles: agricultural production

All of the families in these communities grow both coffee and milpa, and they have very similar amounts of land planted in both types of crops, as Table 2 indicates. By one of the primary measures of wealth in the Rincón - access to land - there is no great disparity between the Fair Trade and conventional producer households. The demographic profile of the two groups - household size and numbers of dependents - is also quite similar for both groups. In short, these are all cash-poor indigenous peasant households who are engaged in subsistence agriculture and small-scale coffee production.

[2] In this chapter I have used pseudonyms for the survey respondents whose words are quoted.

*Table 2. Household size, coffee and food crops (2003).*

| | Fair Trade[a] (n=26) | Conventional[b] (n=25) | Total (n=51) |
|---|---|---|---|
| Household size (members) | 4.68 | 4.27 | 4.47 |
| Age of primary respondent (years) | 44.4 | 47.5 | 46.1 |
| Number of Dependents (ages 0-17, 65+) | 2.12 | 2.24 | 2.18 |
| (1 outlier removed; n=50): | (n=26) | (n=24) | (n=50) |
| Number of coffee parcels | 3.12 | 3.38 | 3.24 |
| Total size of coffee parcels (hectares) | 2.46 | 2.34 | 2.41 |
| Number of food crop parcels | 3.23 | 2.83 | 3.04 |
| Total size of food crop parcels (hectares) | 1.84 | 1.77 | 1.80 |
| Ratio of coffee area to food crop area | 1.37 : 1 | 1.32 : 1 | 1.34 : 1 |

Note: All figures are means.
[a] Members of Michiza and CEPCO.
[b] Unorganized producers, plus members of CNC/Fraternal.

### *4.3. Income and debt*

The most direct motivation for producers to join the independent organisations such as Michiza is access to the higher per-kilo prices conferred by the organic and Fair Trade markets. Table 3 compares gross coffee incomes, harvest volumes, sales and yields for the two groups. As it indicates, members of Michiza in Yagavila and Teotlasco earn significantly more on average from coffee sales (after subtracting the costs of hired labour) - almost four times the earnings of their unorganised counterparts. This is due largely to the preferential Fair Trade prices, but also to the much higher volumes that Michiza producers harvest and sell. Figure 1 examines the specific components of the *gross* household income for these two groups, and Figure 2 shows *net* household incomes, after all expenses.[3]

A few sets of numbers in these tables and figures are worth discussing in greater detail. First, the income from coffee sales does not account for even half of the total cash income of either group, indicating that cash is coming into these families from other

[3] It is important to note that because of the lack of markets for non-organic Fair Trade coffee, all Michiza members are required to enter the transition process immediately upon joining the organisation. Thus, organic certification is 'bundled into' Michiza membership, and all members are either in transition to organic certification, or are fully certified. The figures for the Fair Trade group in this survey show the combined benefit of both the higher Fair Trade price and the small price premium for certified organic coffee (US $0.15/pound, paid to the organisation). While the survey data do not permit disaggregation of the household economic benefits provided by the small organic premium from those of the higher Fair Trade price, producers spend only two years at the 'transitional' price level, so that the large majority of members receive the full combined Fair Trade/organic coffee price.

*Table 3. Coffee harvests, sales and income (2002-2003).*

| | Fair Trade (n=26) | Conventional (n=24) |
|---|---|---|
| Kilograms harvested | 493.19 ** | 321.17 ** |
| Kilograms sold | 410.69 ** | 248.79 ** |
| Kilos sold to coyote | 53.15 ** | 202.33 ** |
| Kilos sold to organisation | 356.19 *** | 46.25 *** |
| Coffee yield (kilograms/hectare) | 213.21 * | 153.01 * |
| Average price/kg from coyote (pesos) | 4.23 ** | 5.74 ** |
| Average price/kg from organisation (pesos) | 14.62 *** | 5.77 *** |
| Average total price/kg received (pesos) | 13.22 *** | 5.74 *** |
| Total received from coyote sales (pesos) | 225 *** | 1,161 *** |
| Total received from organisation sales (pesos) | 5,206 *** | 267 *** |
| Total income from all coffee sales (pesos) | 5,431 *** | 1,428 *** |

Note: All prices in pesos. Approx 10 pesos=1 US$); All figures are means; 1 outlier removed.
* Significant at the 0.1 level; ** Significant at 0.05 level; ***Significant at the 0.01 level.

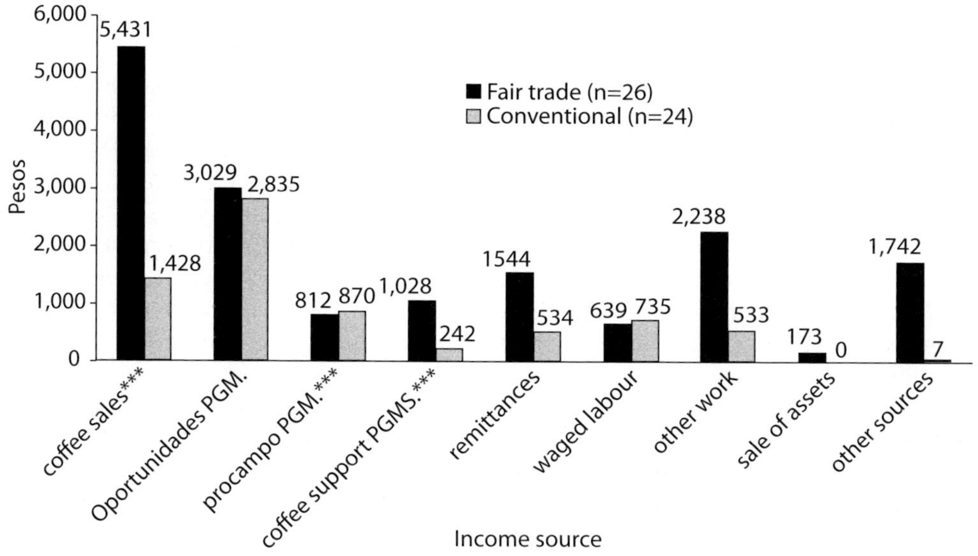


*Figure 1. Composition of household income (2003).*
*All figures are means. *** Significant at 0.01 level.*

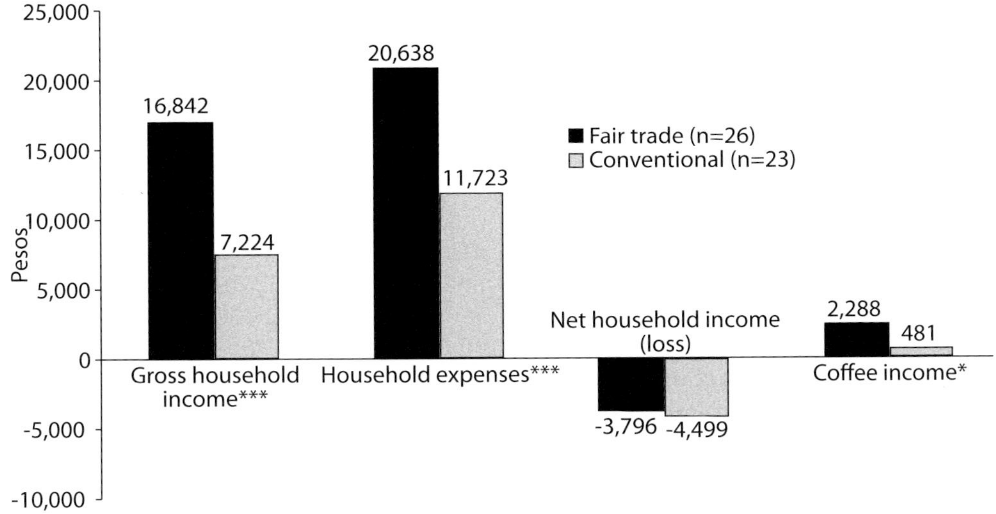


*Figure 2. Household income and expenses, Yagavila and Teotlasco (2002-2003)[a].*
*[a] Coffee income = income from coffee sales, minus cash cost of coffee labour.*
** Significant at the 0.05 level; *** significant at the 0.01 level.*

important sources. Second, it is immediately apparent how modest the income from coffee of even the Fair Trade group is - an average of just over US$ 540, *before* deducting the cash costs of production. The *total gross* cash income of these families is also quite low - 16,842 pesos (US$ 1,684) for Fair Trade households and 7,224 pesos (US$ 722) for their conventional counterparts. Last and most dramatic, as Figure 2 shows, both groups have a *negative net* household income. That is, they are losing money - roughly US$ 379 on average for Fair Trade members and US$ 416 for conventional producers - even as they invest hundreds or thousands of hours of labour to weed, harvest and process their coffee. Only 12 of the 51 families surveyed actually had a positive net income in 2002-2003, eight of whom were Michiza members.[4]

The implications of the data on net household income are troubling indeed. Most families were actually losing money during the crisis, and Fair Trade members lost nearly as much money as their conventional counterparts. At least on the surface, it would appear that participation in Fair Trade in the Rincón does not put member families any farther ahead.

[4] Negative net household incomes can reflect a sudden decline in cash income - such as when crop prices drop precipitously - and can last until families either reduce their expenses, find alternative income sources or take on debt. The families in the survey are adopting a range of strategies to stem the flow of red ink. Nevertheless, a caveat is in order here. It is possible that participants in the survey may have understated their income from certain sources - government support programs or remittances from migrants - potentially based on a stigma attached to dependency on programs, or concerns that showing a higher household income might jeopardise their access to the federal support.

I also examined the levels of household debt. According to a local Michiza leader, 50 to 60 percent of the families in Yagavila take out loans on a regular basis during the 'lean months' (*meses flacos*) of the summer - a time when meager cash income from the spring coffee sales has often run out and the milpa has not yet been harvested.[5] One of the important aspects of Fair Trade is the provision of pre-harvest financing, and Michiza does pay approximately 30 percent of the anticipated final price to its members several months before the harvest. As Annex Table A2 shows, a total of 18 producers (35 percent of the sample) had outstanding debt at the time of the survey. Just over 41 percent of conventional producers were indebted, compared to only 30.8 percent of Fair Trade members. The average loan size for the Fair Trade group is 2,345 pesos, compared to 3,525 pesos for the conventional group. Just over 59 percent of Fair Trade members had borrowed money at least once in their lives, compared to 70 percent of the conventional group. However, producers' *dependence* on loans - that is, the frequency and regularity with which they have to borrow money - shows the most significant difference. Over 57 percent of the conventional farmers say they have to borrow money every year, while only 29.2 percent of the Michiza and CEPCO members do. Exactly one-third of the Fair Trade producers who responded say that they borrowed money for the past coffee harvest, while 83 percent of the conventional producers had done so. The level and timing of their coffee payments appear to give Fair Trade members greater liquidity and lower their dependence on credit from traditional sources. They are not forced into a cycle of debt in order to bring in the coffee harvest, or even worse, to eat.

### *4.4. Family and hired labour*

Hired labour is indispensable for the majority of the families in Yagavila and Teotlasco. Two-thirds of the families in the survey (34 out of 51) hire labourers - known in this region as *mozos* - to help bring in the harvest and maintain their coffee plots. The need to hire *mozos* depends largely on three factors: the number of family members who are available to help with the harvest, the size of the plots, and whether or not farmers belong to an organisation producing organic coffee. As Table 4 shows, both the amount and cost of hired labour are significantly higher for Fair Trade families than for their conventional counterparts. In part this added labour burden is due to the specific plot management techniques required to gain and keep organic certification (which is a requirement for membership in Michiza), and in part to the rigorous quality demands of the European export market, which requires much greater attention to wet-processing, drying and selection. Fair Trade producers in Yagavila and Teotlasco pay for an average of 64 mozo/days per year for coffee, while the typical conventional producer hires mozos for coffee labour on less than 21 days. The average Michiza member spent approximately 58 percent of his or her coffee income on coffee labour, leaving a very modest return of 2,288 pesos (US$ 229) after labour costs for the year's work. However, the conventional producers on average spent 67 percent of their meagre income from coffee sales on labour, leaving the

[5] Gómez Sánchez, M. (2002). Local President of Michiza in Yagavila. Personal communication.

*Table 4. Person/days and costs for hired labour (2002-2003).*

| | Fair Trade (n=25) | Conventional (n=23) | Total (n=48) |
|---|---|---|---|
| Number of person-days for coffee tasks | 64.44** | 20.87** | 43.56 |
| Number of person-days for milpa tasks | 47.92** | 16.91** | 33.06 |
| Total number of person-days | 112.36** | 37.78** | 76.62 |
| Average daily mozo wage paid (pesos) | 47 | 44 | 46 |
| Costs for mozo labour in coffee (pesos) | 3,109*** | 975*** | 2,087 |
| Costs for mozo labour in *milpa* (pesos) | 2,242** | 807** | 1,554 |
| Total Costs for mozo labour (pesos) | 5,351** | 1,782** | 3,641 |
| Coffee labour costs as % of *coffee sale* income | 57.2% | 68.3% | 59.5% |
| **Net coffee income** | | | |
| (coffee sales minus coffee labour costs) | 2,288 | 481 | 1,422 |

Note: All figures are means; 3 outliers removed (n=48).
** = Significant at the 0.05 level; *** = Significant at the 0.01 level.

average conventional farmer with, astonishingly, just 480 pesos - *48 dollars* - for the entire year's harvest. Moreover, these figures do not include or attribute a cash value to the thousands of hard hours of *unpaid* family labour involved in picking, hauling, wet-processing, drying and selecting the coffee.

### 4.5. Food security

In the Rincón as of 2003, each kilo of conventional coffee bought only one-quarter to one-sixth of what it did five years earlier. Getting *enough* food is not a problem in the Rincón, but adequate nutrition is. The normal diet in the region, even in good economic times, is deficient in protein, calories and other nutrients (Tyrtania, 1983; Beltrán, 2000). During the price crisis, conventional producers faced not merely a reduction in food choices, but in many cases they were literally experiencing malnutrition. Researcher Emma Beltrán wrote in 2000 that 'the region presents a marked deficit in standards of infant nutrition, according to the parameters of weight and body size'.

The most important response to the prolonged coffee price crisis by Rincón families was to turn back to the shelter of subsistence that had supported them for millennia. The land area planted in milpa increased notably, while the area in coffee being harvested declined due to abandonment. Anthropologist Paola Sesia describes this phenomenon as a return to subsistence production, a process she terms *recampesinización* - literally, 're-peasantisation' (Sesia, 2002). The ability to transform oneself from small commodity producer back into subsistence farmer is key to survival. Annex table A3 shows that fully two-thirds of the conventional households are planting more milpa in 2003 than five years earlier, before the price crash; only 28 percent of the Fair Trade families give the same response. The increased land clearing for milpa in Yagavila does not typically impact the coffee areas, but rather the remaining forests in the region (Beltrán, 2000). Thus, planting more milpa is also a process with distinct environmental implications.

The concept of food security has become an increasingly common lens with which to look at people's access to food. This useful approach focuses not just on nutrition, but also the policies that affect food availability, how agriculture is organised, and the ways that households make decisions about producing and consuming food (Sen, 1981). The differences between the two groups of producer families in the Rincón extend to measures of household food security. By several measures, the conventional households are in a more precarious position than their Fair Trade counterparts, as Table 5 shows. Two-thirds of Fair Trade families say they always have adequate food to meet the needs of the entire household, compared with only 44 percent of conventional families. Over 83 percent of non-fair-trade families say they experience food shortages during the year, versus only 58 percent of the Fair Trade group. By other measures, too, the distinction is apparent. The purchase of food eats up a far bigger share of conventional households' budgets, accounting for a whopping 85 percent of their total gross income, compared with 59 percent for the Fair Trade group. Food bought with cash accounts for 30 percent of Fair Trade families' total household expenses, compared with 51 percent for the conventional group. Interestingly, despite the greater expansion of milpas among the conventional group, the home-grown maize and beans of the Fair Trade families still lasts them a bit longer on average (7.5 months of the year versus 6.8 months). Finally, the total amount of cash that families spend to purchase food is different - 5,500 pesos (US$ 550) for conventional producers versus almost 7,000 pesos (about US$ 700) for the Fair Trade group, 25 percent more.

*Table 5. Food security overview (2003).*

| | Fair Trade (n=26) | Conventional (n=25) |
|---|---|---|
| Mean household cash expenditure on food, 2002-2003 (pesos) | 6,886 * | 5,507 * |
| Mean expenditures on food as percent of *gross* household *income* | 40.9% | 76.2% |
| Always has adequate food to meet the needs of entire family | 17 ** (68.0%) | 11 ** (44.0%) |
| Always has adequate food to meet the needs of the children [n=26] | 10 (71.4%) | 7 (58.3%) |
| There are times of food shortage in the household [n=50] | 15 ** (57.7%) | 20 ** (83.3%) |
| Family's maize and bean harvests last the entire year | 5 (19.2%) | 3 (12.0%) |
| Mean number of months maize and bean harvests last [n=42] | 7.50 | 6.68 |

Note: * Significant at the 0.10 level; ** Significant at the 0.05 level.

One way to confirm these differences is by looking at the number of meals containing key foods that these families eat. For both meat and dairy, the differences are striking. As annex Table A4 shows, Fair Trade families consume milk an average of 2.53 times per month, compared with less than once (0.83 times) for the conventional families. They consume meat (beef, chicken or pork) 2.05 times a month, versus 1.08 times for the non-fair-trade group, and eat cheese just over three times a month, compared with once monthly for the conventional group. Only when it comes to eggs are the differences negligible.

Overall, then, the members of Fair Trade organisations - and their children - are receiving more protein in their diets than conventional families. They are using part of their higher gross incomes to feed their families better, and are less likely to experience shortages of food or have to go without essentials. They also have a wider range of options for food provisioning (short of going into debt) when their subsistence maize and beans run out, partly because of their greater cash from Fair Trade coffee sales and the distribution of coffee payments throughout the year.

### *4.6. Migration*

According to interviews with community leaders and families, approximately one-third of the residents of both Yagavila and Teotlasco - both single young adults and entire families - have left the villages since the year 2000, both to the United States and to urban areas in Mexico. People in Yagavila and Teotlasco agree that virtually nobody from these villages had ever migrated to the United States prior to the coffee price crash. 'It's because of the low prices', explains Mario, a Michiza member in Teotlasco. 'People lose hope, and then they go. It just doesn't pay to harvest coffee anymore'. While there had been a modest tradition of migration to Oaxaca City and occasionally to Mexico City, primarily for education, neither the 'pull' nor the 'push' factors existed before 1999 or 2000 to send indigenous residents of the Rincón across the border. 'The ones in the U.S., it's because of the low price of coffee', opines Rodolfo, a 32-year old Michiza member in Yagavila. However, while many people have left the community in order to bring money into the household economy, it takes money to emigrate in the first place - a fact that is key to understanding who is emigrating from the Rincón and why. The coffee crisis and the resulting emigration have placed a major strain on both the household economy and cultural integrity of these communities. Migration has especially compromised the key institutions that mobilise communal labour and organise village governance - *tequios* and *cargos* - because of the loss of able-bodies adult members, particularly heads of households.

What role does Fair Trade play in this picture? In Yagavila and Teotlasco, as Annex Table A5 indicates, roughly equal numbers of conventional and Fair Trade families have migrants living outside of the community (two-thirds of each group) and living in the U.S. (27 percent for the Fair Trade group and 20 percent for non-fair-trade households). But here the similarities end. Despite claims by Fair Trade organisations that participation in Fair Trade can or does *reduce* migration[6] - for example, Transfair USA's educational material for cafés states that 'through fair pricing, millions of people around the world are able to stay on their land' (Transfair, 2004) - it is clear that at least in the Rincón, the reverse is true. On average, the Fair Trade families have almost twice as many members living outside the community - 1.88 people per household, compared with 0.96 for their conventional neighbours. They are also sending more than twice as many migrants to the U.S. (0.54 people on average) than the conventional group (0.20 people). The differences continue with the issue of remittances. Nine Fair Trade households - over one-third of the Fair Trade families with at least one migrant - are receiving remittances, compared to seven families in the conventional group (29 percent). Among this group, the difference is great: an average of 4,461 pesos (US$ 446) in remittances for the Fair Trade group and only 1,960 pesos (US$ 196) for the non-Fair Trade households. These remittances account for 16 percent of the average gross family income of the Fair Trade group, but over 22 percent for the conventional families.

This picture at first blush does not seem to square with what many Michiza members say about their more favourable situation, and it also challenges some suppositions about the benefits of Fair Trade. Surely, if Michiza members are in better financial straits, they should feel less pressure to emigrate. However, this phenomenon is explained by a paradox that migration researchers call the 'selectivity of migration' - the fact that the very poorest families are the least likely to be able to migrate. 'The extremely poor', writes development expert Arjan De Haan, 'are generally excluded from migration opportunities' (De Haan, 1999). Rather, it is those with enough resources to send people out of the community in the first place who can take advantage of the migratory option (Durand and Massey, 1992).

These figures also square with what researchers have found in other Oaxacan communities. Lewis and Runsten (2005) conducted a detailed study of coffee labour and emigration in the Mixtec indigenous community of Cabeza del Río, where Michiza also has a presence. They too compared conditions for organised producers and *productores libres*, and found a similar pattern. In sum, it is too facile - and in this case incorrect - to assert that participation in Fair Trade deters migration.

Michiza members appear to be using migration both as a way to leverage further improvements in their quality of life - by sending their children to post-secondary school, by feeding the remaining family members better, and also as a means to sustain their investment in organic coffee production, particularly the costly hired labour and quality improvements it demands. However, many Michiza producers say there is one important difference: as of the time of the survey, the *heads of household* in Fair Trade families had so far not emigrated. According to Jesús, a long-time organisation

[6] Garcia (2004) writes that 'the dignity and personal sovereignty imparted by Fair Trade could make economic migration as a result of free trade policies a thing of the past'. Transfair USA's web page listing the benefits of Fair Trade (Transfair, 2004) also quotes a Mexican producer: 'The more Fair Trade coffee we sell, the more stability we have in our community, and the less we have to migrate'.

member, 'At least the Michiza members are here in the community. They are willing to do the *tequios*, and do the *cargos*'. This is likely because these member heads of household are locked into an investment in organic and Fair Trade certification that bears fruit financially, but must be maintained constantly (Mutersbaugh, 2002). This in turn benefits the whole community because they remain in the village, available to sustain the vital institutions of indigenous communal maintenance and governance.

### *4.7. Environment*

Yagavila and Teotlasco are on the front lines of the struggle to protect shade coffee ecosystems, in a situation that attests to the complex relationship between economic crisis and environmental degradation. Many researchers have catalogued the extraordinary biodiversity that is found in traditional shade coffee plantations (Rice and Ward, 1997). The Rincón is no exception. In a few sample coffee plots, Mario Bolaños Méndez and a team of Oaxacan biologists found 60 identifiable plants and another 30 that could not be identified, more than 100 bird species, 18 kinds of mammals and several reptile species (Bolaños Méndez and De los Santos, 2003).

Using the typology of shade coffee ecosystems developed by Mexican ecologists Moguel and Toledo (1999), the majority of coffee plots in the Rincón are best categorised as highly diverse 'coffee gardens', with a minority of plots in less diverse 'commercial polyculture' and a small amount of the 'rustic' type (Beltrán, 2000). The shade trees in these coffee plots harbour a significant proportion of the original forest biodiversity, above the Mexican average, which in turn is quite high for Latin America. Thus the urgency of keeping shade coffee ecosystems intact is especially salient in these remote Zapotec communities.

In Mexico, only about 10 percent of coffee land has been converted to technified, 'full-sun' coffee, far less than in most producer nations. This is partly because of the land tenure structure in which small peasant and indigenous producers dominate, and in part because of the methods promoted by the state coffee agency Inmecafe from the 1950's to the 1980's. Yet in many areas such as the Rincón, where smallholders have neither the resources nor the desire to convert to full-sun coffee, shade coffee has been increasingly abandoned or – worse - cleared for other land because it no longer brings income for farmers, particularly during the recent crisis. For these small producers, according to anthropologist Mirna Cruz Ramos, to cut down their coffee plants 'is like quitting'. Unfortunately, during the crisis, coffee farmers in Yagavila and Teotlasco began to do just that. Jimena, a 46-year old conventional producer in Teotlasco, says 'many people just leave the coffee and don't weed it, but some people are cutting it down'. Juana, a 29-year old Michiza member in Teotlasco, agrees: 'they are beginning. The [coffee] plants are old, so they cut them down to plant maize'.

In such circumstances, what role does Fair Trade - and the organic and traditional production methods that usually accompany it - play in protecting shade coffee? Can and does Fair Trade, and the organic production methods with which it is linked, help reduce environmental degradation in the Rincón, and even to restore some of the biodiversity and soil fertility lost over the past decades? For the members of Michiza, Fair Trade is intimately linked with the plot maintenance and crop processing tasks required for organic certification. Due in large part to the falling demand for non-organic Fair Trade coffee, the organisation requires that all of its producers begin the transition to organic immediately upon becoming members. These highly labour-intensive tasks—because they immediately affect the production process - constitute the functional meaning of Fair Trade for most members. Zoila, the local Michiza president in Teotlasco, describes some of the practical tasks involved in organic plot maintenance: 'we renew the coffee plots, prepare the compost with ash, [coffee] pulp, manure, maize stubble, and cane chaff … we do pruning, we make live barriers and terraces, and twice a year we weed the land' (Gijsbers, 2003). This extra labour investment has paid off, at least in terms of productivity. The coffee yields of the Fair Trade/organic producers in this survey are 40 percent higher than for the conventional group (213 kilograms per hectare, compared to 153 kilos per hectare). Bray and Plaza Sánchez (2002), in a study of producers in neighbouring Chiapas, concur that coffee yields with organic methods tend to be higher. Almost 90 percent of the Fair Trade producers say their yields have increased at least somewhat since converting to organic methods.

In addition to these members' embrace of conservation techniques, however, an interesting phenomenon is occurring in Yagavila and Teotlasco. The survey found that *conventional* producers are now also widely using several of the specific practices that were introduced to the region by Michiza, in a kind of organic 'demonstration effect'. Table 6 indicates that three techniques in particular - producing compost and applying it to coffee plots, establishing live plant barriers, and building terraces - have been adopted by almost half of the conventional farmers, even though they are not required to do so and have no immediate prospects for organic certification. Two-thirds of the conventional group also say they now incorporate their coffee pulp into compost rather than dumping it; the pulp's value as fertiliser seems to be increasingly evident.

Finally, these organic techniques are not only being transferred from Fair Trade to conventional producers, but they even appear to be making the jump from coffee to food crops. Many Michiza members, especially those most engaged with the organisation, are experimenting with several organic practices on their milpas. Roughly half of the members in these two villages are applying their painstakingly prepared compost onto their maize and beans as well as their coffee, as Table 6 indicates. Close to 60 percent are adding manure to the milpa as well, and 41 percent are planting 'green manure' - a nitrogen-fixing cover crop - on their fallow milpa plots to restore fertility. Mario, a Michiza member in Teotlasco, sows the main green manure species used in this region - velvet bean, known locally as 'Nescafé bean'. He says, 'I use it in places, where I see that the soil requires more nutrients. I harvest it at the moment it is flowering, because that's when it provides the most nitrogen'.

*Table 6. Use of soil conservation, soil fertility and other practices (2003).*

| | Fair Trade (n=26)[a] | Conventional (n=25)[b] | Total (n=51) |
|---|---|---|---|
| **Coffee plots** | | | |
| Compost | 26 ** (100.0%) | 12*** (48.0%) | 38 (74.5%) |
| Live plant barriers | 26 *** (100.0%) | 12 *** (48.0%) | 38 (74.5%) |
| Terraces | 21 ** (80.8%) | 11 ** (44.0%) | 32 (62.7%) |
| Contour rows | 17 *** (65.4%) | 2 *** (8.0%) | 19 (37.3%) |
| Dead plant barriers | 13 *** (50.0%) | 1 *** (4.0%) | 14 (27.5%) |
| Mean times plot weeded per year | 2.00 *** | 1.46 *** | 1.74 |
| ***Milpa* subsistence plots** | | | |
| Apply manure to the *milpa* | 15 (57.7%) | 11 (45.8%) | 26 (52.0%) |
| Apply compost to the *milpa* | 14 * (53.8%) | 7 * (29.2%) | 21 (42.0%) |
| Plant green manure on fallow *milpa* | 11 ** (42.3%) | 1 ** (4.2%) | 12 (24.0%) |

Notes: * significant at the 0.10 level; ** significant at the 0.05 level; *** significant at the 0.01 level.
[a] Members of Michiza and CEPCO.
[b] Unorganised producers, plus members of CNC/Fraternal and new Michiza entrants.

The survey data also suggest that participation in Fair Trade may also be a deterrent to the abandonment and clearing of coffee plots. While nine percent of conventional producers said they intend to raze their plots and plant another crop in the next, none of the Fair Trade members give this answer. Fully 80 percent of the Fair Trade members said they intend to 'plant more coffee' in the future - meaning they intended to replace old plants with new ones, not necessarily to plant additional coffee parcels - while only 54.5 percent of the conventional producers gave the same answer. Fair Trade producers overall appear to hold a more optimistic vision of a viable future in shade coffee production.

Moreover, these Fair Trade organic producers are providing a different sort of 'demonstration effect'. They illustrate to the rest of the community that it is indeed possible to reap a higher economic return for coffee, and that this extra price premium is linked to specific ecological management practices. Several conventional producers whom I spoke with - even if they were not planning to join Michiza at the moment - indicated that they see organic coffee as the only option with any promise. In the words of Alma, a *productora libre* in Yagavila, 'the one who has this kind of coffee [organic] will get ahead. If they comply with everything, in five or six years this producer will get ahead. The one who doesn't follow these steps will be screwed. If I fail to take care of the coffee plots, in the future there will be no hope. The one who sticks with organic will have a future'. Despite all of the challenges involved, then, the extra income generated by Fair Trade plays an important role in sustaining the ecosystem-protecting services of shade and organic coffee production, particularly during a commodity price crisis.

### 4.8. The limitations of Fair Trade

Overall, how do coffee producers in Yagavila and Teotlasco perceive the economic differences between the two groups of households? Interestingly, as Table 7 indicates, conventional producers say that belonging to Michiza makes more of a difference than do the Michiza members themselves. Over 56 percent of the conventional group say Fair Trade members are 'much better off', compared to only 24 percent of the Fair Trade families. Most Michiza and CEPCO members themselves (64 percent) say that they are 'a little better off', compared to 44 percent of the conventional group who give the same answer. And while 12 percent of the families in these two organisations believe that membership makes no economic difference at all, none of the *libres* give this response. Virtually all respondents do note some difference, although the majority say it is a small one. Berta, a conventional producer in Teotlasco, sums up this general sense perhaps better than anyone: '*Los socios de las organizaciones están un poco mejor, pues, pero no muy bien que digamos*' [The organisation members are a little better off, but you wouldn't say great]. Most of these Fair Trade participants are still barely breaking even on their coffee, after labour costs are accounted for. Michiza member Rodolfo puts the situation this way: 'The costs of production are going up, but the Fair Trade price has remained the same for 10 years. Ten years ago, a mozo cost 20 pesos per day, but now they charge 50 pesos. Fair Trade really isn't fair anymore'.

The issue of the declining power of Fair Trade minimum prices - virtually stagnant since the movement's inception in 1988 - is perceived as an urgent one by many producers, and certainly by their organisations. Researcher Christopher Bacon found that the FLO minimum price for certified organic (US$ 1.41 per pound at the time) had an effective value of only 87 cents per pound in 2005, when adjusted for inflation (Bacon and CLAC, 2006).[7]

*Table 7. Producer perceptions of economic differences between Fair Trade and conventional households (Yagavila and Teotlasco, 2003).*

| | Are the members of organisations (Michiza and CEPCO) in better economic conditions than the non-members (*libres*)? * | | |
|---|---|---|---|
| | No difference | A little better off | Much better off |
| Fair Trade (n=25) [a] | 3 (12.0%) | 16 (64.0%) | 6 (24.0%) |
| Conventional (n=16) [b] | 0 (0.0%) | 7 (43.8%) | 9 (56.3%) |
| Total (n=41) | 3 (7.3%) | 23 (56.1%) | 15 (36.6%) |

Note: * = Significant at the 0.10 level.

[a] Members of Michiza and CEPCO.

[b] Unorganised producers, plus members of CNC/Fraternal and new Michiza entrants.

[7] This study used the USA inflation rate as measured by the Consumer Price Index (CPI). However, inflation in most producer nations has been higher than in the USA, causing an even greater loss of purchasing power.

The current Fair Trade minimum prices, then, are inadequate to meet the needs of most small producer families and compensate them for the extra costs of the labour needed for organic production. What would it require for these coffee farmers to feel they are being fairly compensated? When I posed this question to people in Yagavila and Teotlasco, the responses I received give cause for serious reflection about the division of benefits along the Fair Trade coffee chain. Annex Table A6 shows the average amount that each group of producers deems a 'fair' farmgate price for coffee. For Fair Trade members, the figure was 37.72 pesos, or US$ 1.49 per pound. Among the conventional group, it was 21.67 pesos, only 86 cents per pound. Either way, these figures are quite low - between 8 and 18 percent of the average purchase price of a pound of gourmet coffee in the United States.

## 5. Discussion, conclusions and implications

In Yagavila and Teotlasco, the coffee producers who belong to organisations participating in the Fair Trade market clearly receive real and significant benefits - social, economic and environmental - even in the midst of a severe price crisis. Fair Trade is redirecting additional capital to these Zapotec peasant households, and in the process it is buying them, and their communities, some extra financial 'breathing room'. Compared with their conventional neighbours, the Michiza member families who participate in Fair Trade are more food secure, less indebted, have higher gross incomes, engage in more environmentally beneficial organic coffee farming methods (and spread those methods beyond coffee plots to their *milpas*), generate more paid work for local people, and are more likely to continue growing coffee rather than abandoning or razing their shade coffee plots. This does indeed constitute a fairer, more sustainable market.

However, Fair Trade's limitations are also clearly visible in these mountain communities. The minimum prices do not represent a compelling enough incentive for most of the conventional families to persuade them to take on the harder work and higher labour costs involved in joining a producer organisation like Michiza. Fair Trade's guaranteed minimum price does not fully reach producers and has lost a good deal of its value to inflation, and in some cases the amount farmers *do* receive does not even, amazingly, cover their costs of production. Under these conditions, to expect families who are barely breaking even to subsidise organic coffee production from their meagre earnings is surely no recipe for Fair Trade's long-term sustainability. The costs and exigencies of high (and rising) international organic standards are also changing traditional household labour arrangements, communal work patterns, and producer organisations' staff requirements. These and other factors stand in the way of realising the premise that the system provides a 'living wage' to peasant farmers.

In the context of the *Rincón de Ixtlán* region, Fair Trade could be characterised as necessary, but not sufficient. Participation in Fair Trade markets brings many benefits - often significant ones - to member families. Yet at the same time, these benefits are insufficient to persuade many non-member households in the Rincón to participate; they are deterred by the high labour burdens and costs, and the only marginally better net returns, of organic coffee production in independent producer organisations. In this context, Fair Trade does not currently provide a sufficiently compelling alternative for many households, let alone constitute a solution to rural poverty, economic crisis or ecological degradation.

Finally, I suggest a few changes that could move Fair Trade closer to realising that potential. These recommendations range from tinkering to fundamental change:

*Adjust the base price.* The aspect of Fair Trade that coffee producers and their organisations most frequently mention as problematic is the minimum price. The Fair Trade floor price for coffee was established in 1989 and was based on the International Coffee Organization's effective minimum under the old quota regime. It has been raised only twice since then, most recently in 2007 (by 5 cents per pound, and another 5 cents for certified organic coffee). While the current minimums of $ 1.31 or $ 1.51 per pound are certainly higher than the average world price for coffee since 1989, only part of this amount actually reaches farmers. It is clear that the Fair Trade minimum is inadequate to sustain many producers, provide food security for their families, and keep them farming sustainably - or in some cases, farming at all (Levi and Linton, 2003). In the intervening decade and a half, inflation has soared in all producer nations, and both production costs for small farmers and expenses for their organisations have risen along with it. Michiza's costs, for example, have increased two- to three-fold in this period, eating deeply into the proportion of the Fair Trade price it can return to its members. Those members, while getting less for their Fair Trade coffee, have also watched their labour costs double in the past several years, and felt the work burden to keep their organic certification grow considerably.

The Fair Trade base price needs to be re-examined, and raised. Fair Trade organisations must undertake new, comprehensive studies of real production and living costs for small producers in each nation and for each commodity involved in Fair Trade. Based on the study results, FLO should adjust the base price so that it again provides a 'living wage', to be calculated not at the organisational level, but at the *farmgate* - the price the farmer actually receives. Since Fair Trade organisations face their greatest challenges when commodity prices are high, the movement also needs to further widen the differential between conventional and Fair Trade prices so that organisations are able to consistently offer a better price, and producers are less tempted to deliver their harvests to the coyote merely in order to put food on the table.

*Revisit the allocation of benefits.* The sacrifices involved in Fair Trade must be shared more evenly. When Michiza's peasant coffee producers still cannot provide adequate protein in their children's diets after thousands of hours of strenuous labour growing organic coffee, the Fair Trade system is not sufficiently fair. While nobody expects Fair Trade alone to bring the living standards of Ethiopian coffee farmers or Bolivian cocoa growers up to those of Northern consumers, there is ample room in the current commodity chain to return far more income to the people who work to produce these commodities - to allow producers at a minimum to live dignified livelihoods, be fully food secure, and put aside a bit of income to realise improvements in health care, education and housing for themselves and their families.

In concrete terms, the allocation of economic benefits across the Fair Trade commodity chain must be readjusted. A reasonable goal would be to restore the share of the purchase price that is returned to the producer nation (currently less than 10 percent for conventional coffee and about 15 percent for Fair Trade[8]) at least to its level prior to the collapse of the International Coffee Agreement in 1989 - approximately 33 percent. There is no rational or moral justification for the enormous profits that have been reaped by the coffee industry in the post-ICA era, much less during the recent devastating coffee crisis - but the *Fair Trade* system certainly should not be replicating this pattern. Another way to increase the fairness of Fair Trade is to mandate that producers be given an economic stake in the retailing of their products in the North - in other words, a share of the value added. This is the approach of a few innovative Fair Trade initiatives, such as the Day Chocolate Company in the UK, in which the cocoa producers hold one-third equity ownership.

*Address costs and demands of organic certification.* The costs of organic certification and inspection hit small organisations harder than large ones (Mutersbaugh, 2002). Since the environmental services provided by organic production of coffee and other crops, especially tree crops (biodiversity conservation, bird and other wildlife habitat, erosion control, carbon sequestration, etc.) are considered to be so important in global ecological terms, producers and their organisations need to be compensated financially for the additional costs, labour demands, and lost productivity involved in 'going organic' and keeping certification. A comprehensive international system of subsidies should be designed to cover at least the multi-year transition period, during which farmers often see a drop in yields but do not yet receive the higher prices for full organic certification. This recommendation clearly extends beyond the Fair Trade movement - it needs to be addressed by environmental NGOs, international development organisations, and governments alike.

Such substantive changes clearly will necessitate increased dialogue and discussion among Fair Trade movement participants about the nature and purpose of socially just trade. It is my hope that such a dialogue can have the result of making Fair Trade stronger, more effective at actually improving conditions for the disadvantaged producers it is intended to benefit, and – indeed - more fair.

[8] In the case of Fair Trade, this is the amount received by the producer organisation, before costs are deducted.

## References

Aranda Bezaury, J. (2000). *The Mexican Experience*. Presentation at Symposium on 'Reregulating the Global Economy Through Fair Trade' Boulder, Colorado, 17 May 2000.

Bacon, C. and CLAC (2006). *Estudio de Costos y Propuesta de Precios para Sostener el Café, las Familias Productores y Organizaciones Certificadas por Comercio Justo en América Latina y el Caribe*. Coordinadora Latinoamericana y del Caribe de Pequeños Productores de Comercio Justo (CLAC). Unpublished Report.

Beltrán, E. (2000). *Monografía de Santa Cruz Yagavila, Ixtlán*. Oaxaca: Mexico. Unpublished Manuscript.

Bolaños Méndez, M. and J. De los Santos (2003). *Café de Sombra en el Rincón de Ixtlán, Sierra Norte, Oaxaca, México*, 2003. Oaxaca, Mexico: Grupo Mesófilo, A.C.

Bray, D.B. and L. Plaza Sánchez (2002). Social Dimensions of Organic Coffee Production in Mexico: Lessons for Eco-Labeling Initiatives. *Society and Natural Resources* 15: 429-446.

De Haan, A. (1999). Livelihoods and Poverty: The Role of Migration - a Critical Review of the Migration Literature. *Journal of Development Studies* 36: 1-47.

Durand, J. and D.S. Massey (1992). Mexican Migration to the United States: A Critical Review. *Latin American Research Review* 27: 3-42.

Equal Exchange. (2002). *Our Mission*. Available at: www.equalexchange.com/intro/eeintro5.html.

FLO (2004). *Shopping for a Better World: Annual Report 2003-2004*. Bonn, Germany: Fairtrade Labelling Organisations International.

Garcia, S. (2004). *Stop Border Deaths Now*. Latin America Working Group. Available at: www.rtfcam.org/border/deaths071604.org.

Gijsbers, W. (2003). Café y Biodiversidad en el Rincón de Ixtlán. *Noticias*. Oaxaca, Mexico: 8.

Global Exchange. (2002). Fair Trade: Economic Justice in the Marketplace. Available at: http://globalexchange.org/stores/fairtrade.html.

INEGI (2000). *Censo de Poblacion y Vivienda 2000 (Resultados Oaxaca)*. Mexico City: Instituto Nacional de Estadística, Geografía e Informática.

Levi, M. and A. Linton (2003). Fair Trade: A Cup at a Time? *Politics & Society* 31: 407-432.

Lewis, J. and D. Runsten (2005). *Does Fair Trade Coffee Have a Future in Mexico? The Impact of Migration in a Oaxacan Community*. Paper presented at 'Trading Morsels' Conference, Princeton University, Princeton, NJ.

Moguel, P. and V.M. Toledo (1999). El Café en México: Ecología, Cultura Indígena y Sustentabilidad. *Jarocho Verde* 11: 3-12.

Mutersbaugh, T. (2002). The Number is the Beast: A Political Economy of Organic-Coffee Certification and Producer Unionism. *Environment and Planning A* 34: 1165-1184.

Oxfam America and Transfair USA (2004). *Fair Trade Coffee: The Time is Now*. Boston: Oxfam America. (Handbook for Student Organizers).

Porter, R. (2000). Politico-Economic Restructuring and Mexico's Small Coffee Farmers. In: R. Tardanico and J.B. Rosenberg (Eds.) *Poverty or Development: Global Restructuring and Regional Transformations in the U.S. South and the Mexican South*. New York: Routledge, pp. 111-137.

Ransom, D. (2001). *The No-Nonsense Guide to Fair Trade*. London: Verso.

Raynolds, L.T. (2000). Re-Embedding Global Agriculture: The International Organic and Fair Trade Movements. *Agriculture and Human Values* 17: 297-309.

Rice, P. and J. McLean (1999). Sustainable Coffee at the Crossroads. Washington D.C.: Consumers's Choice Council.

Rice, R.A. and J.R. Ward (1996). *Coffee, Conservation, and Commerce in the Western Hemisphere.* Washington D.C.: Smithsonian Migratory Bird Center and Natural Resources Defence Council.

Sen, A.K. (1981). *Poverty and Famines: An Essay on Entitlement and Deprivation.* Oxford: Clarendon Press.

Sesia, P. (2002). Crisis Cafetalera, Familias y Nutrición en la Región de la Chinantla, Oaxaca. *Cuadernos del Sur* 17: 31-42.

Transfair USA. (2004). Barista Quick Reference Guide to Fair Trade Certified. Oakland Ca: Transfair.

Tyrtania, L. (1983). *Yagavila: Un Ensayo en Ecología Cultural.* Mexico City: Universidad Autónoma Metropolitana (UAM-Iztapalapa).

## Annex

*Table A1. Michiza Payments to Producers and Coyote Prices (2002-03, 2003-04 and 2004-05 Harvests)* [a]

| | 2002-03 | 2003-04 | 2004-05 |
|---|---|---|---|
| Michiza: certified organic | 15.0 pesos/kg = US$ 0.68/lb | 17.7 pesos/kg = US$ 0.71/lb | 19.7 pesos/kg = US$ 0.79/lb |
| Michiza: transitional | 10.0 pesos/kg = US$ 0.45/lb | 14.0 pesos/kg = US$ 0.56/lb | 17.4 pesos/kg = US$ 0.70/lb |
| *Coyote* price [b] | 5.0 pesos/kg = US$ 0.23/lb | 5.8 pesos/kg = US$ 0.23/lb | 19 pesos/kg = US$ 0.76/lb |

[a] Exchange rate in May 2003: approx. 10.1 pesos = US$ 1. April 2004-April 2005: 11.3 pesos =US$ 1.
[b] Average *coyote* prices reported in April 2003, January 2004, and April 2005, Yagavila.

*Table A2. Household debts (2003).*

| | Fair Trade | Conventional | Total | N [1] |
|---|---|---|---|---|
| Families with outstanding debt (%) | 8 (30.8%) | 10 (41.7%) | 18 (36.0%) | 50 |
| Mean amount borrowed (pesos) | 2,345 | 3,525 | 2,935 | 20 |
| Mean number of months needed to repay loans | 5.80 | 5.04 | 5.37 | 23 |
| Mean interest level for loans (%/month) | 6.11 | 7.69 | 7.05 | 22 |
| Families who have ever borrowed money | 13 (59.1%) | 14 (70.0%) | 27 (64.3%) | 42 |
| Families who have to borrow money each year | 7 *(29.2%) | 12 * (57.1%) | 19 (42.2%) | 45 |
| Borrowed money for 2002-03 coffee harvest | 4 ** (33.3%) | 5 ** (83.3%) | 9 (50.0%) | 18 |

Note: * significant at the 0.10 level; ** significant at the 0.05 level.
[1] *N* for each question varies because only some respondents answered each item.

*Table A3. Expansion of milpa agriculture (1997-2003).*

| | | Fair Trade (n=26) | Conventional (n=25) | Total (n=51) |
|---|---|---|---|---|
| Are you planting more or less milpa now, compared to when the coffee prices were high (5 years ago)?*** | More | 7 (28.0%) | 14 (66.7%) | 21 (45.7%) |
| | The Same | 14 (56.0%) | 4 (19.0%) | 18 (39.1%) |
| | Less | 4 (16.0%) | 3 (14.3%) | 7 (15.2%) |

Note: *** All differences significant at the 0.01 level.

*Table A4. Consumption of Animal Protein (2003).*

| | Fair Trade (n=25) | Conventional (n=24) | Total (n=49) |
|---|---|---|---|
| Mean number of times per month family consumes meat | 2.05* | 1.08* | 1.58 |
| Mean number of times per month family consumes milk | 2.53 | 0.83 | 1.70 |
| Mean number of times per month family consumes cheese | 3.04*** | 1.04*** | 2.06 |
| Mean number of times per month family consumes eggs [n=48] | 11.08 | 10.70 | 10.90 |

Note: *N=49 unless noted; 2 outliers removed.*
* significant at the 0.10 level; *** significant at the 0.01 level.

*Table A5. Migration and remittances (Yagavila and Teotlasco, 2003).*

| | Fair Trade (n=26 except where noted) | Conventional (n=25 except where noted) | Total (n=51 except where noted) |
|---|---|---|---|
| Mean number of total migrants from household | 1.88 *** | 0.96 *** | 1.43 |
| Mean number of migrants in United States | 0.54 | 0.20 | 0.37 |
| Mean age of all migrants in family (yrs.) | 21.52 * | 24.75 * | 23.14 [n=34] |
| Mean number of migrants sending remittances | 0.88 * | 0.28 * | 0.59 |
| Mean remittance income among families with remittances, 2002-03 (pesos) | 4,461.11 [n=9] | 1,960.00 [n=7] | 3,366.87 [n=16] |
| Remittances as mean % of gross household income of families receiving remittances | 16.55% [n=9] | 21.72% [n=7] | 18.81% [n=16] |
| Number of families with any migrants (and % of all families in category) | 17 (65.4%) | 17 (68.0%) | 34 (66.7%) |
| Number of families with migrants in US (and % of all families in category) | 7 (26.9%) | 5 (20.0%) | 12 (23.5%) |
| Number of families receiving remittances (and % of all families in category) | 9 * (34.6%) | 7 * (29.2%) | 16 (31.4%) |

Note: * significant at the 0.10 level; *** significant at the 0.01 level.
All monetary amounts in pesos. (Approx 10 pesos = US$ 1).

*Table A6. Producers' definition of 'Fair' coffee price (2003).*

| If you could set a producer price for coffee that would be fair, how much would it be? | Mean Price mentioned (pesos/kg) | Equivalent in US$/pound (11.5 pesos = US$ 1) |
|---|---|---|
| Fair Trade (n=25) | 37.72** | 1.49 /lb |
| Conventional (n=16) | 21.67** | 0.86 /lb |
| Total (n=41) | 30.03 | 1.19 /lb |

Note: **significant at the 0.05 level.

# Chapter 10

## Looking beyond the cooperative: Fair Trade and the income distribution

*Robbert Maseland and Albert De Vaal*

### 1. Introduction

We have taken it upon ourselves to look at the impact of Fair Trade from a wider perspective. So far, the impact studies in this volume have illustrated that Fair Trade generally has a positive effect on incomes and/or wealth of the participants. This is perhaps not very surprising. One would expect that organising producers in cooperatives, paying higher prices to these cooperatives, and instigating local development projects (such as schools) brings economic gains to the people involved. More surprising and encouraging is the result that Fair Trade not only brings gains to participants, but also to non-Fair Trade producers operating in the same region. This indicates that Fair Trade can be an effective instrument in regional development.

These positive results notwithstanding, the effects of Fair Trade potentially reach further than the Fair Trade cooperative and its immediate surroundings. There might be unintended side-effects of the implementation of Fair Trade principles in other parts of the economy which are not themselves involved in Fair Trade (Maseland and De Vaal, 2002). Such effects may not be the result of purposeful or strategic interaction of Fair Trade organisations or associated cooperatives, but arise because instigation of a Fair Trade scheme sets off a chain of effects in the world market of which the final outcomes are difficult to predict. What, for example, is the effect of Fair Trade arrangements for producers outside the cooperative or outside the region? What does Fair Trade do for global income and its distribution? This chapter forays into the possible unintended consequences of Fair Trade beyond the arrangement. In contrast to previous chapters, it does so on a wholly theoretical basis.[1] Obviously, such an approach is too abstract to result in any final verdict about Fair Trade, but it does

[1] The theoretical concerns discussed in this chapter could of course be empirically validated in order to assess their relevance in practice. Such an endeavour lies beyond the scope of this chapter, though.

allow us to point out where Fair Trade's potential problems and areas for improvement are. To make the most of this potential, we will adopt a somewhat more sceptical stance towards Fair Trade. By setting ourselves to the task of uncovering the potential flaws of the Fair Trade approach, we hope to increase knowledge about which areas require further attention if we want to maximise the positive impact of Fair Trade.

The structure of this chapter is as follows. In Section 2, we discuss the impact of Fair Trade on producers who are not participating in a Fair Trade scheme themselves, but are confronted with Fair Trade activities in their sector. Section 3 provides a framework for assessing the consequences of Fair Trade premiums for income and its distribution over owners of various production factors. In Section 4, we apply the insights originating from these models to the context of the bulk of Fair Trade arrangements; poor, peasant households producing commodities for the world market. Section 5 concludes.

## 2. Intra-sector analysis

This section assesses the effects the presence of Fair Trade producers may have on other producers in the same sector. In economic theory this is called a partial equilibrium perspective, since it ignores demand and supply linkages with other sectors in the economy. The latter effects of Fair Trade will be discussed in Section 3. We note that when we speak of a producer, we actually mean the producer as an independent entity producing the good. This entity may range from a small local farmer producing output based on self-employment to a large multinational agri-business that hires local labour to generate output.

In the realm of Fair Trade, partial equilibrium may also be given a geographical interpretation; Fair Trade arrangements are often highly localised. But given that Fair Trade produces for the international market, this would clearly be a too limited view. We therefore divide this section in two parts. The first part focuses on the effects on producers of Fair Trade goods, whether they be inside or outside the Fair Trade cooperative, and irrespective of the geographical distance to it. The second part considers the implications for trade.

One of the key elements of Fair Trade is that consumers pay a higher price than for the same non-Fair Trade good (e.g. coffee). Normally this will lead to demand-supply reactions and according price adjustments to retain market equilibrium. We assume that these effects solely occur because of the price premium that is being paid. That is, we assume that the prime function of Fair Trade is to buy coffee from local smallholders and to sell it on Western markets where this was previously done by other trade organisations. As such we assume no direct effect on supply. Paying a higher price, however, has a negative effect on demand, potentially causing oversupply in the market. Alternatively, we could see the introduction of a Fair Trade labelled product as an additional supplier in the market, but this would not really change the analysis. Also in that case, Fair Trade is expected to lead to an oversupply situation and world prices and output must adjust to realign demand-supply equilibrium. Producers not themselves participating in the Fair Trade scheme will therefore be affected by Fair Trade.[2]

### *2.1. What is the effect of Fair Trade on producers not taking part in Fair Trade?*

Fair Trade may cause a negative demand externality for producers outside the Fair Trade cooperative. By partitioning the market in Fair Trade and non-Fair Trade products, demand for output of producers outside the Fair Trade arrangement is reduced, which forces them to lower their prices and reduces profits and income. The extent of this effect of course depends on the relative importance of Fair Trade in the world market of a particular commodity as well as on the extent to which local producers' demand depends on demand at world markets. Producers that only serve local markets, for instance because they fail resources to access the world market, may therefore be hardly affected by this negative externality. Local producers that serve world markets will be affected though. Moreover, they will have to compete for the reduced market share with large multinational corporations (MNCs) active in those markets. In so far these MNCs have market power, especially small local exporters will suffer, who may try to compensate by increasing supply on local markets. Consequently, the negative demand externality will also affect small local producers, whereas also small to medium sized local exporters will be affected.

This situation worsens if producers that are engaged in Fair Trade projects would also produce for the local market. The higher prices they receive due to their engagement in Fair Trade programs will help them to cross-subsidise their supplies for the local market, putting additional competitive strain on the outside local producers. What is more, competition increases because of other aspects of Fair Trade programs, aiming as they do at increasing the productivity of the involved producers. Productivity effects may also arise because of the negative demand externalities themselves. Empirical research in international trade has shown that only firms that are sufficiently productive tend to expand their operations to exporting, while less productive firms settle for supplying domestic markets. From recent theory in this field we may then learn that any effect to increase costs or lower profit margins, implies that the lowest productive firms will exit the domestic market, while firms that were initially just productive enough to export now only start serving domestic markets (e.g. Melitz,

[2] Although negative effects on demand must always be felt somewhere, it is possible to conceive of a situation in which they are felt in different sectors from the one in which Fair Trade operates. It could be that the customers buying Fair Trade bananas, for example, were not buying bananas at all before Fair Trade entered the market, or that these customers are prepared to spend a larger part of their budget on bananas than they previously did. Still, consumers will have to find budget to cover their (additional) expenses on Fair Trade bananas, so spending must fall (or grow less strongly) as a consequence of Fair Trade somewhere. Reduced demand as a result of Fair Trade entering the banana market does not have to be felt in the banana sector, but in that case, it must be hurting producers of DVD players or flowers for example. Such effects are discussed in the next section.

2003). This implies that average productivity in the sector increases – firms should on average be more productive to survive in the market – which may be considered good news. However, it also implies that due to the implementation of Fair Trade programs the producers that must exit the market are forced into marginal existence in the informal sector. As far as we can see, this effect can only be overcome by an expansion of Fair Trade programs, reaching out to those producers that could not face the negative externalities Fair Trade bestowed on them. By offering them a secure channel to export, inclusion in Fair Trade would help the least productive producers to find a substitute market for their lost competitive edge in local markets. Note however that these concerns depend heavily on the local market situation. If access to these markets is restricted, as it is often the case in local coffee and banana markets, the argument raised becomes far less relevant.

The negative competition externalities that we have highlighted so far may, however, not arise in case the producers that join Fair Trade programs operate under conditions of poverty. In that case, supply for the local markets may be high because of low prices and subsistence requirements; a low price means that it is necessary to produce a lot in order to make ends meet. Under subsistence conditions, therefore, Fair Trade suppliers might react to higher Fair Trade prices or improved productivity by contracting supply for the local market.[3] This lowers competition on local markets and prices may go up outside the Fair Trade program as well. The common practice of Fair Trade organisations to target the most vulnerable groups within local communities may therefore be helpful in minimising the negative demand externalities on producers outside their programs.

To see this in more detail, consider the following situation. Assume we have a small local Fair Trade farmer that faces the choice between (a) working on the land to produce Fair Trade goods and (b) any other alternative activity that is useful for the farmer or its household, but does not raise direct income (leisure time, training, house repairs, etc.). Whatever the farmer chooses should however raise an income equal or exceeding a minimum subsistence level of consumption. Since engaging in alternative household activities implies lower farm income, the decision to work on the land or not depends on how much is earned in two ways. First, how much the farmer works depends on the desirability of working, determined by the (expected) yield of working on the land. Secondly, the decision to work or not depends on the farmer's subsistence requirements. More specifically, a farmer cannot spend such amounts of time on alternative activities that income falls below the minimum subsistence level.

The farmer's labour supply decisions are illustrated in Figure 1. The U-curves represent iso-utility curves depicting all possible combinations of alternative activities and farm income that yield the farmer the same level of utility. The slope of the curve in each point gives the marginal rate of substitution of farm income and alternative activities

[3] For whatever reason, for instance because higher prices allows producers to substitute to other important household activities like providing subsistence crops or schooling,

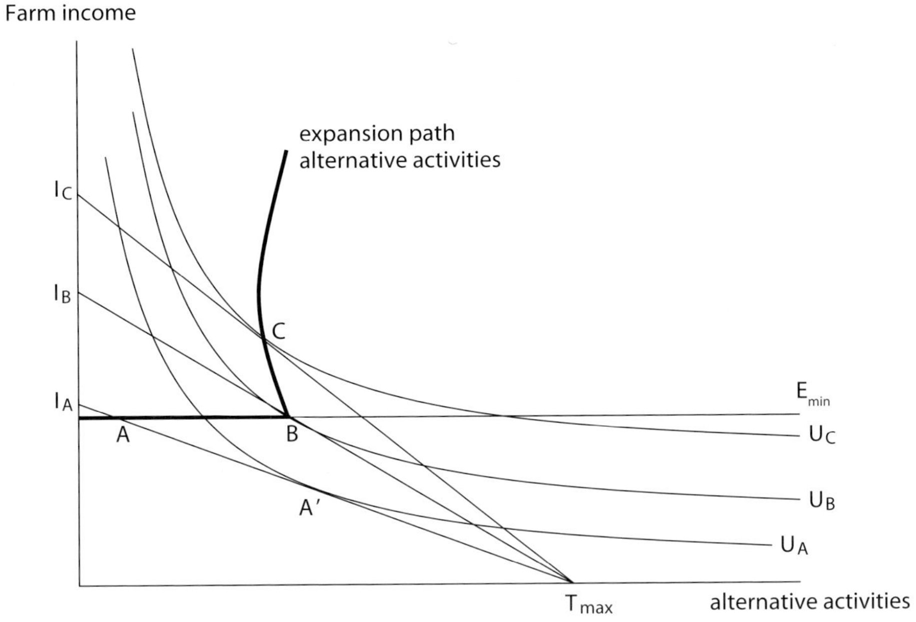


*Figure 1. Labour input decision of small farmers.*

in utility; the steeper the slope, the more the labourer values an additional unit of the alternative activity. This is weighed against the opportunity cost of not working on the land, that is farm income per hour *I*. In the figure, this is represented by the slope of the budget lines $I_zL_{max}$, for $z = A, B, C$. These budget lines give, for each level of time devoted to alternative activities that is physically possible ($T \leq T_{max}$), the income level attainable at the prevailing income rate. Normally, the optimising farmer will choose a 'consumption' basket of alternative activities and income such that the marginal costs of the former equal the marginal benefits, that is: where the budget line is tangent to the highest indifference curve possible. Point B and C indicate such points. Below the income level associated with point B, however, optimisation means to work until income reaches the level of consumption minimally required to sustain the household (the horizontal line $E_{min}$), leaving what is left for the alternative household activities. The low farm income prevents the labourer from choosing the desired combination of work and alternative activities, resulting in a higher than desired rate of work. For instance, for income $I_A$, the optimum choice would be A', yet the farmer must choose A to stay at a subsistence level of income.

Under poverty, therefore, the choice how much to produce is not always what is desired and may be determined by meeting subsistence requirements. In the figure this is indicated by the bold solid line in the figure. Up until point B, any rise in income will increase the possibilities to engage in alternative activities, reducing the number of hours that are spent on the land. But at farm income above $I_B$ the farmer is not longer constrained by the need to survive and the decision how much time to spend on alternative activities is determined by normal marginal cost-benefit analysis. Under such conditions, the optimal level of alternative activities will be lower than upon subsistence, though at income levels high enough it may increase again. This leads to the 'bend' in the curve.[4]

The implications of Fair Trade are then clear. Above subsistence levels of farm income, paying higher prices will increase the time the farmer works on the land, generating higher output and negative supply externalities on outside producers. If, by contrast, the farmers participating in Fair Trade schemes are at subsistence levels of income, paying higher prices causes Fair Trade farmers to spend more time on alternative household activities, keeping their market incomes constant while enjoying higher levels of welfare. For outside producers, this is good news too; the switch to alternative household activities reduces supply of the Fair Trade good, so that no negative externalities are present.

### *2.2. What are the effects of Fair Trade on international trade?*

To analyse the effects of Fair Trade programs on trade, we think of a setting of a rich and a poor country where the rich country is a net imported of Fair Trade type of goods. Fair Trade is interpreted as a scheme in which consumers in the rich country pay a price for the goods produced in the poor country under Fair Trade conditions that is at least as high as the price that would come about on the free market. This situation is illustrated in Figure 2, which depicts a standard partial equilibrium world import demand and world export supply diagram. Without Fair Trade, equilibrium would be where import demand and export supply are equal, resulting in a price $p_0$ and trade volume $q_0$. If the going world market price is however lower than the minimum price Fair Trade organisations pay, that is when $p_0 < p_{FT}$, the situation becomes different. The presence of Fair Trade contracts in the market increases the price at which products are sold in the rich country, reducing the rich country's net import demand for the good to point *a*.[5] At the higher Fair Trade price, *all* producers in the poor country would increase their supply, increasing total export supply to point *b*. If we assume that the supply of the producers inside the Fair Trade program is secured at their initial levels – the idea is after all that they get a higher income – then this must imply that outside producers will have to cut their production levels to settle the balance with an amount of *ab*. Indeed, this higher price applies also for the

[4] That is, we implicitly assume that the income just above subsistence are not high enough to lead to a situation in which it would lead to a lowering of the number of hours worked. The latter phenomenon is a well-known possibility in the literature on labour markets, where it leads to the backward bending part of the individual labour supply curve. It seems a reasonable assumption as backward bending supply curves are usually considered to occur in situations of relative affluence.

[5] To facilitate the analysis we assume that Fair Trade products are perfect substitutes for non-Fair Trade products in consumption. Consequently, prices in the rich country will converge to the minimum price Fair Trade charges. Assuming that Fair Trade goods are imperfect substitutes will not qualitatively alter the analysis, but quantitatively the effects will be less.

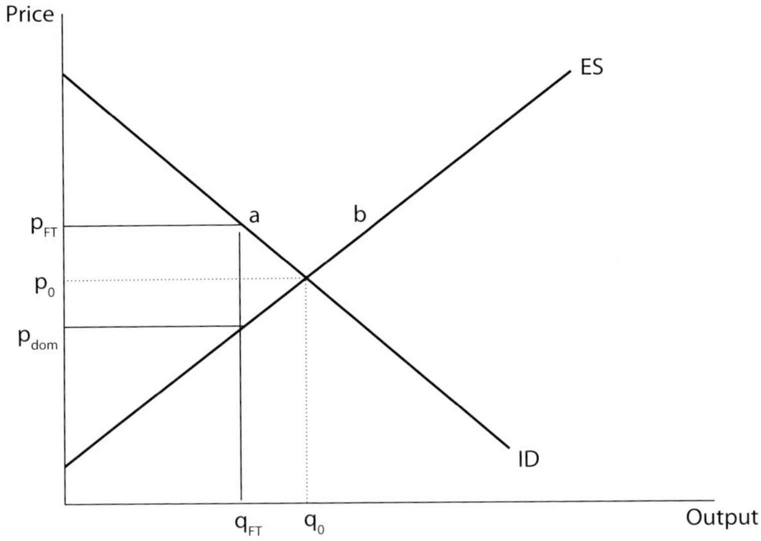


*Figure 2. Effect of Fair Trade on international trade.*

producers in the poorer country that are not directly involved in a Fair Trade scheme and export through different channels. However, those producers that do not export will find that the price they receive on the domestic markets has come down; whatever is not exported gets a price of $p_{dom}$. Effectively, therefore, the situation is as if the rich country imposes an import quota on the Fair Trade good. The quota implies a higher price for those producers that acquired a license to export, but lowers the price for all other producers. The difference is that in the case of Fair Trade the license to export is also related to being in- or outside the Fair Trade arrangement.

The analysis above can of course be qualified in several ways. For instance, the implications on domestic producers rests on the assumption that the output of the Fair Trade cooperatives is large compared to the net export supply of the poor country such that it leads to price adjustments on the world market. Were this not the case, the domestic price would remain the same at $p_0$ and local, non-exporting producers would not be affected by the Fair Trade arrangement. This would also be true if Fair Trade output would be marginal compared to total demand in the rich country. These are considerations that should be taken into account when assessing the impact of Fair Trade on trade volumes and prices. However, the other side of the coin is that if Fair Trade becomes more important, one cannot but conclude that it will lower trade volumes and reduce prices for those producers that cannot (longer) export.

A more fundamental issue is perhaps that the analysis rests on perfectly working markets, including perfectly functioning labour markets. That is, any reduction in output and price must be associated with lower employment and lower wages.

If we loosen this (implicit) assumption and allow for the existence of involuntary unemployment and a limited number of buyers, the impact of Fair Trade on trade becomes more positive. This is the analysis that is proposed by Mark Hayes (2006), arguing that this altered set-up is tantamount to a situation of unequal market power. Suppose we look at the market for bananas. Buyers of bananas have the opportunity to reduce their demand (and thus indirectly employment) and to thereby push down wages and prices. The reason for this is that in a situation of involuntary unemployment, less demand for bananas forces producers into alternative activities that are less productive than growing bananas. If the outside options for banana producers are limited or less attractive, buyers are in a position to exercise pressure on prices and wages. That is, they have monopsony power. Obviously, such a reduction of demand and prices harms producers. This problem is aggravated if the buyer adopts a strategy of price discrimination, whereby separate deals are made with each producer. In normal functioning markets, the price of bananas received by producers is equal for each and every one of them. That implies that those producers who were willing to sell their bananas for less than this final price profit. If buyers are able to make separate deals with producers, for example in the case of middlemen travelling around to buy small quantities of bananas from remote individual farmers, this profit goes to the buyer. The buyer is able to pay each and every producer exactly what (s)he individually minimally requires for the sold goods. This brings down the incomes of producers further, while again raising the incomes of buyers.

Hayes (2006) shows that the creation of a Fair Trade cooperative among producers can address these problems. Such a cooperative can pay its members equally, making discriminative pricing impossible. Also, it can decide to employ the producers leaving the market because of monopsonistic attempts to reduce prices and wages. In both cases, the market power of the Fair Trade cooperation works to negate the market power of the buyers. As a result, Hayes finds that Fair Trade reduces market failures and increases trade in a world that is characterised by unequal market power and imperfect markets.

A similar argument can be made by introducing transaction costs to the analysis. Transaction costs, making it expensive to trade, have a dampening effect on international trade. In the context of Fair Trade production, transaction costs play an especially important role. Lack of physical infrastructure, lack of knowledge of markets, red tape and dependence on chains of middlemen are but a few of the reasons why it can be very expensive for banana farmers in for instance Central America to get their products to Western Europe. Fair Trade programs can act as (subsidised) ways of reducing transaction costs, by linking cooperatives more directly to consumers in developed countries - the so called 'cutting out the middlemen' - or providing producers with relevant knowledge about markets. In this way, Fair Trade can boost trade rather than limit it. With some imagination this can be easily seen in a graph like Figure 2. Suppose that *a* in Figure 2 is the point of intersection of a transaction cost inclusive export supply curve parallel to ES, leading to a trade volume of $q_{FT}$. The difference between $p_{FT}$ and $p_{dom}$ would then be the transaction costs of getting products to foreign markets. If Fair Trade reduces these transaction costs to, say, zero, the export supply curve as depicted in Figure 2 would instead be the relevant one. The price changes to the mutual benefit of consumers and producers, and trade increases.

The Hayes and transaction cost argument have in common that Fair Trade might actually increase trade, which is different from the trade limiting outcome in the standard demand-supply analysis. The arguments, however, not only differ in their conclusions, but also in the aspect of Fair Trade they focus on. The first argument, showing that Fair Trade carries the risk of reducing trade, centres around Fair Trade as a program aimed at higher prices. By contrast, the market power and transaction costs arguments focus on other aspects of Fair Trade: organisation in cooperatives and linking producers to potential markets, respectively. The differential conclusions suggest that the genuinely important element of Fair Trade is perhaps not the price aspect, but the impact on the organisation of production and supply chains.

## 3. Inter-sectoral effects

Until now, we have focused on the income effects of Fair Trade within the sector of the Fair Trade good. Attention has been paid to the likely impact on income distribution between producers in- and outside Fair Trade arrangements. An alternative question is what the impact of Fair Trade is on incomes within society as a whole.

Almost two centuries ago, David Ricardo showed that international trade is generally positive for societies as whole. The basic principle behind this is that what goes for individuals goes for countries as well: specialisation and exchanging with others is more efficient than trying to produce everything one consumes oneself. This is true even if one actor is best at producing any good. Comparative cost differences, not absolute advantages are what matters. In general, therefore, trade between any two countries is mutually beneficial.[6] This basic premise is still theoretically uncontested, but of course there are distribution effects. For instance, while producers in export markets will gain, those in import competing sectors lose. Moreover, trade will harm factors of production used in imports, while those used in exports gain. Inter-sectoral factor mobility may of course redistribute some of these gains and losses, but it is clear that whereas free trade based on comparative advantage leads to gains at a macro level, at the micro level not everyone will gain.

In this section we switch to so-called general equilibrium trade models to analyse these income distribution effects of Fair Trade. We apply a framework that also includes other sectors of the economy, just as it takes into account effects on the rewards for the factors of production that are used to produce each sector's output. Hence, we will

[6] For a standard text book treatment of the Ricardian model of international trade see e.g. Ethier (1995). An advanced treatment can be found in Bhagwati and Srinivasan (1983) and Bowen *et al.* (1998).

address the impact of Fair Trade on the factors of production involved, whether they work in the Fair Trade sector or not.

We will frame our analysis in a setting that should be very familiar to international trade theorists. We see the world as consisting of two countries, where one of these countries is a developed country and the other one developing. Both countries can produce two types of goods by means of employing capital and labour. One of these goods, say manufactures, uses mainly capital, while the other good, farm products, is relatively labour intensive. If we assume that the developing country is relatively scarce in capital compared to the developed country, then the developing country has a comparative advantage in farm products and specialise accordingly. Specialisation is not complete though. Both countries produce both goods, but the developing country relatively more farm products than the developed country. Consumers have similar tastes in both countries, hence there must be trade between the two regions to settle the balance. The developing country will export farm products to the developed country in exchange for manufacturing goods, and vice versa.

The income distribution effects of international trade in such a framework are well-known. Trade increases the price of a country's export good and lowers that of its import good. The production of exportables increases, at the expense of importables production. Demand for the production factor that is intensively used in the export sector increases, increasing its reward in nominal as well as in real terms. By the same token, trade decreases demand for the factor that is intensively used in imports, decreasing its nominal and real factor reward. These effects are known as the Stolper-Samuelson theorem.[7] Applied to the situation at hand, trade will increase the reward of labour in the developing country, while decreasing the real reward of capital. In the following we will use this as a benchmark for assessing the implications of Fair Trade for the income distribution effects.

Free trade increases the real reward of a country's abundant factor of production and lowers it of its scarce factor. The question now is how does the practice of Fair Trade alter this picture? Here we should apply one of the key outcomes of the analysis of Section 2, where we saw that Fair Trade may either decrease or increase trade, depending on which aspect of Fair Trade we focus on.

Suppose we find that Fair Trade reduces trade, emphasising that the effects of paying higher prices for Fair Trade goods in developed countries are similar to imposing an import quota. This implies that the income distribution effects must be exactly opposite to what we have described for free trade. With Fair Trade reducing trade, the

[7] Compared to autarky, the price of exported commodities will rise, whereas the price of imported commodities will fall. As the price of any commodity can be expressed as a weighted average of the price of the factors of production, applying the nominal version of the Stolper-Samuelson theorem implies that the price rise of the exported good must be less than the price rise of the abundant factor, while the price decline of the imported commodity must be less than the fall of the price of the scarce factor. Consequently, also in real terms the abundant factor gains and the scarce factor loses.

production factor that is used intensively in the export sector – in our set-up labour – will lose, while the factor used intensively in the import sector – capital – will gain. On the other hand, if Fair Trade increases trade the income distribution effects are according to a move towards free trade, making capital owners lose and labourers gain. Consequently, to asses the income distribution effects of Fair Trade it is essential to know the impact of Fair Trade on trade.

Whether Fair Trade reduces or increases trade is unimportant for an additional effect that occurs though. In the above, we have ignored that the price premium that is being paid abroad for Fair Trade products generates a rent for those producers involved, to be channelled through to the production factors involved. This is reminiscent of the insider-outsider problem we have touched upon before, but in this case prospects may be less gloomy. The point is that whenever production factors are mobile within an economy, production factors from elsewhere are attracted to Fair Trade programs, implying that factor rewards may rise elsewhere as well. This is a genuine pecuniary externality. It arises because if production factors within Fair Trade cooperatives receive higher rewards, also outside the arrangement there may be no other choice than to pay higher factor rewards. This may help to compensate part of the losses that occur when Fair Trade reduces trade.

Another qualifying point is that the Stolper-Samuelson theorem holds when factors of production can easily move across sectors. If this is not the case, for instance when certain production factors are immobile or of no use in other sectors, the income distribution effects of trade are different. To see this we adapt our framework slightly and assume that the two goods each country produces requires the use of one production factor that is specific to that good. Specifically, we will assume that manufacturing production requires capital and labour, while farming requires land and labour. Capital and land are therefore sector-specific production factors, while labour can be used in both sectors. We still assume that the developing country has a comparative advantage in farming products so that trade and specialisation patterns are as before.

The general outcome is then that trade increases (decreases) the real factor rewards of those factors that are specific to the export (import) sector, while the effect on the reward of the production factor that is used in both sectors is ambiguous and depends on how much is consumed of the import good. The reason is that labour moves to the export sector – here farming – while capital cannot. This mitigates the wage increase in the export sector, making it lower than the price increase of the export good that arose due to trade. Consequently, if labour mainly consumes export goods, it will lose from trade; if it mainly consumes import goods, it will gain. The owners of land, by contrast, will clearly gain. Not only do they face a higher nominal reward because of the increased export price, but also will they face a productivity increase due to higher labour employment in the export sector. By the same token, capital owners in the import sector lose from trade.

If Fair Trade leads to an increase of trade, these will also be the effects Fair Trade implies. Applied to the situation above: because of Fair Trade, capital owners in manufacturing will lose and land owners in farming will gain. Labour, by contrast, only gains when its consumption pattern is such that mainly manufacturing goods are consumed. If, on the other hand, Fair Trade reduces trade the picture is exactly opposite. In that case capital-owners gain and land-owners lose, while the effect on labour is only positive if mainly farming products are consumed.

Also here we have to adjust for the rents that paying a price premium in Fair Trade programs give rise to. However, the potential positive spillover effects of this may be more problematic as these occur mainly due to cross-sectoral mobility of production factors. If this is absent, as we assumed for the specific factors above, a negative spillover effect arises for the immobile productions factors outside Fair Trade programs, in our case capital in manufacturing production. For land owners and labour the externality is positive. Apart from this it depends of course on the extent to which entry into Fair Trade programs is open to labour and land owners outside the program. But this seems not to be a real issue, since closed cooperatives are banned by international Fair Trade standards (Hayes, 2006).

Finally, we note that all of the above can also be given a more regional interpretation. The analysis above highlights the inter-sectoral consequences of Fair Trade when we see countries as one entity. However, also within countries specialisation occurs, which is most eminent in the difference between rural and urban areas. The plausible assumption is that developing country's farm production mainly takes place in rural areas and manufacturing in urban areas. In that case, the inter-sectoral implications we discussed above also have interregional implications, depending on (a) whether or not Fair Trade increases or reduces trade, and (b) whether or not production factors are mobile between sectors and regions. Also inter-regionally, therefore, Fair Trade may have unexpected income distribution effects.

## 4. Evaluation: the impact of Fair Trade on rural poverty

The analysis of Sections 2 and 3 has shown that Fair Trade has generally beneficial effects for producers involved in the program, but is also capable of harming other groups in society. In Section 2, we have shown that Fair Trade may harm non-Fair Trade producers in the same sector; in Section 3, we have focused on the income distribution effects between owners of production factors. The question we seek to address in this section is what this implies for the target group of Fair Trade: poor peasants, producing commodities for the world market.

From the intra-sectoral analysis, we learn that Fair Trade is, under normal circumstances, likely to produce negative externalities for producers not participating in Fair Trade. A higher price for part of the market reduces overall demand. If this reduction of demand is not compensated by a reduction of supply on behalf of those involved in Fair Trade - because of switching to alternative activities for example - prices and incomes in the non-Fair Trade segment of the market must fall. This basic insight seems to be at odds with the empirical observations presented in the previous chapters of this book. There, it has been shown that the implementation of a Fair Trade program generally has a positive effect on prices and incomes in the region, including those involved in non-Fair Trade production. This discrepancy between theory and empirics is something that needs to be explained. One plausible and slightly disturbing explanation for it is that the negative externalities of Fair Trade programs are there, but that they are felt only outside the region. Implementation of a Fair Trade program for coffee producers in Peru might then amount to a redistribution between the global poor. Coffee producers all over the world give in a little, so that producers in Peru can gain quite a lot. This is a real possibility which we need to look into if we want to improve Fair Trade.

Applying the inter-sectoral analysis to the context of poor peasants producing for the world market is slightly less straightforward. The analysis in section 3 is rather stylised, focusing on the effects on income distribution between several production factors (land, labour, capital). In practice, the peasants targeted by Fair Trade programs are usually simultaneous (small) owners of all these production factors. This might trigger doubts about the relevance of the analysis. After all, does it really matter for a small peasant whether income increases because of a higher reward for labour or a higher reward for land? Isn't the fact that incomes rise the only thing that is important? The answer to this question is yes and no. Of course, if Fair Trade raises incomes of peasants it is a good thing. The concern, however, is with the efficiency of Fair Trade arrangements; do they primarily reach those who they intend to reach? Here, some doubts arise about Fair Trade practice.

As mentioned, peasants are owners of land and labour. However, they do not own land and labour in equal proportions. Some are relatively land-abundant, others have a large household with only a very small plot of land. In other words, all peasants are located somewhere on a continuum between 'owning only labour' and 'owning only land'. If Fair Trade raises prices of land-intensive products - agricultural products such as coffee or bananas would qualify - the analysis in section 3 shows that it is likely to increase the reward of land relative to labour. While this is probably an income improvement for all peasants, peasants owning relatively more land benefit from Fair Trade to a stronger extent than peasants owning relatively more labour. In extreme cases - when a household does not produce enough agricultural products to provide for its own needs and is dependent on alternative activities to supplement its income - the effect might even be negative.

The problem is that the amount of land owned is correlated with the income of a household. The larger its plot of land, the more a household is able to produce, and the higher its income. If Fair Trade boosts household's incomes through higher prices for the produced goods, the households capable of producing more goods gain more than those capable of producing only little. Fair Trade thus risks benefiting richer, relatively land abundant peasants more than poorer peasants, who have not much more than their labour to sell. Without any further redistributive measures, rural inequality is likely to increase as a consequence of Fair Trade premiums. Of course, some redistributive measures are possible and exist within Fair Trade cooperatives, but this does not solve the heart of the problem. The question is whether Fair Trade, by 'subsidising' agricultural output rather than wages directly, is not structurally biased towards raising incomes of richer peasants above poorer ones. Like with insider-outsider inequality, this is a real possibility which needs to be investigated. It might imply that Fair Trade would do better to shift its focus towards labour-intensive sectors.

## 5. Conclusion

Fair Trade might be positive, but if one looks beyond the target group of the arrangement, it is by no means automatically so. In this chapter we have tried to show that also with Fair Trade gains for one group typically comes at the expense of losses for another group, whether this be producers in the same or other sectors or the owners of production factors that are not (prominently) used in Fair Trade production. Moreover, we have made an argument that even when looking at the target group of Fair Trade alone – poor peasants – Fair Trade may have unexpected consequences, for instance benefiting richer, relatively land abundant peasants more than poorer peasants.

Essentially, these outcomes all have to do with the fact that the arguments why Fair Trade would be a good thing have their grounds in correcting for market failures. Only if markets fail, intervention can lead to net societal welfare gains, providing room to compensate the losers of policy actions. That triggers the question if Fair Trade is the best way to resolve the problems. It shows that Fair Trade should be based on a thorough analysis of the market situation of the sector in question, rather than to be taken as an approach that is always positive.

We conclude by saying that our outcomes are mainly based on a standard trade framework, which is geared towards the analysis of the question trade or no trade. Fair Trade has been assessed in this way through this framework; as a program potentially limiting trade, distributing resulting rents. Strictly speaking, such an analysis does not do justice to what to many practitioners is probably the essence of Fair Trade: Fair Trade is not about trading more or trading less, but about trading in a different manner. Economic theory (as it is) is not really equipped to deal with that aspect, since it is built around certain assumptions about how people behave vis-à-vis each other. Such a theory only leaves room for a discussion of how to manage such (opportunistic, utility-maximising) behaviour optimally, not about how to behave. It leaves such questions to moral and political philosophy. For a more definitive verdict on the Fair Trade, one should perhaps turn to those disciplines.

## References


Bhagwati, J.N. and T.N. Srinivasan (1983). *Lectures in International Trade*. Cambridge, MA: MIT Press.

Bowen, H.P., A. Hollander and J.M. Viaene (1998). *Applied International Trade Analysis*. London: MacMillan.

Ethier, W.J. (1995). *Modern International Economics*. Third Edition. New York: Norton.

Hayes, M. (2006). On the Efficiency of Fair Trade. *Review of Social Economy* 64: 447-468.

Maseland, R. and A. De Vaal (2002). How Fair is Fair Trade? *The Economist* 150: 251-272.

Melitz, M.J. (2003). The impact of trade on Intra-industry Reallocations and Aggregate Industry Productivity. *Econometrica* 71: 1695-1725.

# Chapter 11

## Is there a moral case for Fair Trade products? On the moral duty for consumers to buy and for governments to support Fair Trade products

*Jos Philips*

### 1. Introduction

Could there be a moral duty for consumers to buy Fair Trade products? Even more dramatically, could there be a moral duty for governments to support Fair Trade products? This contribution argues that the answer to both questions may well be affirmative – where I am thinking of consumers and governments of (relatively) affluent countries such as Western countries. In relation to the first question, the existence of a moral duty to buy Fair Trade products goes against the idea that, in their consumer behaviour, individuals are morally free to choose as they please or prefer. In relation to the second question, the existence of a moral duty for governments to support Fair Trade products goes against the idea that governments should not interfere with markets, among other things because these markets are thought of as devices that give voice to consumer preferences. In this chapter, I will try to show why despite such doubts, there may still be a moral duty for consumers to buy and for governments to support Fair Trade products. By Fair Trade products I shall mean products that take account of some minimal standard of protection for producers, and possibly also for the environment.

The chapter is structured as follows. In the remainder of this introduction, some doubts will be dispelled as to whether morals or ethics is a subject about which sensible things can be said at all (section 1). In section 2, I will argue that individuals may well have a moral duty to buy Fair Trade products. This argument sets the stage for the next section (section 3), which argues that governments may well have a moral duty to support Fair Trade products. Where sections 2 and 3 consider two prominent moral approaches - contractualism and consequentialism - , section 4 offers some arguments as to why a prominent different moral approach could also agree with our conclusions. On all three approaches, then, it seems that moral agents are not acting as they should, and the question arises as to why not: why, for example, do Fair Trade products not have much larger market shares? The Chapter will end with some remarks concerning this admittedly complex issue.

By way of preliminary remark, then, let us consider the view that there are really no meaningful things to be said about morals or ethics, that is, about such issues as what is good and bad, and what it is right and wrong to do. This view, which one may call sceptical (or, somewhat less appropriately, subjectivist, or relativist), holds that morals or ethics are what someone pleases (or not) to make of them: there is nothing real to talk about here. I take it that this view is ultimately entirely indefensible, and that its indefensibility is best shown not in a theoretical but in a practical way. The point to emphasise is that (virtually) no one accepts the view's practical implications, such as that it is perfectly all right for people to severely harm someone just because they feel like doing this. Such an implication is surely absurd, and it becomes even more unacceptable to most of us if *we* are the ones who might suffer the harm: when we ourselves are wronged, who of us believes that ethics is nothing real and just whatever one likes it to be? (cf. Nagel 1971: 145) These considerations suffice to show that, when discussing morals and ethics, we do have a meaningful subject on our hands. Now, let us see whether a moral duty to buy Fair Trade products is defensible.

## 2. Is there a moral duty for consumers to buy Fair Trade products?

Modern ethical thought has generated two main broad approaches for determining what moral duties certain agents have. One approach, called (broadly) 'Kantian' because it is inspired by the great 18th century philosopher, Immanuel Kant, asks whether a certain course of action is one that would find universal acceptance, or, put differently, whether it is a course of action that no one could reasonably reject.[1] I will extensively discuss this approach, and come to the other main approach – which is commonly called 'consequentialist' – only at the end of this section.

If we apply the Kantian approach to our question, the following may be the main questions to consider: could the peasants who produce Fair Trade products reasonably reject a permission for Western consumers *not* to buy such products? And, could Western consumers, in turn, reasonably reject that there *is* a duty for them to buy Fair Trade products? I will now, without striving to be complete, discuss some important issues that bear on these questions.

For the peasants who produce Fair Trade goods, like coffee, things may seem straightforward. What is at stake for them is their ability to live in minimally

[1] The latter formulation is freely inspired by T.M. Scanlon's contractualist theory (1998, especially Chapter 5). This kind of contractualism is often considered the most important form of present-day Kantianism. Due to lack of space, I try to apply Scanlon's approach without further discussion of its theoretical features.

acceptable conditions, which have to do with housing, sanitation, with the education for their children, and with healthcare for themselves and their families. However, more complex goods and values may also be involved, like their ability to participate in the community, and their self-respect and dignity; and these complex goods, in turn, serve to remind us that even apparently simple goods (like food or healthcare) can involve a lot of complexity... Nevertheless, there will be wide agreement about the importance of (many of) the goods that are at stake for the peasants, and justifiably so, if only because such goods as decent housing and basic healthcare are plausibly preconditions for almost any other goods that people may value.

Of course, if we say that for the producer-peasants such goods as basic health care are 'at stake' in decisions of Western consumers to buy or not to buy Fair Trade products, there is the question of what good individual Western consumers actually do or can do by buying Fair Trade products; and not only the question of what good they can do to the producer-farmers, but also the question of whether they harm third parties by benefiting these farmers, in which case such third parties might reasonably reject a duty (or even a permission) for Western consumers to buy Fair Trade products. A large part of the issues involved in answering these questions is empirical, and I will not consider it in this chapter; in what follows I will just assume to be talking about Fair Trade products which bring great benefits to producer-farmers (also in the long run) without substantially harming others.[2] Another part of the issues involved does have a less empirical (and more philosophical) side, namely those issues concerning how to determine and morally to evaluate just how much good (if any) individual contributions to cooperative projects do: is my purchase of a few kilos of coffee of any help to the success of a Fair Trade project, or is its effect really negligible or inexistent? If it is negligible, would there still be a moral case for my contribution? Such questions have sparked sophisticated debates, which I cannot pursue here; suffice it to say that in the face of such complications, many philosophers (e.g. Parfit 1984: Ch. 3; Cullity, 2004: Ch. 4) have seen no reason for scepticism about the effect and/or about the moral case for individual contributions. (One kind of argument that has figured prominently in the pertinent debates is the usefulness and the moral obligation of an individual contributing their 'fair share'). Therefore Fair Trade farmers can, as before, reasonably reject (systems of) moral principles that do not specify a duty for Western consumers to buy Fair Trade products.

Let us now turn to Western consumers: why could they reasonably reject a duty to buy Fair Trade products? They can say that if they had such a duty, they would face greater expenses - inasmuch as Fair Trade products are more expensive - and thus be left with less money and, consequently, with less choice in their lives. It will of course depend whether it is reasonable for consumers to reject a principle on these grounds; the crucial issue here seems to me to be that finances and an array of choice are, *to a certain extent*, needed if one is to live at all and even more so if, very generally speaking, one is to flourish to some minimal degree. More particularly, they are needed if one

[2] The other contributions in this volume show that Fair Trade products generally meet these conditions.

is to be able to live one's life to some minimum degree by one's own light; and the importance of being able to live in this way has generated endless comment but seems rather nicely captured in the following famous quote from Isaiah Berlin (a quote which also involves much else):

> *'I wish my life and my decisions to depend on myself, not on external forces of whatever kind. I wish to be the instrument of my own, not other men's acts of will ... I wish, above all, to be conscious of myself as a thinking, willing, active being, bearing responsibility for my choices and able to explain them by reference to my own ideas and purposes'* (Berlin, 1969: 131).

It is important to add, however, that often a reduction of funds and of choices does not credibly jeopardise the ability of consumers to live by their own lights, let alone their ability to have minimally decent living conditions (cf. Philips, 2007: Ch. 6). Often, it is more plausible to say that what they give up when buying Fair Trade products (if anything)[3] is just some extra money and some luxuries, without which they can still – even if plain and simple luxuries are surprisingly hard to think of - do very much everything that matters to them.

Having seen the matter from two sides, that of the producer-farmers and that of Western consumers, the question is how we should balance these against one another. I mention three considerations that are relevant here. First, although it is plausible, as said, that individual contributions are meaningful contributions to Fair Trade projects, one may have some doubts as to just *how* meaningful they are. Sometimes supporting some faraway project does seem to bring great and immediate good (frequently, projects set up by someone you know personally spring to mind), but often the suspicion is that the good that projects do is mitigated by all kinds of middlemen, siphons etc. In such cases, it may be thought that even the sacrifice of relatively clear luxuries for the sake of supporting Fair Trade projects, may be resisted.

However, I think that this is not so. To show this, I would appeal to a second consideration, namely, that it is extremely hard to believe that the global institutional arrangements that we, as Western individuals, have allegedly upheld and that we have in any case benefited from, are morally defensible. If they are not, then we owe those who were not benefited but harmed as a result, some compensation.[4] For this reason, there is a case that Western consumers should contribute to Fair Trade projects, i.e. buy Fair Trade products, even where middlemen and other efficiency-reducing complexities are involved in getting consumers' contributions to these projects.

---

[3] They may also *gain* in certain ways when buying such products! (cf. DeCarlo, 2007)

[4] This would remain true even if (as very probably ought to happen) these structures were reformed right now; it would only not be true if such immediate reforms included due compensation for past harms. For extensive development of the theme that the global institutional order harms the poor, see the work of Thomas Pogge (e.g. 2002, 2007).

There is, however, a third important consideration. Whether it is reasonable for Western consumers to reject a duty to buy Fair Trade products will certainly also depend on the other duties of equal or greater stringency these consumers would have. However, the urgent nature of the goods served by buying Fair Trade products, coupled with the thought just mentioned about compensation for past harms, make it clear that the case in favour of having to buy Fair Trade products is a very weighty one.[5] Accordingly, only if there were very weighty countervailing reasons could a duty on the part of consumers to buy Fair Trade products be reasonably rejectable. It is unlikely that Western consumers could point out that such countervailing reasons apply to them. There may be some exceptions, as firstly, where there are undoubtedly good causes other than 'Fair Trade' to which consumers can contribute clearly more effectively; and secondly, where consumers are unemployed, single mothers or in similar situations. But otherwise it will be hard for Western consumers to find good countervailing reasons. This will obviously be especially hard for products where there is a wide choice of Fair Trade products (as in the case of coffee) and where Fair Trade products are not much, if at all, more expensive than non-Fair Trade varieties (as is sometimes the case for chocolate).[6]

I want to leave the argument here as to why Western consumers may well have a moral duty to buy Fair Trade products, and turn to the duty that Western governments may have to support Fair Trade products. Before doing so, however, it is important to note that, where we have been pursuing a broadly Kantian form of moral reasoning, an argument to the same effect can be made in the other main contemporary style of moral reasoning, which is called consequentialist, because it holds that moral agents should always choose the course of action which, of all those courses of action available to them, promises the best results or consequences. I shall be very brief here, because I have extensively pursued a consequentialist style of moral reasoning elsewhere (see Philips, 2007: esp. Ch. 6). Inasmuch as very basic goods are at stake in supporting Fair Trade projects, and inasmuch as Western consumers can expect to reasonably effectively be able to contribute to the realisation of these goods, there may, for a consequentialist, well be a moral duty for these consumers to do so - and there is certainly such a duty whenever, in buying Fair Trade products, only relatively clear luxuries are 'sacrificed' and where there is no clearly urgent cause in sight that allows for contributions more effective than those made though buying Fair Trade products.

[5] Of course, it is not as if compensation for past harms could only take the form of buying Fair Trade products. However, buying Fair Trade products seems one credible form it could take.

[6] For Fair Trade products where these conditions are not fulfilled, one may argue in favor of a duty for consumers to campaign for their becoming available. However, I will not develop this point here.

## 3. Is there a moral duty for governments to support Fair Trade products?

Could there be a moral duty for governments to support Fair Trade products? We could proceed here as we did above: we could ask whether a duty on the part of governments to support Fair Trade products would be reasonably rejectable, from the standpoint of fair-trade farmers or consumers, or from the standpoint of some other party. By 'supporting', I mean reducing value added taxes on Fair Trade products or similar measures. Fair Trade farmers could plead in favour of a duty to support their products for the reasons we saw in the previous section: they could point out that for them, such a duty serves a number of vitally important goods. However, the objections that Western consumers could have to such a duty will be somewhat different from the objections they could have to a duty for themselves to buy Fair Trade products. On the one hand, it is not so likely that, for reasons of finances or choice reduction, they could have credible objections against a government duty to support Fair Trade products. For, with the exception of those consumers whose income depends on products that compete with Fair Trade products, government support for Fair Trade products does not cost consumers any money. Now it could be the case that such support is paid for by an increase in taxes, and then it seems that it does cost consumers money. However, government support for Fair Trade products could also take the form of lowering value added taxes on such products, in other words, it could take the form of decreasing tax revenues. Alternatively, government expenditure could be shifted from elsewhere to the cause of supporting Fair Trade products. It is true that such ways of financing, too, may be cast as costing consumers money. However, the story that would need to be told here is not very straightforward, but very complex, and it would be a story in which every decision on public policy would imply costs for consumers – which is questionable. Furthermore, a government does, by supporting Fair Trade products, not usually radically change the range of options that consumers can choose from. It only makes some alternatives, in this case Fair Trade products, more attractive *vis-à-vis* others. Such government support does not, by itself, force consumers to buy Fair Trade products, nor does it entail a moral requirement for consumers to do so.[7]

It could be objected that government support for Fair Trade products, as described above, still constitutes an 'interference' with free market structures and that as such it requires justification. This objection can be construed in at least two ways. The first way to take it is as saying that those who interfere with market structures, interfere with consumer freedom – or rather, with consumer preferences[8] - and should therefore be able to produce good reasons for doing so. The first and most obvious reply is that actual markets, perhaps unlike the markets that figure in economic textbooks, do not

[7] If governments should have a moral duty to support Fair Trade products, how would such a duty affect the possible individual moral duties to buy such products? In part both duties go together - we still need individual duties to buy the products that receive government support. One other possibility is that supportive measures by the government may make the existence of individual duties superfluous. However, I suspect that much of the reasoning in the previous section would remain intact even if such supportive measures were taken.

[8] Shortly, we shall come back to this equation of consumer freedom and consumer preferences.

always protect consumer preferences. However, let us for the sake of the argument assume that actual markets do protect consumer preferences. Then the reply to the objection can be, on the Kantian line of argument that we are pursuing, that consumer preferences as such do not bear much moral weight. Some things that do bear much moral weight, we have said above, are the opportunity to have fulfilled one's basic living conditions, and the ability to live one's life, in important respects, by one's own lights. The latter ability offers a much more plausible interpretation of what it is that matters about freedom or autonomy than would be offered by pointing to the (mere) ability to have one's preferences fulfilled as much as possible.[9] (Besides, keeping in mind someone's ability to live their lives by their own lights also helps to illuminate why supporting Fair Trade products, as I have understood it, is morally much less problematic than *prohibiting* the sale of non-Fair Trade varieties).

However, all this is compatible with holding that there is *some* value in (mere) preference fulfilment, because such fulfilment will figure to *some* extent in a conception of what it is to live one's life by one's own lights. Therefore *some* justification should be offered for interference with consumer preferences. To this it may be added that the justification had better be a good one, since very many causes for interference suggest themselves, so that the situation readily arises where interference does touch on morally weighty values, such as the ability to live one's life importantly by one's own lights. However, in the present context the important point is that for supporting Fair Trade products such a good justification is certainly available. It is available, that is, if, as we have supposed, Fair Trade products do lead to substantial improvements in the living conditions (and freedom) of farmers, without clearly harming third parties.

The second way of taking our objection that interference with markets should be justified points out that markets constitute efficient and effective devices for producing goods. The first thing to say in relation to this construal of the objection is that reasons of efficiency and effectiveness are not, as such, credible reasons that consumers could adduce in order to reject a duty for governments to support Fair Trade products. Consumers (or others) must show that to accept losses in efficiency or effectiveness means, in effect, to compromise their basic living conditions, their freedom to live by their own lights, or other important goods. Now in principle a lack of efficiency or effectiveness might indeed compromise such goods. However, it can be added as a second point that insofar as actual markets do make for efficiency – which in at least some cases, as with regard to public good, they notoriously do not - these beneficial effects will largely be preserved even if support for Fair Trade products was introduced, whenever such support leaves large parts of the workings of markets untouched. Furthermore, and this is a third point, such support would be in line with a history of interfering with markets for the sake of weighty causes. Not only are

[9] This is admittedly - and in the present context unavoidably - very brief. The attractiveness of seeing the good for a person as a matter of preference-fulfillment, i.e. subjectively, resides among other things in the risks of defining the good for a person in a way that has no principled link with what they themselves regard as good, i.e. of defining it objectively. However, stressing the importance of someone being able to live by their own lights alleviates this risk to some extent.

actual markets, as is all too well known, complex institutional arrangements that can only exist and survive in complex interplay with governments (and other institutional agents), but more particularly have governments always interfered with markets, on the one hand in order to create an environment where production of goods could become (somewhat) efficient and effective at all - through antitrust legislation, and through the provision of security, infrastructure, basic sanitary conditions etc. -; and on the other hand governments interfered to protect labourers, consumers, and the public at large. Grades and standards for food safety provide an important example here. Such grades and standards (which, again, are evidently forms of governments interference in markets) are widely accepted.

Supporting Fair Trade products, then, may, given the vital goods that are at stake here for fair-trade farmers, be seen as just another natural area where market forces cannot be left to what they would otherwise do. Once again, one may rightly demand that interference with markets be justified and that the justification be a good one; but, as also said above, such a good justification is available for supporting Fair Trade products. It may be added that nothing we have said is to deny that support for Fair Trade products can have unintended and undesirable consequences, such as the overproduction of certain goods (like coffee or cocoa). The possibility of such consequences does not, however, speak against support for Fair Trade products in the sense discussed above. Rather, it indicates on the one hand the possible need to introduce other measures *in addition*, and on the other hand the need to carefully monitor the supportive steps that are taken as well as whatever other measures are taken. The details of the measures to be taken in favour of Fair Trade products are necessarily dependent on hosts of empirical questions, which this paper cannot address. But what has been said should be enough to show that a permission and even a duty for governments to support Fair Trade products cannot be reasonably rejected by consumers on the basis of considerations concerning the role of markets in securing certain kinds of freedom and in securing efficiency and effectiveness in the production of goods.

How would consequentialists regard government support for Fair Trade products? At first sight, it may seem that consequentialists would oppose measures that constitute interference with markets, inasmuch as consequentialists regard those measures as morally required which maximise fulfilment of consumer preferences and inasmuch as free markets are thought to maximise such fulfilment. However, the first point to make in reply is that – as already noted above – actual markets differ from markets in economic textbooks in that they do not always fulfil consumer preferences. Indeed, they leave some preferences – like those of the farmers who would benefit from support for Fair Trade- manifestly un- or underfulfilled, and thus it is very well possible that such support would be advocated from the perspective of overall fulfilment of preferences. Secondly, although all consequentialists would hold that there is a moral requirement to do what has or promises the best results, not all consequentialists agree about what *constitutes* the best results. Some would say that the good result that matters is the fulfilment of preferences; others would say that it is pleasure and the avoidance of pain; and still others would say that the attainment of a variety of goods matter, and that the attainment of certain urgent goods, such as the fulfilment of basic living conditions, matters especially. These last forms of consequentialism would say that the fate of the poor farmers who would benefit from government support for Fair Trade products, has a great deal of weight. Therefore, the government may well have a moral requirement to support Fair Trade products.

We started this chapter with two critical considerations that at first sight tell against a moral duty for consumers to buy and for governments to support Fair Trade products, namely, firstly that in their consumer behaviour, individuals are free to choose as they prefer, and secondly that governments should not interfere with markets, since markets give voice to consumer preferences. It is clear that the theoretical approaches that we have taken to see whether there is a moral case for buying or supporting Fair Trade products, do not take consumer preferences and free markets as sacrosanct, but assess their value in a broader framework. This does not mean, however, that the mentioned critical considerations are not taken seriously. Consumer preferences and free markets are seen as valuable, among other things because of the links that they have with freedom; and free markets are also instrumentally valuable to the degree that they provide a relatively efficient and effective way to produce many kinds of goods.

In closing this section, one further objection should be addressed. To say that the government should support Fair Trade products is to say that the government can have moral duties. But can a *political* entity have *moral* duties? I would defend that the answer is affirmative. Politics, after all, is done by politicians, and for them – like for anyone else - the most important thing would in the end be to live by their moral values; or so I will shortly argue. Of course, if these moral values are sound, they will prominently include values which are often called political values, like the values of maintaining peace and order and the values of respecting those with whom you disagree and of seeking common ground with them when making decisions. Here, we may also add the value of only referring, when justifying political decisions, to grounds that everyone can be expected to acknowledge (cf. Rawls, 1993).[10] (One meets this last requirement if one justifies support for Fair Trade products by referring to forms of freedom and elementary flourishing that are widely seen as very important.) Thus, politicians can and indeed should make a lot of room for so-called political values, but this does not imply that such values are beyond moral assessment. Rather, the proper place of political values is best discovered and appreciated from a larger moral perspective.

[10] Emphasizing this value can be regarded as insisting that a government should in important respects be 'neutral'.

## 4. To conclude

Why should we care about doing the things that the approaches to morality that we have so far considered, tell us to do? There are at least two ways of taking this critical question. The first is to ask whether there could not be different approaches to morality, which would lead to very different conclusions with regard to our questions concerning support for Fair Trade products. The second way is to take the criticism as asking why we should act morally at all. I will take these two interpretations in reverse order.

For many religious people, the question why one should act morally was not a very difficult question to answer; it was a divine commandment to so act. But a well-known doubt about this kind of religious motivation for being moral is that it actually boils down to being moral for fear of punishment. Anyway, for many people this alleged religious motivation is no longer available and a different story needs to be told. I can only be very brief here, but I think that what is most important is to observe that moral behaviour is, in the end, behaviour that can be justified to some larger audience than myself. Now the point is that most of us, religious or not religious, do care a lot that our behaviour is justifiable to a larger audience, and not just to ourselves and in terms of our own interests. Indeed, we care so much about such broader justifiability that, whenever certain behaviour is not so justifiable, we commonly see this as a *decisive* reason not to perform it.

However, even if people see the importance of behaving in a morally acceptable way, we may ask whether the content of moral demands may not be fleshed out in a different way than done above (in the contractualist approach that we outlined, and in the consequentialist approach). Although the two approaches that we have discussed are probably the two most important, there are of course others. To end, I will have a brief look at just one different approach to individual morality, Bernard Williams's, which is very different from the approaches above and which is influential (it has a number of similarities with ancient virtue ethics). As I will argue, however, this approach still yields very nearly the same conclusions as we have reached, and thereby suggests that very many different moral outlooks can agree about these conclusions.

Now, what does Williams say? He is suspicious that there could be any general moral theory that could have the authority of telling us what to do. For him, what moral requirements there are issue from the consideration that 'each person has a life to lead' (Williams 1985, p. 186) and must therefore be able to rely on certain things: not to be killed, not to be assaulted, and, positively, to be helped in certain cases of immediate need. However, there is, according to Williams, no general obligation to help people; such an obligation would easily come to overshadow the helper's entire life. Yet I would think that even Williams's outlook is friendly to admitting that there is a strong moral reason for Western consumers to buy Fair Trade products, at least under the conditions that obtain for many of us, specifically: where buying such products does not in any serious way cause problems for the life that we are living. Still, Williams might require in addition that there is a salient relationship between us, as Western consumers, and the beneficiaries of Fair Trade products (cf. Williams, 2005: 146). But it could be argued in a number of ways that such a relationship does exist, e.g. because of the active contributions that we Western citizens make, through our consumer and voting behaviour, etc., to the predicament of the world's poor, and/or because of the multiple global connections that exist between people worldwide in an age of globalisation. Finally, these same reasons that speak in favour of a moral duty for Western consumers to buy Fair Trade products could also serve as reasons for them not to oppose (rather to advocate) government support for such products.[11] This discussion of Williams's views is of course very brief. Nevertheless, what has been said suffices to show that a moral case for Fair Trade products might be made even from rather unexpected directions.

At this point, we are left with a puzzling question. If morality is generally recognised as providing important reasons, and if moral approaches usually see strong moral reasons in favour of buying and/or supporting such products, why then are we not buying many more Fair Trade products, and why does their market share remain so small? Very formally speaking, there are two possibilities. Either we do not agree with the above picture and do not see the moral reasons that we have according to this picture. Or we do see things this way but our actual motivations come from elsewhere than from assent to these reasons. Those readers for whom the latter is the case should, I think, admit that they *could* act more in accordance with what they recognise to be their moral reasons to buy Fair Trade products. In the former case, by contrast, it would be interesting to see where readers disagree. If it is true that we can buy many more Fair Trade products that seriously improve the living conditions of many farmers without jeopardising our autonomy or our essential flourishing in any serious way, and if the case for buying Fair Trade products is further strengthened by the fact that Western consumers were and are implied in the hardships that many farmers in the South face, then there is a strong case for a moral duty to buy Fair Trade products. This is so on many different moral approaches.

That is the story for the individual consumers. The moral case for governments to support Fair Trade products draws on somewhat different considerations, but here again considerations concerning the autonomy and essential flourishing of Western consumers and farmers in the South will be important. I have argued that consumer preferences *as such* and market freedom *as such* do not make for convincing arguments: while not totally devoid of importance, these considerations cannot be given some immediate sacrosanct status, but need to be backed up and explained further. The considerations that will emerge if we try to do this will again have much to do with autonomy and essential flourishing; and on these grounds, we will find more to say in favour of a moral duty to buy Fair Trade products (for consumers) or to support them (for governments) than against such a duty.

[11] Concerning Williams's views on government support, one must make some guesses. His thoughts on political issues were only published posthumously and remain rather fragmentary.

## References

Berlin, I. (1969). *Four Essays on Liberty.* Oxford: Clarendon Press.

Cullity, G. (2004). *The Moral Demands of Affluence.* Oxford: Oxford University Press.

DeCarlo, J. (2007). *Fair Trade.* Oxford: OneWorld Publications.

Nagel, T. (1971). *The Possibility of Altruism.* Princeton: Princeton University Press.

Parfit, D. (1984). *Reasons and Persons.* Oxford: Oxford University Press.

Philips, J. (2007). *Affluent in the Face of Poverty.* Amsterdam: Pallas Publications/Amsterdam University Press.

Pogge, T. (2002). *World Poverty and Human Rights.* Cambridge: Polity Press.

Pogge, T. (2007). *Freedom from Poverty as a Human Right.* Oxford: Oxford University Press.

Rawls, J. (1993). *Political Liberalism.* New York: Columbia University Press.

Scanlon, T.M. (1998). *We Owe to Each Other.* Cambridge MA: Harvard University Press.

Williams, B. (1985). *Ethics and the Limits of Philosophy.* Cambridge MA: Harvard University Press.

Williams, B. (2005). *In the Beginning was the Deed.* Princeton: Princeton University Press.

# About the contributors

**Ruerd Ruben** is professor in development studies and director of the Centre for International Development Issues (CIDIN) at Radboud University Nijmegen, the Netherlands. He holds a PhD in economics from Free University Amsterdam and has published widely on cooperative development and rural organisations, agro-food supply chains and networks, rural land and labour markets, microfinance and sustainable development, including recent articles in *World Development*, *Food Policy*, *Agricultural Economics*, *Journal of Agrarian Change*, *Journal of Chain and Network Science* and *Supply Chain Management: International Journal.*

**Ricardo Fort** is a researcher at the *Grupo de Analysis para el Desarrollo* (GRADE) at Lima, Peru. He holds a MSc in Agricultural Economics from the University of Madison, Wisconsin (USA) and a PhD degree in development economics from Wageningen University (The Netherlands). His PhD thesis '*Property rights after market liberalization reforms: land titling and investments in rural Peru*' is published with Wageningen Academic Publishers (2007). He has recently published articles in *Agricultural Economics* and *Wageningen Journal of Life Science.*

**Guillermo Zúñiga-Arias** works as training director of La Catalina R.L. in the cooperative sector in Costa Rica. He is also a consultant in agribusiness for EARTH University and for the Inter-American Development Bank (BID) on supply chain analysis in Central America. He obtained his PhD degree in development economics from Wageningen University, the Netherlands, with a study on '*Quality management and strategic alliances in the mango supply chain from Costa Rica: An interdisciplinary approach for analysing coordination, incentives and governance*' (Wageningen Academic Publishers, 2007). Recent articles are published in the *Journal on Chain and Network Science* and *International Journal of Quality and Management Reliability.*

**Fernanado Sáenz-Segura** is director of research at the Centro Internacional de Política Económica para el Desarrollo Sostenible (CINPE) at the National University (UNA), Heredia, Costa Rica. He obtained his PhD degree in development economics from Wageningen University, the Netherlands, with a study on '*Contract farming in Costa Rica: Opportunities for Smallholders*?' Recent articles are published in the *Journal on Chain and Network Science* and the *European Review of Latin American and Caribbean Studies.*

**Lucie Van Schendel** is a graduate student of the Research Master in Comparative Social Science Research at Radboud University Nijmegen, the Netherlands. She conducted field studies in Ghana and delivered her thesis research on the comparison of Fair Trade and non-Fair Trade plantations in Eastern Ghana.

**Thomas De Hoop** is a PhD candidate at the department of Development Studies at Radboud University Nijmegen, the Netherlands. He obtained his MSc degree at Free University Amsterdam and is currently involved in participatory impact studies of health care, water and sanitation, and microfinance programs in Peru, Ghana and India.

**Leonardo Becchetti** is professor of Economics at the University of Rome, Tor Vergata, Italy. He obtained his MSc. Degree in Economics at London School of Economics (1992-93), a D.Phil. from the University of Oxford and a PhD. in Economics from the University of Rome 'La Sapienza'. Recent articles are published in *World Development, the Review of Industrial, Applied Financial Economics* and *Weltwirtschaftliche Archiv.*

**Marco Costantino** is graduated in Economics from Bari University, Italy, and has a master degree in Development Economics and International Cooperation at University of Rome 'Tor Vergata'. He is actually attending a PhD. in Economic Geography at University of Bari and works at the Youth Policies Department of Regione Puglia (Regional Government). He is involved in research on Fair Trade issues for CTM Altromercato (the leading Italian Fair Trade import consortium) and co-authored the study '*Il commercio equo e solidale alla prova dei fatt*: *Dai gusti dei consumatori del Nord all'impatto sui produttori del Sud del mondo*' (B.Mondatori, 2006).

**Luud Clercx** is staff member at the Agrofair Foundation for Assistance and Development (AFAD) in Barendrecht, the Netherlands. He holds a MSc degree in anthropology from Utrecht University and has worked extensively in Central America in a wide range of rural development programs for peasant and cooperative production, sustainable resource use and rural poverty alleviation.

**Dario Cepeda** is a PhD candidate at the University of Paris, France and researcher at the *Sistema de Investigación sobre la Problemática Agraria del Ecuador* (SIPAE). He is co-author of the study '*Mega diversidad agraria en el Ecuador: disciplina, conceptos y herramientas metodológicas para el análisis-diagnóstico de micro-regiones*' (Institut Français d'études andines - IFEA, 2007) and '*El dilema constante del productor bananero en tiempos de brete: ¿asociatividad o individualismo?*' (SIPIA/IFEA, 2007).

**Daniel Jaffee** is an Assistant Professor in the Department of Sociology at Washington State University, USA, and author of the book '*Brewing Justice: Fair Trade Coffee, Sustainability and Survival*' (Berkeley: University of California Pres, 2007). His research examines the effects of economic globalisation and neoliberal policies on social and environmental conditions for rural communities in the global South, particularly Latin America. Additional interests include social movements around sustainable agriculture and resource use in both North and South; the effect of global trade rules on environmental protection and regulation; and issues of access to and privatisation of commons resources

**Robbert Maseland** is a senior researcher at the Department of Political Science, Radboud University Nijmegen, the Netherlands, where he also obtained his PhD in economics with a study on the political economy of development and reform in Malaysia and the Philippines. His current research focuses on economic institutions, cultural values and economics, economic geography, political economy and Fair Trade. Recent articles are published in *Third World Quarterly*, *De Economist* and *Journal of International Business Studies*.

**Jos Philips** is an assistant professor at the Ethics Institute and in the Department of Philosophy at Utrecht University, the Netherlands. His research interests are related to global justice and in the ethical aspects of poverty. He holds a PhD in Philosophy from Radboud University Nijmegen with a study on '*Affluent in the Face of Poverty: On What Rich Individuals Like Us Should Do*' (Amsterdam University Press, 2007).

**Albert De Vaal** is associate professor in Economics at Radboud University Nijmegen, the Netherlands. He holds a PhD in economics from Erasmus University Rotterdam. His current research activities are focused on the effects of international trade and foreign direct investments. Recent articles are published in *Journal of Development Economics*, *Journal of International Trade & Economic Development* and *The Journal of Economic Inequality*.